A Question Mark

An Investigation into the Mysterious Death of Elliott Smith

Alyson Camus

Los Angeles, California USA

A Question Mark

Published by:
Genius Book Publishing
31858 Castaic Road #154
Castaic, California 91384 USA
https://GeniusBookPublishing.com

ISBN: 978-1-947521-68-1

Library of Congress Control Number: 2021947161

211017

"Convictions are more dangerous enemies of the truth than lies."
Friedrich Nietzsche

"Life is not a problem to be solved, but a reality to be experienced."
Søren Kierkegaard

"History is the lie commonly agreed upon."
Voltaire

"It is perfectly true, as philosophers say, that life must be understood backwards. But they forget the other proposition, that it must be lived forwards."
Søren Kierkegaard

"What I seek to accomplish is simply to serve with my feeble capacity truth and justice, at the risk of pleasing no one."
Albert Einstein

"Once you label me you negate me."
Søren Kierkegaard

Contents

"Everybody gets a tag. If you listen to a Velvet Underground record, you don't think, 'Godfathers of Punk.' You just think, 'This sounds great.' The tags are there in order to help try to sell something by giving it a name that's going to stick in somebody's memory. But it doesn't describe it. So 'depressing' isn't a word I would use to describe my music. But there is some sadness in it—there has to be, so that the happiness in it will matter."

—Elliott Smith

Preface

This book has been a journey of several years that started on October 21, 2003, when singer-songwriter Elliott Smith died of two stab wounds in the chest, allegedly self-inflicted. Two stab wounds in the heart.... The gruesome event shocked the Los Angeles music scene, and the case is still open eighteen years later. This story is addressed to the people who have always been interested in the search for truth and justice, and it is especially dedicated to people who have always been suspicious of Elliott Smith's alleged suicide.

This has been a long journey, a lonely ride. During all these years I have received the support of many people, but I have also endured harsh criticism and even derogatory comments from others. Many people regularly ask, "*Why is it so important to know how Elliott Smith died?*" Isn't it obvious? Aren't the circumstances of someone's death always relevant when we think about a deceased person? People sometimes say, "*We want to celebrate his life and his music and not his death....*" But isn't death part of life? Elliott Smith's death is attached to his life and his death does affect how people perceive his music and time on earth.

Death is definitive and death closes life. It always has the last word, and last words are important. Happy endings only occur in Hollywood movies, but happy endings set a tone and taint the entire story, once we know about them. It is the same for life, and a life which ends with suicide is examined through this specific lens. And if you are an artist, it is even worse; your entire body of work is also reanalyzed through the terribly narrow lens of suicide. Too many people are in love with the simple equation "*sad lyrics = suicide*," no matter how many times the artist has said that his songs were not his personal diary. Countless times I have heard, "*Of course he killed himself, have you read his lyrics?*" or "*His final album was basically an extended ode to suicide.*" It becomes a cliché, and the artist's work and life, all intertwined and confused, become a cliché. The tortured artist has committed suicide, it is that simple.

In life, however, things are rarely simple. Life is a convoluted and complicated train wreck with plenty of unexpected detours, and no one-line equation can sum up anybody's life. It would be a lazy and especially unrealistic biography.

Of course, challenging the narration that Elliott Smith committed suicide opens another problem since it brings suspicion on another person, and stops many people in their tracks with the "*innocent until proven guilty*" declaration, which only applies in the courtroom; not only do we have the right to express an informed opinion outside of it, but we should, expressing and writing what we think is part of our rights, especially when our opinion is based on solid evidence. We should not fear free expression of opinion or speculation. I have encountered many people afraid to express an opinion, visibly scared to be caught judging. Many of my sources have desired anonymity, which certainly doesn't serve my credibility. But, in the pursuit of truth, I was left with no other choice. And what if I had gathered enough discrepancies and inconsistencies to have an opinion about the case and to question the suicide theory? I am not in a courtroom. I am not sitting at the jury table. I am not sending anyone to jail. I am just expressing a very informed opinion in a free society, and the "*innocent until proven guilty*" statement does not apply here.

If this book often sounds like a character assassination, it is because it may very well be one, as there is no other way to convey my in-depth research about Elliott Smith and the events surrounding his death, although it is very important to highlight the differences between facts, hearsay, and opinions. "*You seem to have a very good grasp on what is interpretation, opinion or speculation, and what is a provable fact,*" LAPD homicide detective J. King once wrote to me. "*Please know that I'm always grateful for the information you provide, so do not be deterred.*" This has been encouraging, to say the least, because I have not only been deterred, but I have also been discredited, denigrated, and slandered. Expressing skepticism toward the mainstream suicide narration has often been interpreted as pointing the finger at someone. Questioning the narration is sometimes rejected as a "*lunatic conspiracy theory.*" However, if the authorities have never decided one way or the other, if the coroner and the police have never been able to determine the manner of death and left the case open, my declaring Elliott Smith's death suspicious is not a conspiracy theory.

Then there is the "*we will never know*" crowd, which strikes me as the apotheosis of political correctness. This is a crowd too afraid to take a stand, afraid to be accused of misogyny in this specific case. Misogyny? Pure nonsense. In the politically correct era, doubting and going against the popular opinion is regarded as having the plague was in earlier times, but it's also labeling someone, and people have often discredited my research under the cover of "misogyny," a label so ridiculous and so weak that this seems to be the last refuge of someone who has no argument left and is ignoring the facts. As a truth seeker, I have looked at the facts, but I have never cared about political correctness. Above everything I have never had an agenda, and I have nothing to gain at proving one thing over another.

I realize I have not taken an easy road. The suicide narration is a path of least resistance and expedited closure. Those hurt by it cannot speak against it because they are either dead or unwilling to acknowledge it and challenge it. It would also be misleading to say that I have chosen a path; the evidence has led me. There was no choice, as it certainly is the most difficult road.

My goal is not necessarily closure; it simply aims at the truth. We should not even ask ourselves if this matters. "*Telling accurate stories is crucial,*" said remarkable neurobiologist Oliver Sacks in one of his last interviews.

Should we even ask ourselves whether justice matters? Justice has many aims but one of its ambitions is the investigation of truth, seeking the reality of what happened in order to determine if a just or unjust act has been committed. Justice is often portrayed as a blindfolded woman, so that she cannot be corrupted by what she sees, carrying in one hand a set of scales—so that she can weigh both sides fairly—and carrying in the other hand a sword—so that she can act once having made her judgment. This is the only true portrait of justice. It is the epitome of truth and the exercise of fairness. True justice is necessary for a fulfilled life, the Just lives better than the Unjust.

My goal, however, is not necessarily justice. Charging someone with murder and proving someone's guilt beyond a reasonable doubt is actually a very difficult thing to do, and that's why justice fails repeatedly. I have mostly been doing this research to change the narration that has been accepted by the vast majority of people because of some repeated sloppy journalism and an initial misstep in the police investigation. Many articles have stated Elliott committed suicide without any doubt, while the case has been left open by the LAPD for 18 years. How can popular opinion close a case when the police have not? I aim to expose the complicated truth behind the simple explanation that purportedly tied up this mysterious death years ago.

This story is told by Alyson, a half-fictional character who has witnessed true events. I am Alyson as I have lived everything she is reporting. But this is also not my real identity. Alyson is a necessary character to tell the story and connect the different actors. She is a stratagem to take a step back and see the research through fresh eyes. She tells the story, meets people, witnesses many events, asks questions, and takes action by consulting experts, talking to the detectives and journalists. But she is first of all an Elliott Smith fan, and this is why this research exists in the first place. Also, please know that while Alyson is somewhat fictionalized, all of the facts, quotes, and other collected data is entirely true.

Chapter 1: Memories, this is all we have

I read the news today, oh boy

On Tuesday, October 21, 2003, Alyson was having a brief lunch break as she often did at that time, a short trip to the grocery store to grab a salad and a cold drink, and to sit for a few minutes alone in her car, eating quickly while listening to the radio. It was a very hot day for October, and the Santa Ana winds were blowing dry. She can still recall plenty of details of that day.

Alyson didn't learn about the terrible news until she went home and checked the internet. It was a pre-iPhone, pre-Facebook, pre-Twitter era, which is a bit difficult to imagine in these days of instant information. If Elliott's death had happened today, everyone would have learned about it instantaneously, but back then, it took a while for the news to hit, but then it rapidly spread all over her favorite music-related sites. Alyson remembers being in total disbelief. Singer-songwriter Elliott Smith had been found dead in the house he was sharing with his girlfriend, Jennifer Chiba. Dead? How? What had happened? The Elliott Smith message board, where fans were exchanging concert photos and analyzing the meaning of his songs, was exploding. It was even down for a while, when nothing was working, then it reappeared. Alyson became frustrated because she could not get more information. She thought it was some stupid hoax for a while, but hoax it was not. It became official, and she could not think about anything else for the entire night.

Eighteen years later, Alyson still clearly remembers this sad day. Memory is strange, but some events make indelible tattoos when strong emotions are attached to them. This is why she still sees herself lying on her bed, grinding her brain over what could have happened. Elliott Smith was by no means what we can call famous; he wasn't the voice of his generation, he wasn't really in the mainstream radio circuit, he wasn't even a celebrity, but he had some exposure in 1998 with an Academy Awards nomination for his song "Miss Misery" in the movie *Good Will Hunting*, followed by a few MTV appearances. However, his music had been a part of Alyson's life's soundtrack since August 2001, when she had seen him play at a street fair on Sunset Boulevard. The strangest thing was that that concert was far from being his best. She even had heard rumors that he was going through a really bad time during this period, that drugs were ruling his life. Watching him, it was obvious; he couldn't remember his songs during this 2001 performance, and he did look broken, strung out, and almost ashamed of himself, constantly apologizing and aborting songs. He had his Willie Nelson braids and his Shiva T-shirt to protect him, but he struggled terribly throughout his set. Alyson still remembers the scene: a girl in the crowd had kneeled to reemerge with a similar hairdo. In five minutes, she had managed to braid her hair to look like him and she was singing the lyrics that he couldn't remember. But it was that night when, despite the drug haze and Elliott looking so out of it, the magic had operated. People were asking for their favorite songs, and he couldn't play any of them, but people loved him no matter what.

All these concert memories are fading away

Since that day in August 2001, Alyson had been on a quest. She had been determined to know more about Elliott Smith and his music, and eventually bought all of his albums, one by one, attended many of his concerts, and even traveled to just outside San Diego to see him on a weeknight. She saw him nine times altogether and had a ticket to see him again on November 9, 2003, when Elliott was on the bill of All Tomorrow's Parties curated by the famous cartoonist Matt Groening, a music festival headlined by some of Elliott's idols, including Iggy and the Stooges. Tragically, Elliott died a few days before the performance. At the show, Iggy dedicated "Dirt" to him, and everyone was crying.

Ten years later, the mythology had started its devastating warpath that Elliott had become this cursed poet haunted by death and suicide, destined to kill himself, a myth slowly built by many people with the help of his last girlfriend, Jennifer Chiba, but also from professor W. T. Schultz, a psychobiographer and personality psychologist, who published an Elliott Smith biography in 2013.

Years after his death, everyone wanted a piece of him, but the Elliott Smith myth, like any myth, has always suffered from a lot of misinformation, misconceptions, and misinterpretations:

"*Elliott was a sweet, sweet human,*" said Flaming Lips' Steven Drozd to Alyson several years after Elliott's death, and Elliott certainly sounded like a kind and humble person when she had the chance to talk to him in 2003. In describing Elliott, musician and friend Jon Brion said:

"*He was also very talented as everyone knows, and he knew that. It's possible to be humble but know at the same time that your art is not crap, right? He was quite uncomfortable in his own skin but confident with his art; he was this intense combination of heaps of self-doubt and self-assurance.*"

Elliott didn't care about fame, because of the deceptive way fame affects people's lives, and he didn't consider himself famous, so you could talk to him after a show, ask him anything, and he would pay attention to you. He didn't want to perform at the Oscars, but he begrudgingly accepted when the Academy Awards producers threatened to use someone else instead—pop star Richard Marx. Elliott wanted his music to reach a lot of people, and he admired giant rock stars like Paul McCartney, so, in a way, he wanted to be famous. That was the paradox, the Elliott paradox.

Elliott hated the "*fucking*" Eagles, but he loved the Beatles, Big Star, the Kinks—and Supergrass too. The British invasion. He covered many songs, from many artists he revered, from Neil Young to George Harrison, who was one of his favorites. One of his friends said that Elton John's "Goodbye

Yellow Brick Road" and Phil Collins' "Against All Odds" made him cry. He had Stevie Wonder, Willie Nelson, and Hank Williams T-shirts. He met Celine Dion and found her nice, but he once refused to meet Paul McCartney, who was visiting the small club Largo, because it was just "*too much*" for him.

Elliott used to ask at concerts, "*Do you want to hear a sad song or a happy song?*" and people would scream "*happy!*"... "*sad!*" and he would laugh, and any song he played would always end with both of these feelings, happy and sad at the same time. His songs were about nuances of feelings, sad and happy impressionistic touches in the same song, encapsulated best by the word melancholy. Elliott liked the dark because it made us see the light. He despised boring performances, aborted songs when he was not in the mood to sing them, and apologized plenty of times.

He also joked a lot during shows. He wove in stories of wigs and basketball games, pirate hats, and eye patches, both during concerts and in recording sessions.

Elliott was often changing his mind. He was such a complex human being that he almost became a different character depending on who was describing him to Alyson. He didn't want to hurt others, although he probably hurt many. But who didn't? He didn't always make the right decisions. But who did? He was often caught between please-everybody and fuck-everybody. He could be abused and abusive. But he was also very generous. He had a great sense of justice too, like the time he tried to intervene with security when he saw a kid being harassed at a Beck/Flaming Lips show. He also had a good bullshit detector, a good people radar. Unfortunately, he may not have used it all the time.

After his death, casual fans often pigeonholed him as a "*sad sack troubadour*," a cartoonish tortured/tormented artist that the media adored. It was the perfect marketing for someone who wrote self-deprecating and self-destructive lyrics, but he made it clear before his death that he hated that idea. One of the last songs he recorded gave part of the answer. In the song "Suicide Machine," Elliott explained through his lyrics that the rough patches had a tendency to be better documented than the bright ones, and that this is how we build the myths of doom. He had taken the habit to draw "*Kali the Destroyer/More Kicks Than Pricks*" tattoos on his arm with a Sharpie to hide some of his bad reminders with more cryptic thoughts.

Elliott was often intense. He was a stay-up-all-night character, doing his punk-rock thing, finding the courage to share these intricate tales of depression, drug addiction, and cursed relationships through beautiful and profound metaphors wrapped in rawness and pain. A fearless freak, taking all the risks and playing with the idea to refine his Figure 8—what was to become his next album.

"*Perfection is not my ideal. It's an insult to the gods,*"[1] he once wrote while signing (h)hhelliott on Sweet Adeline's fan message board.

Elliott often participated in his own mythmaking, a romantic myth of self-destruction. This may have effectively been written all over his lyrics before he actively practiced it. On the other hand, he was offended at the idea of adding another layer to the doomed Elliott Smith story, refusing to wear a white T-shirt artistically spattered with fake blood for a photoshoot.

His songs were not autobiographical. That is a misconception because they were sung in the confessional and intimate tone that they should have been, and it was an idea that Elliott found insulting and repulsive. He said it would have been the equivalent of self-pity, something he hated. He probably would have also hated the suicide as self-prophecy theory that came after his death.

Elliott's dream-inspired songs were complex, multi-faceted, layered with meaning, and always brilliant and intelligent. Plenty of people find them sad and depressing, but he often described them as "*abstract movies*" or "*moods,*" in a way of using sadness-to-bring-joy kind of way. His songs went to hell and back, providing an invitation to travel without a precise destination. They were proof of his resilient survival. And they were surely heartbreaking… in a good way. "*I am way more robust and resistant than my songs,*"[2] he once said in an interview.

Contrary to what many people think, he used drug metaphors in his lyrics long before taking hard drugs. Elliott had a particularly difficult time with drug abuse in 2001 and 2002, but he was resilient. Those drug-infused years were his worst times. He was aborting his tunes or not completing entire songs during shows. Mr. Misery was truly feeling miserable. When he took drugs, he burned many bridges, and many of his friends had made their goodbyes those two or three years before he died.... A few weeks before he died, he wanted to reconnect with his friends—at least this is what many have said.

Before he died, Elliott was hoping to release a double album; instead, we got the posthumous *From a Basement on the Hill.* He left us with many projects in the works. In addition to the double album, he was planning a tour and festival performance (a slot just before his idols Iggy and the Stooges), a movie soundtrack (Mike Mills' *Thumbsucker*), a new recording studio, a charity for abused children—and this is only what we know of. After his death, Beck alluded to having a possible project in the works with Elliott: "*We even talked a few times about getting together and making some music when I got off tour.*"[3]

The last time Alyson saw him in concert, Elliott was performing at a tribute for the Kinks, and his smile seemed to say, "*I still have some more work to do, I'm gonna hang around.*" He was not done.

At the end of 2002, and until his death in October 2003, Alyson was certain Elliott got better and better, healthier and healthier, contrary to the myth or the vague idea that people now have of that last year. Memory has a tendency to compress time and the further we drift from specific periods, the closer together they seem to be. Who can, today, still distinguish between August 2001 and August 2003? This is unfortunate, but it is essential to the story.

In the late summer and fall of 2002, Elliott disappeared for a while to undergo a controversial detox treatment under the supervision of the enigmatic Dr. Hit, but he reemerged toward the end of 2002, still fragile and thin, even out of shape, but apparently clean. Alyson saw him on October 1, 2002 for the first time after his treatment. He still looked broken down, walking with his head down, looking at the sidewalk, like a character in one of his songs, while his new female companion, Jennifer Chiba, was following him like a loyal companion. At that moment, Alyson worried about his mental and physical condition. But then when she saw him on stage at the Echo, he played a great set and was in a good spirit, joking around, and finishing all his songs.

During the following months, Alyson saw him many times in several clubs around town, where he played many gigs. She felt he looked better and tougher each time. He sold out two consecutive nights at a larger Hollywood theater, the Henry Fonda (then called the Music Box). Despite people reporting that he was mumbling some incomprehensible monologue between songs, he was making sense if you had the chance to be close enough to hear him. Alyson was in the front row and she could see everything. She was not in denial. There were still problems, big ones, and his drug use and treatment had taken a toll on him physically, but those two January/February shows were far from the sad train wreck people had witnessed at the Sunset Junction Fair in 2001.

Alyson thought that Elliott looked really great at the two last shows she attended a few months later. They both took place at the same intimate venue, a small Los Feliz club called the Derby, now defunct. In May, he played a few new songs with friends and musicians, among them Robin Peringer, a bass/drum player who seemed to be always at Elliott's side during his last year on earth. It was as if he had become Elliott's best friend. Alyson had the pleasure of having the longest conversation she had ever had with Elliott that night, and asked him about his projects, about touring. He said he definitely wanted to tour, especially Europe. "*Paris is my favorite city when I tour in Europe,*" he said, his face lighting up. He also mentioned his charity for children, something he had put on hold during his detox treatment. He said he was ready to start it again. But before anything, he wanted to finish his latest album, which could be a double album. But, he said, he was not sure of anything. He was constantly changing his mind. Alyson wanted to know more but it was at that moment Jennifer Chiba decided to interrupt. "*She wants to leave,*" said Elliott with almost some regret in his eyes… or maybe that was Alyson's imagination. She was so thrilled to have had this conversation backstage that she didn't even pay attention to Jennifer Chiba's alleged impatience.

A few weeks later, Alyson ran into Elliott, or rather he passed next to her when she was attending a concert at the Troubadour on the west side of town, where one of Elliott's friends and ex-bandmates, Neil Gust, was playing with his band.

Alyson saw Elliott one last time at the Derby. That night several bands were playing a tribute to the famous band of the '60s, the Kinks. Alyson almost didn't recognize him. He had changed for the better; he looked healthy and almost happy. He played a few hits from the great British band with a renewed energy, even going behind the drum set and jumping around, looking so far from the empty ghost he used to be.

That same night, Alyson also met a French guy, a super-über-fan of Elliott's named François, who had traveled throughout Europe to follow him on tour back in the day. He told Alyson about a French woman that Elliott had met when he was on tour. Strangely, she was one of the first people Alyson heard from when Elliott died. François could not stop talking about the French girl and the big impression she had made on Elliott. He even told Alyson that Elliott had probably written an unreleased song, "Place Pigalle," about her. It could even have been the working title of his last album, which ended up being renamed *Figure 8* because Place Pigalle was judged to be too obscure or foreign by his label. François had met Elliott several times, but many years had passed, and a lot of things had happened since. Knowing about his struggle with addiction, François was not sure Elliott would recognize him after all this time. Nevertheless, "*Hello François*" was the first thing Elliott said when he did see him. François and Alyson didn't know it was the last time they would see Elliott.

Chapter 2: Is there life after death?

In the months following Elliott's death, his passing was all over the news and in magazines. During one morning talk show, Alyson even heard the host mentioning Elliott's suicide while contending that it was a bit expected, since it was common knowledge that he had problems with drugs and depression. Still, everyone was horrified by the terrible method he had picked to go out.

Soon, the gruesome details of his death were everywhere: Elliott had stabbed himself in the chest, in the heart… twice. Actually, this important "*detail*" did appear in the news a bit later, but it was a fact that he had received two deep wounds in the chest. How could he have possibly done that to himself?

Deanna and the first revelations

Alyson had met a few people during Elliott's concerts including Deanna (not her real name). She was always there, more or less in the front with a few others, and she was a major member of the Elliott Smith online community, constantly posting on the message board. For some reason, she always seemed to be in the know, feeding fans with information, while often being a bit cryptic. She had been an aspiring musician within the Seattle music scene in the early '90s. She had had quite a life, and was a bit older than most of the rest of the fans. She had even met Kurt Cobain and his bandmates before Nirvana grew to fame. She had problems with heroin and was not completely over it. Elliott Smith's death had, unfortunately, put her in a deep depression and she fell back into drug addiction for a while.

During the months following Elliott's death, Alyson had long talks with Deanna on the internet and in coffee shops, and now regrets not having taken all the notes she could have. At the time, Alyson had no idea of the importance of these conversations. How could she have guessed that Elliott's death would be something she would continue to pursue 18 years later? In 2003, Alyson was far from guessing that this story would have taken such a path, but Deanna was certainly the first person who planted suspicions in Alyson's mind. Since the two women hardly knew each other, Deanna's desire to confess everything was somewhat bizarre but she probably needed to relieve herself; she knew too much, yet she didn't know enough, and certainly didn't say everything she knew.

Deanna admitted to Alyson that she had been in communication with Jennifer Chiba for the strangest reason: "*Chiba had never paid attention to me when Elliott was alive,*" Deanna told Alyson one day, "*but she talked to me when she saw me at the wall that night.*"[4]

"*I know one thing for sure, Chiba is lying to everybody,*" Deanna had told Alyson very early on, even before the autopsy report was made public. "*She has stories all over the place, and they are all different… I have been able to find out a bit of what she said to Charlie.*"[4]

Charlie was running Sweet Adeline, Elliott Smith's official website[5] and message board, and he had had several close encounters with his hero. He was in awe of him and, needless to say, was completely devastated by his death.

"*She told Charlie about their love and how they were going to be married,*" continued Deanna, "*and yet she says she was trying to break up with him to others and that's why he killed himself.*"[4]

Nothing was making any sense. Alyson had no idea if she could trust Deanna, but she was giving her all this information and she even showed Alyson an email she had received from Jennifer Chiba:

"*I have heard she has been advised by her lawyer not to speak to the police, and there are three stories which are circulating regarding the hospital trip. 1. She drove him to the hospital. 2. An ambulance took him. 3. She drove him to a hospital, and he was transferred to another hospital.*"[4]

Nothing of these different versions ever surfaced in the official news.

Christine Pelisek of LA Weekly

New information was not coming fast enough, and the message board seemed to be the only source of news that fans could access at the time, but it was also the site of a lot of speculation and drama. Eventually, new information was introduced by *LA Weekly*, a local paper that had even organized the *LA Weekly* Music Awards and rewarded Elliott with "*best songwriter*" that year. Journalist Christine Pelisek, who was working for *LA Weekly* at the time, broke the story[6a] that not only were Elliott and Chiba arguing the day of his death, but Chiba had admitted to having removed the knife when he was still standing. Pelisek wrote two more updates[6b,6c] following this story.[6a]

Alyson was a routine reader of *LA Weekly*, and when she saw the article by Christine Pelisek, she posted it on the Elliott Smith message board prior to leaving for work. When she came back, it had disappeared because it had been judged too controversial by the moderators of the board. How could the truth be too controversial?

The Smoking Gun

A part of the autopsy report was made public on The Smoking Gun[8] in early January 2004, along with a few pages of the police report. Although some found it voyeuristic, Alyson immediately looked at it, and read:

"*On October 21, 2003, Elliott and Jennifer Chiba were having an argument and during the argument, Chiba locked herself in the bathroom. While she was in the bathroom, she heard the decedent scream, she came out and found him standing with his back to her. When he turned around, Chiba saw a knife sticking out of his chest, he was standing up, conscious, and gasping for breath. Chiba pulled the knife out of the decedent's chest and saw 'two cuts' on his chest. At this time the decedent walked away and Chiba followed him to where he collapsed. She called 911 at 12:18 pm, requesting medical assistance at her house. The LAFD paramedics arrived and found Elliott with two stab wounds in the chest, then transported him to the hospital emergency room at 1:10 pm, where he died shortly after, at exactly 1:36 pm.*"[8]

The cause of Elliott's death was two stab wounds in the chest, possibly consistent with self-infliction, but the absence of hesitation wounds, as well as the presence of possible defense wounds and stabbing through clothing, were declared atypical of suicide. Toxicology tests had revealed no illicit substances, no drugs or alcohol, but the presence of different medications including antidepressants at therapeutic or sub-therapeutic levels. The coroner declared:

"*The mode of death is undetermined at this time. While his history of depression is compatible with suicide, and the location and direction of the stab wounds are consistent with self-infliction, several aspects of the circumstances (as are known at this time) are atypical of suicide and raise the possibility of homicide. These include the absence of hesitation wounds, stabbing through clothing, and the presence of small incised wounds on the right arm and left hand (possible defense wounds). Additionally, the girlfriend's reported removal of the knife and subsequent refusal to speak with detectives are all of concern. Since a complete knowledge of the circumstances surrounding the stabbing is lacking, the mode will remain undetermined until such time as sufficient additional information becomes available.*" [8]

It was official: the cause of death "*could not be determined.*" A few weeks later, the LA Coroner's spokesman confirmed the ambiguity of the results:

"*The trauma that he sustained could have been inflicted by him or by another and the coroner has not been able to make a determination [as to cause of death].*"[9]

The police report mentioned the existence of a possible suicide note, written on a Post-it, and reading: "*I'm so sorry–love, Elliot [sic] God forgive me.*" The Smoking Gun specified that the misspelling of Elliottin the report was not a misspelling on the note itself but an error made by the person who had typed the police report. The medical examiner had also noted that Chiba's "*reported removal of the knife and subsequent refusal to speak with detectives are all of concern.*"[8]

"*She spent a lot of time referencing songs, the album cover that looks like somebody's jumping,*"[4] Deanna learned from Chiba, and in turn told Alyson. "*Also, she was an art therapist. She pulled the knife out of his chest. If nothing else that killed him.*"[4]

A few months later, the investigation was going nowhere, no update had been published anywhere, and the case was bound to remain unsolved and open forever unless additional information surfaced.

For years, Alyson trusted the police; the police would eventually solve the case and bring an answer, right? Had Elliott killed himself or…? What else could have happened? On the fan message board, people were divided on the subject of his death, and every discussion and speculation about it was immediately censored, under the pretext it was not respectful to Elliott and his family. Alyson was deeply disturbed by this; she was not satisfied by the tribute shows and homages that kept happening. None of them were bringing an answer since the question mark around Elliott Smith's death was too big to ignore.

Sad parties & tribute shows

Just a few weeks after his death, The All Tomorrow's Parties festival did happen without Elliott, and a tearful Jennifer Chiba sang along while surrounded by a group of friends. It was in fact the first one of the series of tribute shows to come. Chiba had asked musician Lou Barlow (of Dinosaur Jr., Folk Implosion, and Sebadoh fame) to perform the set that Smith was going to play at the festival.[10] The singer-songwriter stepped up and performed Elliott's set, but it was a strange and very sad feeling. Several of Elliott's old and new acquaintances were on stage, except for his long-time friend and musician Mary Lou Lord, who was nowhere to be seen even though she had been a very close supporter of Elliott's and had played an important role at the beginning of his career.

"*Mary Lou Lord was told by Robin to stay home during the ATP memorial,*" said Deanna, who has had a long friendship with Mary Lou, "*because Chiba was afraid of her!*"[4] she added.

Alyson could not comprehend why Chiba would have been afraid of Elliott's friend; nothing was making sense.... However, Chiba's behavior got stranger and stranger in the following days and months.

In November, Elliott's sister organized a tribute show at the Henry Fonda/Music Box, the same theater Elliott had played right before his death, and many indie musicians from Beck to Berth Orton were added to the bill, although at the last minute a few of them (Conor Oberst of Bright Eyes, for example) did not show. Alyson still remembers the image of Autumn de Wilde, Elliott's close friend and photographer, crying in the lobby of the theater. Although Alyson doesn't remember seeing her, Chiba was once again there, attending the show with Weezer's frontman Rivers Cuomo, her 10-year on-and-off boyfriend before her relationship with Elliott, if you believe what she said later.

The Figure 8 wall

The Figure 8 wall was a famous red, black, and white mural on Sunset Boulevard that Elliott Smith had used for a photo shoot and had become the artwork used for the cover of his last album *Figure 8*. It had become a memorial for Elliott's fans, and Alyson had spent some time over there, looking at all the flowers, candles, and notes left by other heartbroken fans. The wall was soon covered with graffiti and messages, and although she never stayed there very late, many people would gather every night till the wee hours, singing Elliott's songs while crying. The place had become quite depressing, but people kept coming back. Deanna was there almost every night.

The second night after Elliott's death, Deanna and a few other fans ran into Chiba and Robin Peringer and a couple of their friends at the wall. Chiba was speaking with fans and giving away copies of Elliott's freshly pressed last single, "Pretty Ugly Before/A Distorted Reality is a Necessity to be Free." Deanna wrote:

"*The memorial is beautiful, lots of candles, flowers, lyrics, letters, candy, photos. When I first arrived, there were a bunch of people, sitting in a circle playing guitar and singing. I was trying to paste together a collage that I wanted to make so I really wasn't paying attention,*" she explained to fans on the message board, noting her conversation with Robin that night. "*Robin wanted me to let you know that they had been practicing every day for 7 hours a day, preparing for the Iggy and the Stooges and the ATP show, which was supposed to happen on November 9. He also wanted me to let you know that Elliott was very happy, always laughing, very upbeat, cracking jokes all the time. There was no sign, what-so-ever of anything like this happening.*"[11]

Was it a consolation to know that Elliott was happy? This statement made things even less comprehensible.

"*Robin said that, two days before it happened, they were sitting on Elliott's porch talking about growing a garden, making plans for the records,*" added Deanna. "*It turns out they were going to release one and then another one instead of a double record and then they were going to continue releasing two records a year as the Beatles did.*

"*I was sort of shocked to hear Robin's voice coming up from behind me and asking me how I was doing, considering he was very good friends with Elliott, and I had only spoken to him a couple of times. But everyone seemed to feel the same exact way. Shock. Confusion. Is this real?*"[11]

"*I was definitely surprised to see Chiba,*" said Deanna to Alyson privately. "*I myself would have been heavily sedated at home or with friends whereas she was hanging out at the fan memorial late at night? She had never spoken to me before.*"[11]

At this time, Deanna didn't know that Robin and Chiba had been quite busy before stopping at the wall.

Caroline

Robin and Chiba were driving a jeep that night. They came to the Wall straight from the valley, from Elliott's studio, where they had done some strange business. Fans, including Alyson, learned about it a few weeks later when Caroline, the renter/owner of the recording studio next to Elliott's, posted some disturbing messages on the fan message board:

"*I knew she [Chiba] would come before the family, I just knew it, and the second night after Elliott's death at about 12:00 am in the morning she came, in a jeep with two guys. My partner saw them come, and I had gone outside to say goodbye to him [my partner] and upon hearing my voice she [Chiba] went back inside and didn't come out for twenty minutes. I sat in the car with my partner, directly facing their car and finally she came out and put many boxes into the car with the help of the guys. I felt like protecting Elliott, what if it's his music or writings, what if it's something that people need to see. We stared at them as they filled the back of the car. I wanted them to know that I was watching, I wanted to scream you did it, you killed him, I knew you were a dark force, and I wasn't afraid of her anymore, but I didn't say anything because I really didn't know what the truth was, as I don't know today.*"[12]

Caroline wrote other very long and emotional posts on the fan message board, she was visibly suspicious of what may have happened and she greatly disliked Chiba. She could not even call her with her real name—she had given her the dramatic epithet of "*dark force,*" since the two women had experienced a few negative interactions that last year and had even had some harsh words over a parking space in front of the studios. "*It was around May or June I believe. A regular customer came in screaming at me that she [Chiba] was calling him names and yelling at him to get out of the bleeping parking space,*"[12] explained Caroline.

Caroline said that Chiba had acted this way a few times, and she apologized each time.

"*She seemed arrogant and entitled and that made me uncomfortable,*"[12] wrote Caroline. The next time a customer parked at the place, Chiba called Caroline to get the person to move out of the space, and the next morning, Caroline received a call from Elliott's lawyer to tell her not to park in his spot anymore.

To her great surprise, a few weeks before Elliott's death, Caroline said that Chiba had hired a security guard to patrol up and down the sidewalk in front of the studio. "*What could have been the danger?*" wondered Caroline, whose anger at Chiba grew every day.

Caroline admitted that, out of exhaustion, she had insulted Chiba one day, calling her offensive names, but she immediately felt badly about it. Caroline, who had the most respect for Elliott despite Chiba's presence, wanted to apologize, but a few days later she got a typed note on her car, basically telling her she was a jerk:

"*I'm sorry Caroline but it is none of your business if Elliott is in danger or not, or whether there is a mad killer out to get us and could go by your address instead, I am sorry Caroline but the sidewalk is eminent domain and doesn't belong to you. We are trying to create a creative nurturing environment and we don't need your angry aura ruining it.*"[12]

After Elliott's death, Caroline felt protective of his work and belongings; she didn't want Chiba to take everything, so she called the landlord.

"*I felt just an urgent need to protect Elliott's things from Chiba, I don't know why, I knew he had a family and those things belonged to them. Besides feeling immense grief, it was the only practical things I could do for Elliott then. I called the landlord and told him we should put another lock on so that no one but Elliott's family could get in. He didn't seem to want to do this. Apparently, Elliott had a meeting with the landlord one week before this happened and informed him that he was no longer doing business with his lawyer and that Chiba was now his manager.*[12]

"*I didn't believe Elliott killed himself,*" added Caroline. "*Gentlemen don't stab themselves in the stomach or heart or wherever, they don't do that, he said he wasn't depressed, he was finishing the album, it was obvious [he was in a good place] those last two weeks.*"[12]

For Alyson, these posts were disturbing and came from someone who had direct contact with Elliott and Chiba, but they did not prove anything.

Several years later, Alyson had an exchange with one of the people taking care of the studio after Elliott's death, and she realized that not everyone was ready to trust Caroline, as this person was less than thrilled about Caroline's character. He admitted to having "*several nightmare years dealing with Caroline and her recording artist and husband.*"[13] He was very critical of Alyson's inquiring mind and laughed out loud that she could even consider "*the farce that Caroline posted*" as "a testimony," or "some sort of evidence." Alyson did not consider Caroline's posts evidence, but they were certainly the very definition of potential testimony.

"*I could go through that thing line by line and give you a very different perspective on it than what she portrays. Calling her rant 'testimony' is a stretch from my perspective,*"[13] he wrote to Alyson. While he had a problem because it was "hearsay" and only Caroline's perspective, it didn't take long for Alyson to realize that Caroline and her neighbors were not getting along, to say the least. He said:

"*I'm sure there are elements of truth to it, but she was loud, brash and obnoxious from the first day we met her!*" this person continued. "*We still have a crazy obnoxious note from her that she left on a friend's car. We kept it because it was so off the handle!*"[13]

There was obviously some real animosity between the new occupants of the studio and Caroline's family, but it was not Alyson's role to find out who was right. All she knew was that Caroline had witnessed Chiba and her friends taking belongings from Elliott's studio in the middle of the night, just two nights after his death, and that Caroline had been one of the first persons to ask questions regarding the circumstances surrounding his death. She had had the courage to post her view on a public forum just a few weeks after Elliott's death, even using her real name. She had nothing to gain from this so it was safe for Alyson to assume she was not lying.

Nevertheless, the new studio owner had remained very vague regarding Chiba's raid at the studio. He said he had no idea what Chiba and her two helpers may have taken that night, while also saying that Elliott had been working at home more and more.

"*I understand that he had equipment at home including a computer, tape machine, and multiple people have told me that he had a smaller Trident console at home. Many of his first recordings were done at home and he continued that even after he bought the studio. I found one CDR at the studio that seemed to have rough mixes on it, and I can only think that Chiba had/has plenty of access to all of the archives that he must have had at home as well. Without talking to whoever went with her to remove whatever she took from the studio, it's hard to say for sure the source of the things that she later released. I guarantee she had access to plenty of things at home as well.*"[13]

Whether Chiba had access to equipment at home or not, it didn't stop her from going to the studio, in the middle of the night, and packing the trunk of a car with some items. To Alyson, that was the only thing that mattered. Nevertheless, the man admitted a bit later:

"*We found everything but hard drives or a CPU. Either the family or Chiba took them. We still have his monitor, track ball, and all the other accoutrement that once went with the CPU. I don't know if there's any way to solve these mysteries though unless Chiba or her helper(s) talk.*"[13]

He was finally recognizing there were some things missing, and the fact that he added that he kept the emails he had exchanged with her "*to protect ourselves, in case she came after us*" said a lot about his relationship with Chiba.

"*One last thing,*" he said. "*She and her helpers had not come with any car, but some Jeep-type car [not Chiba's regular car, she had a Subaru?] probably with the goal to be able to load it. You'd need a mack truck to really make a dent in all the gear there, so the night she filled the 'car' with stuff I have a feeling it was personal items and computers,*"[13] he added.

Just like Deanna, Ruth (not her real name) was a fan who wrote on the message board frequently. She was living on the Northwest coast and had been communicating with Elliott's family, although the details of her access to the family have never been very clear to Alyson. Ruth confirmed that Chiba had taken some of Elliott's personal belongings and that she had "*all that stored away.*" There were even some discussions about the artwork chosen for his posthumous album, a photo by Renaud Monfourny showing Elliott sitting on the steps of a New York Brownstone. This was not the artwork he had intended for the album, as he had instead bought a drawing from an artist showing geometric shapes that resembled a building on top of a hill. According to Ruth, Chiba had been holding back the artwork and had never told the family about Elliott's intentions regarding the album cover.

More suspicions

The partial coroner report posted online raised suspicions in the minds of many people. The forensic details were troubling because, let's admit it, most deaths due to stabbing are homicides not suicides. At that time, Alyson started to browse forensic literature related to stabbing, and her suspicions grew with each article. Although suicides by sharp force injuries were not unheard of, they only accounted for 2% of all suicides, and the articles were saying that suicides by stabbing were unusual, and commonly done in the neck, stomach, and abdomen, but rarely in the chest. Then there were all the other disturbing forensic findings. Elliott's stabbing had occurred through his clothes, which was unusual for suicide since most people who want to stab themselves usually remove their clothes in order to find a spot to plunge the knife.

Alyson had stumbled on the following quote in the Association of periOperative Registered Nurses journal:

"*It is much easier to stab someone else than oneself; therefore, suicide by stabbing is uncommon. Most deaths due to stabbing are considered homicides. Stab wounds showing minimal penetration or wounds that barely break the skin usually identify self-inflicted stab wounds and are known as hesitation wounds. Stab wounds seen in people who have committed suicide vary in size and depth with usually only one or two 'final' ones entering the chest wall or an internal organ. It is a rare individual who can self-inflict stab wounds without any evidence of hesitancy.*"

Hesitation wounds/marks around the main stab wounds would have been a strong indicator of suicide, but were absent in Elliott's case, and this was another disturbing feature. In addition, the small fresh cuts on his palms and upper right arm had been described as possible defense wounds, and defense wounds are strong indications of homicide. Plus, Elliott and Chiba had been fighting; she had admitted it to the police, and the neighbors had heard the couple slamming doors and screaming at each other.

Chiba claimed she was tired of the fighting and wanted to isolate herself, Chiba said she had locked herself in the bathroom for a few minutes—she actually would give the time range of 5-10 minutes in Gil Reyes's documentary, *Searching for Elliott Smith,* which was released in 2009. How many people stab themselves in the middle of a fight or even shortly after a fight? And in comparison, how many people are stabbed following a domestic fight?

Alyson was haunted by several comments but especially this one, from an anonymous source posted on a website, commenting on the results of the autopsy:

"*I'm an MD from PDX and have been thinking about this. He may have been a cutter. But the pattern of knife wounds on both palms and his upper R arm writes itself as 'defensive.' Two smooth penetrations of the chest wall in the absence of hesitation marks is suspicious if not damning. If this was a suicide, it was a technical first. It broke my heart.*"[14]

Another fact was still weighing very heavily in the already disturbing list of inconsistencies: Chiba had removed the knife from the wound when

Elliott was gasping for air and still standing, this despite her being a licensed therapist who should have been trained against doing exactly that in any basic first aid course.

Jennifer Chiba, a Loyola Marymount University Licensed Marriage and Family Therapist since 1995, had been practicing as an art therapist and mental health worker[15] in different institutions. Just a few years after Elliott's death, she claimed 15 years of experience on her resume, working as a therapist for a number of non-profit community mental health organizations, including Five Acres,[16] a school for abused and troubled children. Another therapist confirmed to Alyson that Chiba should have known better:

"*I cannot stress this enough: Anyone who takes a Basic First Aid class, even the people who sleep through it, are scared straight from any idea of removing an impaled object of any kind. It creates a second trauma and increases the bleed. You leave it in and wrap it to staunch the bleeding. This is particularly stressed in training for clinicians who work with children!!!*"[17]

If panic could not have been excluded, a simple email addressed to Robin Smith Jurado, Assistant Director of Human Resources, Volunteers and Recruitment at Five Acres, returned an answer confirming that Chiba had been trained in CPR: "*Thank you for your email, All of our direct care staff, including our therapists, is trained in CPR and First Aid.*"[18]

For years, Elliott had been projecting an image of the most depressed singer-songwriter of the century—although there are numerous artists who could claim to be on the same list—having struggled with depression and drug addiction. There was no doubt that suicide ideation had been a common theme in his life and could have been perceived all over his work. Still, this particular type of suicide would make this an incredibly odd case.

Months passed and the media were not updating the story much. Fans were waiting for some kind of development, which was apparently not coming. The Smoking Gun had revealed in January that Elliott had no illegal drugs or alcohol in his system, just therapeutic or sub-therapeutic levels of different prescription medications, making the mystery even thicker. Fans were proud of Elliott for being clean, but certainly stunned that he could have stabbed himself twice without any pain killers. There were nevertheless questions about the prescription medications he was taking and their potential effect on his psyche. Meanwhile, his image of the sad depressed sack meant many were ready to accept the story as it was.

MTV declarations

Chiba must have felt some pressure from the suspicions weighing on her, so she decided to break her silence:

"*Up until now I've chosen to remain silent because I want to maintain some sense of privacy for Elliott and his family and myself in this really difficult time,*"[19] she declared to MTV. "*And I want people to know that I'm not keeping quiet because I have anything to hide. If I were a suspect, I would have heard from the investigators, for one thing. Another is that his sister and his parents and everyone close to him knows the truth, so I'm not worried about it.*"[19]

She added that she felt "*Elliott's privacy and dignity were violated*" when the coroner's report was published, and that some magazines and publication were "*just looking for some sort of sensationalistic angle that will sell their publications.... In my mind, there's no question to what happened and there's no need to put that kind of spin on it. It's absolutely not my fault. I know that, and people close to Elliott know that.*"[19]

There were several problems with her declaration. First, the police report clearly stated that she had refused to speak with the officers in charge, while she was now speaking to the press. Second, Elliott's family had yet to speak to the public. That is until they heard Chiba's statement. Their lawyer issued a statement saying that no one should speak for Elliott's family regarding his death, which continued to be investigated by the police:

"*Elliott's family has every confidence that the ongoing investigation will determine the actual circumstances of his death. Until such time as their investigation has concluded, however, and especially in light of the recently published coroner's report, neither Elliott's family nor anyone else can claim to know 'the truth' about his death, and any statement to the contrary mischaracterizes the family's position.*"[20]

It was clear that, after this, everyone became aware that the family didn't want to have anything to do with Chiba's assumptions. But, to be honest, the family didn't want to have anything to do with anybody and stayed totally silent in the months and even years following Elliott's death.

Starting that day of the MTV interview, things changed in Alyson's mind, as she was starting to understand that the family was not getting along with Chiba, and that they were not supportive of her posing as a victim of a loved one's suicide. And why should they be? She was declaring, "*It's absolutely not my fault,*" when she had locked herself in the bathroom at the most dramatic moment of their fight, and she had removed the knife, an act which certainly precipitated Elliott's death. Chiba had been with Elliott for a relatively short amount of time (barely a year) and hadn't even met his family while he was alive. According to a female neighbor who attended Elliott's funeral in Portland, Chiba actually met Elliott's father for the first time on that sad day.[39]

Alyson was starting to picture the family, or rather the divided family. Elliott's parents (Bunny Kay Berryman and Gary Mac Smith) had divorced when Elliott was just six months old, and the two sides of the family were not on very good terms. Bunny had remarried Charlie Welch and they had two additional children, Ashley and Darren Welch. Gary had remarried Marta Greenwald and they had two daughters, Rachel and Sophie Smith. Elliott had spent his early childhood with his mother and stepfather in Texas, but since he and Charlie didn't get along, he moved to Portland, Oregon to live with his father when he was 14. During Elliott's last years, Ashley apparently got closer to her half-brother despite a seven-year age gap, as she moved to Los Angeles to live in an adjacent neighborhood.

Over the years, Alyson learned that there was poor communication between both sides of Elliott's family. The declaration in response to Chiba's MTV interview was coming from Elliott's father, or rather from his second wife, Marta Greenwald, who was now the administrator of Elliott's estate.

Astonishingly, the family stayed extremely quiet in the following years, and this MTV declaration may have been the only one they ever rendered in public. The only other example Alyson could think of was an article published by *The Oregonian* in 2010 (an article now offline), entitled "The truth about Elliott Smith." It was the first time she read a comment from Marta Greenwald regarding Elliott:

"*He did struggle with those things [drugs, alcohol, and depression]. That's all true. But other things that have been written are not true. He was a really complicated guy, but he wasn't just a sad sack. He had a great sense of humor, and some of his music is very light.*[21]

"*People like to construct a personality, particularly after someone has died,*" she added. "*They like to be simplistic and say, 'This led to this, which led to this, which led to that.' But that reduces the complexity of who they really were.*" Marta even commented on his death: "*The coroner's report ruled the death inconclusive. There's an open police case; it was never ruled a suicide. They couldn't determine if it was homicide or suicide.... That's important to the family.*"[21]

Chiba in London

In the months following Elliott's death, Chiba flew to the East Coast, then to Europe and other exotic places where she continued communicating with Deanna, among others. She stayed in London for a while, apparently still haunted by that horrific day, but her words were a bit confusing, coming from a person who had been through such a dramatic event:

"*I really can't worry about what people say about me, I know the truth of what happened and what we had together and that is enough for me,*" she wrote to Deanna from London. "*I still believe he didn't mean to hurt anyone and that he was out of his mind when he did it. Because of the fucking drugs (medication, too much fucking medication).... I want to stay here. I miss all my friends and my cat but I feel safe and secure here because no one knows me and what I'm going thru. There is a freedom in having people not look at you with either sympathy or suspicion.*"[22]

Chiba was now blaming medications for Elliott's death, where she had not exactly expressed the same feeling when talking on the phone with recording engineer Larry Crane just after the tragedy. Crane, who was supposed to help Elliott finish his album, had written on his Tape Op message board that Chiba had called him and declared: "*I don't understand, he was so healthy.*"[45]

In her email to Deanna from London, Chiba also said she was happy to go to shows and meet with Elliott's old friends like Mary Lou Lord:

"*I saw Mary Lou Lord play a few weeks ago. She played and I cried. I finally got to meet her after bugging the shit out of Elliott all those years to introduce me and he didn't, I always put that song on the setlist to remind him that I wanted to meet her and because it is a beautiful song.*"[22]

"*She is in London,*" Deanna said to Alyson. "*What is with this 'years and years of wanting Elliott to introduce her to Mary Lou Lord'? I asked her three times to see Mary Lou Lord here and she never expressed one bit of interest at all. She never even mentioned her back to me at all!*"[22] Deanna continued with anger not-so-subtly growing in her tone.

Chiba's declaration was quite confusing. Deanna had said that Chiba was afraid to meet Mary Lou Lord at All Tomorrow's Parties because she might have been suspicious of. According to another email she sent, Chiba allegedly said she had been trying to contact Valerie Deerin, Elliott's previous girlfriend, but Valerie didn't want to have anything to do with her. Deanna, Mary Lou, and Valerie.... Why was Chiba suddenly so eager to connect with all these women she had pretty much ignored or avoided when Elliott was alive?

The lawsuit

It is unclear how Chiba sustained her living abroad, but when she came back to the states, she delivered a big surprise in the form of a lawsuit against Elliott's estate.[23] Alyson read it on the message board or in the news, she doesn't remember which, but she does remember she was stunned. A lawsuit? This was July, nine months after Elliott's death, and Chiba was suing the estate, claiming that Marta Greenwald had breached the oral agreement Chiba allegedly had with Elliott by refusing to pay her for performing her contracted services, and she was asking for $1 million for said services.

Like anybody among the fans, Alyson was astounded by this move. How could anyone sue a grieving family? For $1 million? Was Elliott even that rich? Chiba was bizarrely claiming that she had entered into an oral agreement with Elliott, that they were living as husband and wife, and that Elliott had allegedly promised to provide for Chiba's "*financial needs for the rest of her life,*" since she had supposedly agreed to become his "*manager and agent.*"

It was a punch in the stomach for the grieving family, as they were still in shock and didn't expect this. Elliott's finances were not even in good shape; he had invested in his studio and had not really toured since 2000, after the release of his album *Figure 8* that same year. Chiba amended her lawsuit several times in the following years and finally lost the case in 2007. Despite her persistent efforts, she failed to be recognized as a licensed talent and therefore had no enforceable rights. This came to a close almost four years to the day after Elliott's death.

Besides, if someone was within his or her own right to sue, shouldn't it have been the family? Shouldn't they have filed a wrongful death suit against Chiba? Whatever had really happened on October 21, 2003, she had certainly accelerated it by removing the knife, and the family had some solid grounds for a suit, unlike Chiba, who would never be able to prove the existence of an oral agreement, with no witnesses, in court.

Deanna told Alyson during another stop at the coffee shop, "*Chiba got the idea to sue Elliott's mother after she released that statement in the press saying nobody could claim to know 'the truth' about Elliott's death. Elliott's mother is the administrator of the estate, and Chiba doesn't like her at all!*"[4]

This aggressive behavior was echoed by one of the new owners of Elliott's studio who had met with Chiba several times after the studio had been sold. Despite his previous unfriendly tone when commenting about Caroline's posts, he had told Alyson:

"*At first, she [Chiba] was antagonistic and made it clear she felt the studio should be hers.*" This sounded like a bold move, to say the least. "*She told us that her ex-boyfriend Rivers [name-dropping is a theme with her] had her back and would support her financially in a suit against Elliott's family. We instantly felt threatened. After putting up every penny we had to buy the place, she made it clear that she would try to take it away from us,*" he added, confirming Chiba's litigious nature.[13]

More revelations with Ruth

Meanwhile, Deanna was thinking about moving out of town, perhaps to Portland to live with Ruth for a while. Deanna's current roommate was doing too much heroin and she wanted a fresh start, to get away from the drug scene. Ruth, an avid Elliott fan who was living like a sort of recluse in Portland, was hanging out on the Elliott Smith forum all the time. It was obvious she knew a lot about the story; just like Deanna, she consistently dropped pieces of information here and there. Ruth had already been doing a lot of talking and she was one of the fans raising controversy all the time while making good points: Ruth wrote:

"*I'm still stunned that she [Chiba] could say she had nothing to do with Elliott's death, most people who've lost someone to suicide would never say this. Everyone I know who has lost someone that way, feels unbearable guilt and she was even fighting with him when he allegedly killed himself!*"[24]

Ruth kept a timeline of the events and she seemed to know her stuff. She noticed a lot of oddities or plain lies in Chiba's lawsuit. "*The lawsuit says they met in the summer of 1999, they fell in love, and started a romantic relationship?*" noted Ruth. "*But I have a completely different timeline.*"[24]

This was Ruth's timeline: In 2000, Elliott began a relationship with Valerie Deerin. Prior to that, he had had a long on-and-off relationship with Joanna Bolme. During his time with Valerie, Margaret Mittleman was his manager, and tours were arranged by her. Later, when Margaret was replaced, Valerie helped set up tours. Ruth didn't know why Elliott had broken up with Valerie, but in the fall 2002, after undergoing a painful rehabilitation treatment, he moved into Chiba's house and they lived together for barely a year before his death.

According to Ruth, Chiba's claim in the lawsuit about a romantic relationship since 1999 did not make any sense, considering Elliott's chaotic love life between 1999 and 2002: Joanna, Valerie, and Chiba. And where did the French ("*Place Pigalle*") girl even fit in the picture? Ruth didn't know anything about her at all, as she had never been mentioned in conversations. But Ruth was positive Elliott had moved in with Chiba after his treatment because she had offered to help him, and Ruth even suggested that their real "*romantic*" relationship had only begun around March 2003.

Alyson was surprised, how did Ruth know all this?

Chapter 3: Just before rehab

Elliott's drug problem reached its peak in 2002. Alyson had seen his disastrous performance at the Junction Street Fair in August 2001, but there had been other sad gigs. There were a lot of stories floating around about his health and possible addiction, and he had been heavily criticized for strumming the opening chords of songs before aborting them and mumbling half-remembered lyrics during the few shows he had played in this period. He even had a total breakdown when he opened for Wilco in Chicago in early May 2002.

Valerie

Elliott decided to try a new treatment in August 2002, and he checked into a neurotransmitter restoration clinic in the wealthy part of town. Despite the controversy surrounding this treatment, Elliott had apparently gotten clean with it. Incomprehensibly, he and Valerie had separated during one of the last weeks of his treatment. Or had they?

In early August, as Elliott had just started his detox program and was already feeling better, he posted a message on his fan message board under Valerie's account:

"*I've had a sick feeling for a long time, but you will see LP6, IN LEGAL FORM (not that I care if people bootleg it). also, thanks for the photo album of letters and 2nd double disc. some of you sing better than me, of course. this record is not being held up by my (quite good) management or, some kind of corporate crap. I'm getting healthy after a bad time. 2 songs left to pick now from 40. i haven't died, y' know? (wished I had for a while.) THIS MESSAGE APPEARS COURTESY OF THE BLETHER, but is from (i am not the blether, but i know...them.) sure seems like a lot of people on this thread running around with arrows in their hats. love to you all, m' friends. peace, (h)hhelliott (elliott).*"[25]

Somehow, this enigmatic message revealed that things were improving little by little. A few fans who had seen him in concert seemed to believe that Valerie was very supportive

During his last interview with Under the Radar (March 2003), Elliott, now living with Chiba, mentioned the treatment program he had attended:

"*Then, I went to this place called the Neurotransmitter Restoration Center. It's not like a normal rehab. What they do is an IV treatment where they put a catheter in your arm, and you're on a drip bag, but the only thing that's in the drip bag is amino acids and saline solution. I was coming off of a lot of psyche [*sic*] meds and other things. I was even on an antipsychotic, although I'm not psychotic.*[26]

"*I am getting healthy after a bad time... I haven't died.*" These words were haunting, but did his life really look better? Were things really easier? Nothing was simple in Elliott's world, especially in his love life.

Nelson the poet

Elliott had met poet Nelson Gary during a stay at another clinic owned by a drug counselor named Jerry Schoenkopf. They had become close friends and Elliott was even thinking about using one of his poems for a song on his new album. The song in question, "Coast to Coast," originally called "Circuit Rider," had cryptic lyrics but, according to Gary, the song was about Elliott's love for two women. In an article for Lummoxpress,[27] Gary wrote:

"*[Elliott] also explained to me that the circuit rider, who the song is about, is in love with two women. The circuit rider feels extraordinary guilty and depressed with his heart severed in two, but he is also elated with the amount of love he shares with these women. We had this conversation without Val in our company. He confessed to me that the song's central complexity of emotions was autobiographical.*"[27]

Gary, who had written this after Elliott's death, also confided more details, expressing doubt about Elliott's alleged suicide, even though he had met him when he was so "*tore-up*" that he had not recognized him when Elliott introduced himself:

"*Ten days before Elliott died (with Val, who was a major force in helping him in his healing process, no longer by his side), many of my friends, including Jerry, saw Elliott,*"[27]continued Gary in this same article. "*By all accounts, he was doing well. He had come out of the darkness to twilight, then his life tragically ended. There were no narcotics in his system according to the autopsy report. When the police report is examined in full, as it can be on many internet sites, not only the detail of there having been two stab wounds through his clothing, it is astonishing that a more thorough investigation has not been conducted. The first time I heard the album it was hard for me emotionally, still grief-stricken over the dismal turn of events.*"[27]

A few years after Elliott's death, it was clear that Nelson Gary was not convinced that Elliott's death was a suicide, although it was of course impossible for him to point the finger at someone just based on the impression that Elliott was doing well before his death. Nelson was also correct regarding the investigation, that even if Elliott's death had first been reported as a suicide, the results of the autopsy had made the police declare that they were going to open a full investigation into his death. However, considering their lack of new information this was hard to believe.

"*Elliott was a complex person,*" Gary once said to Alyson. "*His relationships with Val and Jennifer [Chiba] added considerably to the complexity of his life. He had a choice about the people with whom he involved himself, and he made them. NO one forced him to be with Jennifer. Most of the people I know preferred Val. I liked Val. I never knew Jennifer.*"[28]

Elliott's life couldn't have been more complex. Alyson learned through different sources that Chiba had assumed the role of girlfriend when Valerie was in Europe sorting out some visa problems. The more people Alyson talked to, the more girlfriends/female friends she seemed to uncover, and the more complicated the unfolding drama became.

The young Elizabeth

Elizabeth (not her real name), a young aspiring musician, was also attracted to Elliott around that time, but between Valerie and Chiba, she never got the chance to seriously date him. Regardless of who was there, either Valerie or Chiba, Elliott was totally out of reach, as neither of the two wanted him around any other girls.

"*Valerie and I got into a fight,*" Elizabeth once said to Alyson, who had met her at a concert. "*She would basically call every girl that was his friend prior to her groupie stalkers,*" she said. "*I went off on Chiba once and told her she's not doing Elliott any good locking him up in her birdcage and then I punched a table she was sitting at in the bar and stormed out. It was always drama back then.... I had my own connection with him... and I felt he was dragged away by these succubus bitches, I have never dated him, though.*"[29]

Whatever anyone was willing to say, Alyson was all ears. It may have sounded like pure gossip, but she might get to the truth one day.

Elizabeth continued: "*We were friends for a while, see each other at bars and clubs and always have a hug, a laugh, sometimes go back to his place afterwards, and then he got with some girl [Valerie], and she was possessive and jealous and hated any female, and I lost touch with him. Then he resurfaced a bit when Chiba stole him away. I would leave him voicemails he never got. Mind you, I was seriously in love with him at the time, wrote some songs about him that he really liked, and we had a really nice connection, but it got ugly with me and Chiba and she kept him away. A year later, right before he died, I was at this club, up in the smoking section with my boyfriend. Elliott came up to me with those braids in his hair looking really ragged, and he said this. 'I really miss when I met you at the bar, the times we used to hang out, but I'm trapped in somebody's life and I don't think I'm going to get out.' And then he mumbled something about cops being after him... and that he really hoped to see me again.*

At that point I was like… whatever vibe to him 'cause I was just like, I have a dude now and you've been a real jerk letting that girl control your life."[29]

Alyson was slowly coming to realize just how complicated Elliott's love life must have been at the time. "*There even were a few other girls,*" said Elizabeth. "*Alex, whom he dated for a while, and Michelle, who got really close but got pushed aside when Chiba came around.*"[29]

It seemed to Alyson that when Elliott's drug problem got worse, only Valerie seemed to have stuck around.

Chapter 4: A studio in Malibu

Satellite Park Studio

Nobody knows exactly what happened to Valerie, who was last seen by fans around 2002. She was very present in Elliott's life when he was recording at Satellite Park in Malibu, a studio owned by singer-songwriter Josie Cotton, best known for the early '80s hit singles "Johnny Are You Queer?" and "He Could Be the One."

Some of the songs that were supposed to be included in Elliott's next album, like "True Love," had already been recorded in 2001 with Jon Brion. But, after a fallout between the two men, Elliott now wanted to work with ex-Goldenboy David McConnell, who was Josie's boyfriend at the time.

In April 2001, Elliott drove up to the studio in the middle of the night with his girlfriend Valerie driving another car, both cars full of his belongings, guitars, keyboard, and amps, as well as clothes, books, toys, medications, and various other things. He had decided to stay there for a while. He also had the two-inch reels, the recordings he had been working on with Jon Brion that he wanted to remix and re-work.

That recording period became very dramatic for both men, as Elliott was at the peak of his drug consumption and wasn't sleeping for days, according to a few accounts. But it was also a very creative period; he was recording his next album, *From A Basement on The Hill*, and it was about to become epic.

Plasticsoul

During that time, Elliott may have come close to overdosing on several occasions, voluntarily or not. His drug use and life during that time has always been vague. The Elliott mythology, with the help of David McConnell's input, has taken over. However, it was clearly a time of torment and craziness: Elliott was experimenting with massive amounts of drugs, mixing crack, heroin, different prescription drugs, and alcohol. Each morning he could not believe he was still alive, and he started to think he had become immune to drugs. If there were suicide attempts during that time, they have to be perceived as experiments.

Elliott had lost a lot of weight, and he didn't look very good when musician Plasticsoul met him. When Alyson got the chance to talk to Plasticsoul, who was at the studio to work with David McConnell at the time, he admitted to having almost been scared by the nightmarish vision that Elliott had become. The first encounter between them did not go well. Plasticsoul entered the house and Elliott got really angry, asking him, "*What are you doing here? You shouldn't be there!*"[30]

At this point, this type of scene was not uncommon, as Elliott had become a victim of paranoia. He even tried to start a fight with Plasticsoul, who may have been twice his weight. Fortunately, Valerie was there and was able to intervene and prevent the fight.

Elliott was also hallucinating all the time because of the crack he was taking, and Plasticsoul saw Elliott, visibly under the influence of hallucinatory substances, burn his arm with a cigarette, trying to kill imaginary insects and worms crawling on him.[30] This may have explained the ovoid marks Elliott had on his left arm when he died, a sad memory he was often trying to put behind him by drawing Sharpie tattoos over it in 2003.

Elliott and David were working long hours on the album, recording many outtakes and experimenting with the sound. Sometimes the sessions turned into therapy sessions, as Elliott was doing improvisations, making up new songs, and talking. Talking about his label's executives, his intentions for the new record, his stepfather who had most likely abused him badly. The nature of that abuse has always been unclear. It had even been claimed to be of sexual nature, although nobody ever had any confirmation on this, and stepfather Charlie Welch has always denied it.

Elliott used drugs to stay up all night, several nights and days, and this period was also becoming very emotional for David. Plasticsoul told Alyson that David was calling him on the phone every night, crying and sounding totally lost. Elliott and David had a verbal agreement, but nothing was ever made public of these sessions. They were not included in the posthumous album, despite David's claim that the songs he recorded with Elliott were much better and closer to Elliott's intentions than the ones featured on the released *From a Basement on the Hill.*

"*David cut ties with everyone,*"[31] Josie Cotton told Alyson a few years later. Things turned sour and Elliott suddenly fired David. Plasticsoul never knew exactly what had happened, as David gave him some ridiculous and bizarre reason, a story about Josie stealing some stuff. But Plasticsoul, like Alyson, has always thought this was complete nonsense.

Josie had the chance to share her impression about Elliott during an interview with *Magnet* magazine in 2009:

"*I was in awe of his talent, so it was a little awkward. He recorded in my bedroom for a while. I'd fall asleep and wake up and there'd be Elliott Smith, singing across my sleeping body.*"[32]

When Alyson got the chance to talk to Josie, she said she knew about Elliott's huge substance-abuse problem, and that she had a very skeptical view about his bizarre passing: "*I've never talked about it and no one ever asked, but it's very mysterious the way he died,*"[31] she said to Alyson. It was very clear that Josie had seen the worst of Elliott, and could have easily bought the suicide story; however, she didn't. She even said that Elliott "*did talk about suicide a lot,*" something Alyson had heard before, but explained that Elliott was very upset with his label DreamWorks and was sending them suicide threats. Despite the drugs, the stay-up-all-night-and-all-day to record with David, despite the constant suicide threats to his label, Josie Cotton called Elliott's death "*mysterious.*" And she even knew a few more details:

"I'm sure you know he was horribly abused by his stepfather and was doing an insane amount of drugs. Everyone was terrified he would die of an overdose. I don't know if they ever did an autopsy, but I can't imagine why someone would want to take him out unless it had to do with money. He had someone who handled his finances. I think Elliott was on some kind of allowance."[31]

Alyson told Josie that an autopsy had indeed been done. After sharing a few details regarding the unsolved circumstances of his death, Josie added:

"It's very strange about the stabbing too, I read that it takes a lot of strength to stab yourself in the chest even once… but to do it twice is almost unheard of. So that stands out to me. It kind of makes me want to be a detective!!"[31]

Josie also shared her opinion about Valerie, who stayed with Elliott at Josie's studio:

"Valerie stayed with him at the house the whole time he was with us. She was down to earth and tough-minded. Lively at times. Very Scottish. But she worried about him a lot. A couple of times she threw herself in front of his car when he was on his way to get his drugs down on Venice Beach."[31]

Elliott was obviously not well at that time. He felt a furious paranoia against his label, enhanced by his large drug consumption. In fact, his label had been trying to help him with his drug addiction and had hounded him at the beginning of his drug use. In the end, Elliott might have had very good reasons to develop this paranoia, but his crack use had led him to imagine he was being followed by helicopters and white vans everywhere.

According to a friend, Elliott was so paranoid that he thought the record company had bugged his home, the plants in his lawyer's suite, and the studio where he was cutting his demos. Elliott thought that they had even tapped his phone

Whatever really happened between Elliott and record label DreamWorks, it is difficult to know where the truth ended and the paranoia started.

Valerie had stayed at Elliott's side during his descent into hell, helping him, feeding him, trying to shake him out of his drug craziness. But she knew she was failing. In her attempt to save him from drugs she was trying to isolate Elliott from his friends, who in return were beginning to hate her. There was even a lot of pressure on Elliott to break up with Valerie, who was allegedly even becoming suicidal herself.

Chiba was around at that time too, as she had been following Elliott for years like a groupie and had eventually provided drugs to him, according to some sources who talked to Alyson. It had been her own way of gaining his attention. Elliott may have stayed friends with Chiba because of the drugs, or because of other reasons, but, regardless, the idea of drug use was highly repulsive to Valerie.

The fight

On many occasions, Alyson heard that there had been a confrontation between Valerie and Chiba one night in a club where Elliott used to play. Alyson heard several times that Chiba had been involved in getting illegal drugs for Elliott, and that Valerie hated Chiba because she had introduced him to crack cocaine. Valerie was tired of the situation, and she was tired of seeing Chiba around. This allegedly ended up in a big fight between the two women, making Elliott very uncomfortable as he totally shut down, huddled in a fetal position, terrorized by the two women fighting.

Valerie was about to give up, and for Elliott this situation was just becoming too complex. He was feeling extraordinarily guilty and depressed, and submerged in a load of complicated feelings. He didn't want to hurt anyone, but he could not make a decision. This fight sort of decided his fate, as some of his so-called friends convinced him that Valerie was a crazy and even a dangerous woman.

A confrontation between the two women was also mentioned by Andrew Morgan, an indie artist who had recorded an album at Elliott's studio in 2002. During an episode of his "*spoken words*" that he posted on Soundcloud,[33] Andrew Morgan even talked about an "*alleged knife attack in a cab*," mentioning Valerie as the alleged attacker and simply "*another woman*" (but probably Chiba). Unfortunately, he never agreed to share more details with Alyson, possibly because he didn't know more, but the fact that he had mentioned a fight confirmed what Alyson had heard before. In his version of the story, the attacker was Valerie and, incredibly, there was a knife involved.

Around that time, Valerie fled back home to Europe, while Chiba fully entered Elliott's life just after his detox treatment.

Chapter 5: More mysteries to add to the pile

A few years after Elliott's death, there was even more confusion. There were contradictory stories from many people, declarations about Elliott's mental health, and it wasn't making sense at all. Alyson knew Elliott had been dangerously paranoid during his recording session at the Malibu studio, but he seemed to have been doing much better since his reemergence on the scene after his treatment. Was the paranoia still there? Were people who had seen him during the hard times confused and not aware he had made progress? Elliott had been through a lot in just a few months in late 2002, from an intense drug binge period to a sort of renaissance. But later, it was easy to meld everything into a big mess, confusing everyone.

The Beck-Flaming Lips incident

A notable incident had happened during a Beck/Flaming Lips concert on November 25, 2002. Not only did Alyson hear about this incident, she had actually been at the concert in question herself. She had ended up sitting a few rows behind Elliott, his sister, and Chiba. Just after the Flaming Lips' set, she saw Elliott and Chiba leave their seats, probably to get something to drink but, to her surprise, they never came back.

The story of what really happened during the concert was revealed later on when, on April 26, 2003, Elliott had to cancel a show in California due to an adverse reaction to painkillers he was taking. The following was posted on his website, Sweet Adeline:[34]

"*Elliott suffered a severe injury in November which has progressively gotten worse. He has continued playing shows despite the chronic pain and subsequent treatment issues. He recently had an adverse reaction to a new medication prescribed to him and he is now undergoing [a] different treatment for this injury. At this time, he is hesitant to reschedule or schedule any shows until he feels confident that the treatment is healing him and that it will enable him to play shows. He would like to express his sincere regret for any inconvenience that the canceled show caused anyone. He will reschedule, it's just a matter of when, and that is better assessed with the help of his doctors in the next month or so.*"[34]

It turned out that Elliott had gotten injured at that Flaming Lips concert. In January, two months after the incident, when he was playing a show at the Lit Lounge, Elliott explained to the audience between songs that he had been beaten by cops to the point that "*blood came out of my ear.*"

According to the reports, some security guards, who were actually off-duty police officers, dragged a man out of the concert for refusing to leave a seat that wasn't his. Elliott had approached the guards, who were trying to handcuff the man on the ground, and after refusing to obey them, he had been involved in a bad brawl, getting pepper sprayed and severely beaten.

According to some people, Elliott had just seen a single man being hassled by some guys and had decided to intervene, without knowing they actually were police officers. After being arrested by the LA Sheriff's Department and charged with unlawfully obstructing a peace officer, he and Chiba had spent the night in jail.

The beating had been so serious that months later Elliott was apparently still complaining about it to one of his friends, Ross Harris, who had directed some of his videos including the one for *Miss Misery.* According to Ross, less than two weeks before his death, Elliott was still in severe physical and emotional pain. Ross said that Elliott had had his collarbone broken and was hurting when swallowing, speaking, and breathing.[35]

For Alyson, some of this did not make sense. If Elliott's collarbone had been broken during the police beating, it was highly improbable it was still broken a year later. Since The Smoking Gun article, Alyson had been able to buy the full autopsy report, done by Dr. Scheinen, from the coroner, and there was nothing about a broken collarbone in it. Since Dr. Scheinin had done a very detailed examination, she probably would have noticed a broken bone. Alyson had no way to know if X-rays had been taken during the autopsy, but X-rays may have been done to determine the depth and the direction of the stab wounds. In that case, a fracture would have been noticed. Plus, a fracture experienced on November 25, 2002 would have healed by October 2003, and it was hard to believe that Elliott could have still suffered from a broken collarbone almost a year later.

The biggest mystery was that Alyson had seen Elliott play on January 12, 2003, a month and a half after the incident at the Flaming Lips concert, and he probably could not have played guitar with a broken collarbone. Alyson even had asked a doctor:

"*Fractures in general are painful and clavicle fractures are very painful, there would be a sagging of the arm involved (down & forward), lifting the arm would have been difficult and excruciating, not to mention the bruising and swelling. Left or right side is pretty much irrelevant because I'm not sure he'd be able to play but if somehow he did, he would have run the risk of shifting the bones ends enough to damage nerves and blood vessels that could result in permanent impairment.*"[36]

What is known is that Elliott had suffered from the beating for a long time, was haunted by the incident during the last months of his life, and was even worried about going to jail because of it. How much of it still haunted him just before his death was a mystery.

SPIN Magazine

A year after Elliott's death, Jennifer Chiba certainly did not disappear from the scene. While her "*subsequent refusal to speak with detectives*" was still looming in the police report, she had not lost any time with the press. The fans received new pieces of information from a long article written by Liam Gowing published in December 2004 by *SPIN* magazine.[37]

Each time she visited the message board, Alyson saw that fans had split into two camps, the "*murder theorists,*" or at least the ones who were seriously questioning Elliott's "*suicide,*" and the ones who had no doubt he had killed himself. Actually, there was another camp, the forever neutral people who never stopped repeating we "*will never know what happened*" and we "*should just focus on the music.*" Eighteen years later, things are pretty much still the same.

"Mr. Misery,"[37] Liam Gowing's piece for *SPIN*, triggered a series of reactions, and at one point even Elliott Smith's sister Ashley registered on the fan message board to share her take on the story. Gowing, who had first written his piece for the *LA Weekly* but had been rejected by the paper because it was too long, was quite proud of his research. As he shared with Alyson during a phone conversation a few years later, he thought he had done a very comprehensive investigation with many interviews, including family members and people who had never talked to anyone before as well as Jennifer Chiba, who had not spoken since her declaration to the press.

A few months before the publication of the article, Chiba shared with Deanna that "*a friend was about to write an article about me with good and bad things.*"[4] Alyson has always thought this friend was Liam Gowing. Nobody else interviewed Chiba at that time, and she had declined being interviewed by Christine Pelisek of the *LA Weekly*.

Gowing declared to Alyson that he and Chiba were not really friends: "*As for my relationship with Jennifer Chiba, she went from a friendly acquaintance I knew through Elliott to a very heavily scrutinized interview subject during the writing of the SPIN article.*"[38]

Nevertheless, the two had certainly been connected on social media for some time. Plus, years later, Alyson saw photos of Gowing attending a gathering to celebrate Elliott's life, organized by Chiba and held at her home in October 2004, just a few months before the release of his *SPIN* article in December 2004.

There was no denying that the two had some sort of relationship.

On the phone with Alyson, Gowing was very eager to defend his article and Chiba, and he sounded like someone who seemed to be convinced that Elliott had indeed committed suicide. He said he had met two different kinds of people, those who knew Chiba in 2000 and had only bad things to say about her, and those who knew the couple at the end of Elliott's life and had positive things to say about her sweet and loving nature, and that she was, of course, incapable of murder.

This was certainly Alyson's experience, although she had encountered more individuals from the first group. Gowing thought it was more reasonable to believe the second crowd because the first group hadn't had any contact with Elliott and Chiba at the end, so they did not have a fair opinion about their relationship.

Gowing said he had interviewed plenty of people: Valerie Deerin, Joanna Bolme, Elliott's stepmother Marta Greenwald, Elliott's stepfather Charlie Welch, Elliott's sister Ashley, Rob Schnapft (one of Elliott's producers)… at least this is what he claimed to Alyson on the phone: "*I can tell you I had more than 30 on- and off-record sources.*"[38]

However, not all of those interviews showed up in his article, and in particular there was no mention of Valerie who had, according to Gowing, declined to be quoted.

The story according to Gowing was that Valerie was a jealous woman who had blamed Elliott's drug use on Chiba, when in reality Elliott had tried drugs before. And Valerie had yelled at Chiba and even attacked her. Chiba had been the good nurturing girlfriend in the story, and Elliott, who had cleaned up right before his death, had been struggling with withdrawal until the end.

Gowing, who also knew about the beating by the police at the Beck-Flaming Lips concert, insisted that Elliott was still in great pain at the end and even had a sharp pain over his heart. He even suggested to Alyson that Elliott may have stabbed himself in that area in an attempt to kill this pain. To Alyson, this was a very strange declaration. Plus, there was a paradox to this statement. If the pain had been coming from a badly healed broken bone (as Ross Harris had suggested), how could Elliott have found the strength (and the courage) to stab himself twice? Stabbing yourself requires great strength. His power would have been somewhat incapacitated because of the possible broken bone. The pain would certainly also have been unbearable.

A neighbor who had befriended Elliott when he was living in the Disney Cottages before he moved in with Chiba had also told Alyson that "*Elliott was such a wuss!*"[39] For her, it was very difficult to imagine that this gentle, needy friend could have done this terribly violent thing to himself. "*He was shy and peaceful, he let people lead.*"[39] And this echoed what photographer Autumn de Wilde had once declared to NME: "*He was always such a chicken about getting hurt!*"[40]

On top of the physical pain, Gowing also mentioned the child molestation allegation, saying that the memories of child abuse had resurfaced because of a family Thanksgiving dinner with stepfather Charlie Welch. In sum, Gowing was claiming that Elliott had a lot he was dealing with in October 2003: the excruciating pain above the heart, the previously repressed child molestation memories, his recurrent depression, the rehab treatment. While his article both blamed the drug intake and the drug withdrawal, Gowing claimed that Elliott had so much on his plate that there was no doubt he had committed suicide.

Gowing said that, as a matter of fact, Dr. Scheinin had actually told Gowing that suicide was her "*gut feeling.*" When Alyson spoke to Gowing, he said: "*She told me, 'My gut feeling is that it was actually a suicide,' but explained that it was her job to pick up on anything—even the slightest detail—that might be useful to the police if they decided the homicide angle was worth pursuing.*"[38]

At the time of the conversation, Alyson had not talked to Dr. Scheinin yet. She had just exchanged an email with her, and the doctor had answered with a very neutral declaration:

"*In the Smith case, there were certain things—both anatomic findings and circumstances—that were suggestive of suicidal death and pointed down that road, while there were other things that were less consistently associated with suicide and suggested the possibility of homicide. There was nothing that tipped the scales one way or other.*"[41]

Thus, we were very far from "*the gut feeling it was a suicide,*" Gowing claimed Dr. Scheinin had said to him. Plus, do doctors really talk about "*gut feelings*"? To Alyson, this sounded almost unprofessional.

Gowing also said he had talked to the police and had even interviewed David Campbell, the official spokesman at the coroner's office, who had "*downplayed the possibility of Elliott's death being a homicide,*" and had even justified Chiba's removal of the knife: "'*If you saw someone who was still alive and they have a knife in their chest, what would you do? The first thing you'd want to do is to stop the bleeding and you can't do that if the knife is still there.*'"[38]

You had to wonder whether Campbell knew about Chiba's first-aid training.

Alyson learned later, from someone who had had a phone conversation with Campbell, that he had not been involved with any of the investigative process in Elliott's case, including the psychological assessment. Instead, he had only worked in the capacity of media spokesperson. Campbell had immediately brought up to this person that the LA Coroner's case was inconclusive and could only be closed pending further evidence.

So, no matter how Gowing had been framing Campbell's answer, it had to be speculative.

Finally, Gowing also insisted that the family had full interest in keeping the investigation open, even pushing for the theory of murder. To him, it was the best way to avoid the child abuse story from resurfacing in plain light. Gowing told Alyson several times that Marta wanted Elliott's death to be ruled a murder, although the family had refused to be interviewed for the article.

Gowing seemed to have had it all figured out: The family had been avoiding the truth (a suicide) because of a bad skeleton in their closet, and Chiba had been Elliott's patient companion, good to him, caring for him during his last days, and extremely misjudged by plenty of people. And there was no doubt she had been telling the truth because she had admitted embarrassing, illegal, and professionally ruinous behavior in the process, like her own past drug use and depression issues. Gowing even had an explanation for each one of her actions and downplayed every oddity of the case. Chiba's raid to the studio in the middle of the night? It was "*to make sure Elliott's songs were not stolen, to protect his music.*" Her removal of the knife? It was because "*she did not necessarily know about knives.*" The possible defense wounds? Gowing claimed that Scheinin had told him that "*they were actually 'very small,'*" and that the one on the hand was "'*a little poke—could have come from handling the knife the wrong way.*'"[38]

Then there was even something bizarre in Gowing's article, something that unfortunately came to Alyson's mind after talking to Gowing, so she never got the chance to ask him about it. Gowing reported a conversation between Dr. Stanton, Elliott's new psychiatrist, and Elliott's father, Gary Smith:

"*In the course of a conversation with Dr. Stanton, a suspicious Gary Smith [also a psychiatrist] asked the doctor if she thought Chiba was capable of murdering his son. Without hesitation, Dr. Stanton told him, 'No.'*"[37]

Psychiatrists never talk about their patients, so Stanton couldn't have reported this to Gowing, and Gowing had certainly not talked to Gary Smith as he had written in an email: "*As for the Smith/Welch family, they first 'declined to be interviewed,' then told other contacts not to speak to me based on the questions I'd been asking.*"[38]

So how could Gowing have known about this conversation between Stanton and Gary Smith? This may have come from Chiba herself, and if so, it was misleading.

A bit later, Gowing revealed two things: First, the family threatened to sue *SPIN* for libel if they published the article, although they never pursued the lawsuit. Second, Gowing had had a personal experience with suicide since his roommate had killed himself in 2001, just before New Year's Eve, and Gowing had found the body on the floor when returning home. For Alyson it was an important point, as it very probably had been a traumatic experience which could certainly have affected his judgment, as if he thought he had walked in Chiba's shoes. Saying he had put a spin on the story would have been almost too no-pun-intended.

Searching for Elliott Smith

Gowing's article was the first wave of impunity, but more media projects were about to follow, such as Gil Reyes's documentary *Searching for Elliott Smith* in 2009.[42] In the documentary, Chiba gave a long and tearful interview, talking about the events of that tragic day, looking as raw and miserable as you can imagine.

The documentary, which had been described at the time as a vehicle to vindicate Jennifer Chiba,[43] had obviously not been approved by the estate and didn't feature a single interview of a family member, who had already been burnt by Gowing's previous reportage.

Reyes had definitively opted for the depressed side of the tortured songwriter, while trying to present at the same time a complete vindication of Chiba in the last part of *Searching for Elliott Smith,* even attempting to justify the findings of the autopsy report in Chiba's favor.

According to the documentary, the "*possible defensive*" cuts were explained by Elliott's cutting behavior, rehashing the same story that Chiba had already told Gowing: Shortly before Elliott's death, Chiba had gone to see a movie (*Lost in Translation*) and had found Elliott lying in bed with his arm bleeding when she returned home.

This story had already been reinforced by Robin Peringer, also very present in the documentary, and always eager to take Chiba's defense. He had already declared to Gowing that Elliott had "*three tremendous knife wounds on his left arm… deep, like he had to go across a couple of times or have the sharpest, biggest knife to do it.*"[37] In the movie, Robin also justified Chiba's removal of the knife.

In the documentary there was even a strange declaration by Steve Hanft, a film/video director who had directed the 1998 fiction short *Strange Parallel,* featuring Elliott. You could watch Hanft suggesting that Elliott was wearing leather wrist bands to "*cover something.*"[42] The problem is that the autopsy report had not revealed any tremendous cuts, or any cuts as a matter of fact, on Elliott's arms and wrists, besides the small cut on his upper right arm, and it stated that there were no fresh or old scars on his wrists. Reyes and Hanft clearly had never bothered to check such "*details*" before insinuating that the possible defense wounds could have been due to self-harm.

A long-time therapist at Cedars-Sinai who talked to Alyson made an interesting remark:

"*People who cut themselves don't do it with a kitchen knife, they use a razor. So for Robin to say Elliott took the biggest knife was a way to dramatize it, and to possibly make the connection with the final act. A kitchen knife doesn't sound like the behavior of people who are self-cutters.*"[17]

"*Plus,*" added the therapist, "*people who cut themselves don't commit suicide; these are two completely different behaviors. This [cutting] is serving their agenda; they over-dramatize to serve their story.*"[17]

As for the removal of the knife, Reyes would even claim later that during a phone conversation with the editor of the music website RockNYC: "*Whether or not Jennifer Chiba knew it would harm or even kill Elliott to remove the knife from his chest, she still did not do anything wrong.*"[44]

Searching for Elliott Smith was screened at various film festivals. Alyson attended one of them, but she got especially interested when she heard that the movie would be followed by a Q&A with Reyes, Goldenboy's Shon Sullivan, and Jennifer Chiba. Chiba was introduced as one of the founding members of the Warlocks, a family therapist, and Elliott's fiancée, and it was even announced that she was writing a memoir about her time with Elliott. However, many years later, nothing of this sort has ever surfaced.

Chiba was there for the questions, what else is a Q&A for? But Alyson seemed to be the only one wanting to ask relevant questions. People were sitting in front of Chiba, the last person who had seen Elliott alive, the person who had removed the knife from his chest, and they were asking about her favorite song.

Questions were fusing in Alyson's head, but she couldn't ask all of them. Why were there no fingerprints on the knife? With two stab wounds, shouldn't the knife handle have been covered with blood and able to retain recordable fingerprints? Had the blood been wiped out from the handle? Had the handle been washed? How long had they been fighting? What time did the police come to the house? These thoughts were way too forensic-precise and bold, but Alyson finally decided to ask two questions, braving the judgmental looks of the few people in the room: Why had Chiba removed the knife? And how was she planning to help the police close the case? Alyson didn't expect too much from her questions, but she tried anyway, and she effectively didn't get very much. Chiba answered that she "*didn't know*" about the consequences of removing the knife, just as she had said in the movie. As for the second question, she was positive she had talked to the police, and that she had told them her story over and over.

There was another important point discussed at length during the Q&A, Elliott's mental health. "*His girlfriend, Jennifer [Chiba], called me [that] last week [of Elliott's life] and asked if I'd like to come to help mix and finish his album,*" recording engineer Larry Crane had written on his message board. "*It seems surreal that he would call me to finish an album and then a week later kill himself. I talked to Jennifer this morning, who was obviously shattered and in tears, and she said, 'I don't understand, he was so healthy.'"*[45]

So why had Chiba been insisting so much on Elliott's paranoia during this Q&A? The commentator always has the last word and, year after year, the story was changing and evolving. We were going from a "*I don't understand he was so healthy*" declaration made at the spur of the moment to a "*he was talking about killing himself constantly,*" or "*he was seriously mentally ill,*" or "*he was flaky and self-centered,*"[46] which were some of the declarations made by Chiba at this same Q&A. Alyson was seeing history being rewritten in front of her eyes and people were acquiescing to it without blinking.

It was even reported to Alyson that Chiba had declared she had "*regretted not allowing Elliott to write a will because a lawsuit would have never happened.*" She was now saying that she had refused to let him write a will because "*it would have given him more of a license to kill himself.*"[46]

Alyson found this statement quite ridiculous on many levels. First, Elliott was only 34 and had just been through a tough rehab treatment in an effort to turn his life away from drugs and addiction—he was clean the day he died—so it was difficult to think that a will would have been in his mind. Second, her statement would have meant that Elliott had become a dependent and obedient childlike person who would have needed Chiba's approval to write a will. This was not the first time she displayed this condescending attitude. Chiba had told a member of Elliott's close family she felt guilty she had left the knife out that tragic day… as if she had to keep sharpened objects out of Elliott's reach as if he had been a toddler?

As Alyson was about to discover, there was more to the story, as well as many variations of it, which was making the truth harder and harder to decipher.

Chapter 6: An interview with Dr. Scheinin, and other forensic experts

Dr. Lisa Scheinin

In the middle of 2011, Alyson decided to talk to Dr. Scheinin, who had performed Elliott's autopsy about seven years earlier. If Liam Gowing, the author of the 2004 *SPIN* article, had already interviewed her, Alyson wanted to ask her own questions. After a short introduction, Dr. Scheinin, who said later she had never talked to Elliott's family, wanted to know more about Alyson. Was she related to Elliott? Was she just a friend? Since the coroner was charging the copious amount of $300.60 per hour, Alyson was ready to get to the essentials, and she talked with her for about 20 minutes.

Throughout the interview, Dr. Scheinin stayed very neutral, not leaning one way or the other toward suicide or homicide, although she would repeat several times that the absence of hesitation wounds was very unusual. When asked whether the directions of the wounds was more consistent with suicide or murder, she replied, "*Either way, there is no way to tell.*"[47]

When asked about the depth of wound #2—which didn't necessarily occur after wound #1, as there was no way to know the order of the wounds—Dr. Scheinin said she was not too surprised by its depth (between 5-7 inches), since "*the hardest part is to cut the skin, but once it's done, there is little resistance.*"[47] She added that both wounds were potentially fatal because they had penetrated the chest cavity, although only wound #2 had penetrated the heart.

Dr. Scheinin became guarded when Alyson mentioned possible "*defensive*" wounds, as if she didn't seem very eager to confirm that these wounds were, indeed, of a defensive nature. In the autopsy report, Dr. Scheinin had described "*a small slight laceration*" on "*the palm of the left and right hand*" and "*another slight laceration under the upper right arm as well.*"[48]

Next, Alyson asked about the nature of the wounds. Without any hesitation, Dr. Scheinin confirmed that the cuts were fresh and definitively not compatible with self-mutilation. "*It's not self-cutting,*"[47] said Dr. Scheinin, insisting that these wounds did not show the pattern of self-mutilation. They were not consistent with hesitation wounds either. Nevertheless, she was not excluding some eventual cutting by accident, or the possibility that Elliott could have mishandled the knife just before the stabbing. Alyson was satisfied by this response, as it dismantled the little charade orchestrated by Jennifer Chiba and Robin Peringer and their attempt to turn the wounds into self-harm.

Dr. Scheinin also confirmed there were absolutely no traces of the "*three really tremendous knife wounds on his left arm*"[37] described by Peringer in *SPIN* magazine, no traces of the alleged self-inflicted cuts mentioned in Reyes's movie, the ones described by Chiba when she came back from seeing the movie *Lost in Translation*. Since that movie had been released on October 3, 2003, about two weeks before Elliott's death, scars of those "*tremendous cuts*" should still have been visible. Even if Robin had exaggerated, it usually takes several months for cuts, even superficial ones, to heal completely.

Scheinin had also noted well-healed pale scars in the autopsy report and described ovoid marks on Elliott's arm. They had been present since at least 2002, even visible on some concert photos, and Alyson still had in mind the story that musician Plasticsoul had told her—that while under the influence of hallucinatory drugs, Elliott had burned himself with a cigarette, trying to chase away insects and worms crawling on his arm. While she was most likely unaware of this story, these marks made Dr. Scheinin think that Elliott had probably been harming himself, but "*not in a typical or classical cutter way*."[47]

Dr. Scheinin also reconfirmed to Alyson that Elliott had no scars on his wrists, and no track marks, as you could read in the autopsy, and this refuted all the rumors of Elliott collapsing in the bathroom of a Silverlake bar with a needle in his arm.

If Dr. Scheinin's interview did not bring the answers Alyson was looking for, it had nevertheless cleared up a few things. The possible defense wounds were fresh and not compatible with self-mutilation or hesitation marks. There were no traces of the wounds on his arm described by Peringer or Chiba. And Elliott's case had several atypical aspects of suicide by stabbing, such as no hesitation marks and stabbing through the clothing, as well as the fact that suicide by stabbing was considered a rare form of suicide in the first place.

While Dr. Scheinin affirmed suicide in this case was not impossible, as some people "*go against the grain*,"[47] she didn't recall talking about a "*gut feeling*" leaning toward suicide, as Gowing had claimed. During the interview, Dr. Scheinin gave the impression of a woman who had avoided displaying any personal emotions, so she certainly didn't look like the kind of person to talk about gut feelings. However, Dr. Scheinin seemed to express a bit of nervousness toward the end of her discussion with Alyson, saying, "*That was easy*,"[47] as if it was sort of a relief when Alyson ended the interview.

Don't mess with forensic science

The fact that suicide by stabbing was such a rare and difficult thing to do had been in Alyson's mind since the beginning, especially after reading quotes like this one from Lanny Berman, the director of the American Association of Suicidology: "*Suicide by stabbing is very rare, and it's particularly rare for someone to stab themselves in the torso*."[49] The statistics for the year 2005 were very telling: Out of the 32,637 people who had committed suicide in the United States, only 590 had done so "*by cutting or piercing, and of those deaths, most were slashing or cutting to the wrists and, to a lesser degree, the throat.*"[49] So the thorax was clearly not the first choice for these types of suicides.

In the years following the interview with Dr. Scheinin, Alyson continued to consult a lot of forensic literature and even sent the autopsy report to a few forensic experts. She surprisingly found out that many people were happy to comment on the autopsy report, free of charge, whereas the LA Coroner had charged her to talk with them.

Kaitlyn (not her real name), a forensic behavioral psychologist with a BA in cognitive psychology who had worked on enough homicide cases to be rather adept at autopsy interpretation, became interested in Elliott's case. She herself contacted Alyson, and had some clever comments to make, particularly regarding the general lack of people's involvement in the investigation:

"*People are surprisingly trepidatious about involving themselves in homicide investigations, not just because they don't want to be caught in the middle of it all, but because they often genuinely question their own judgment about whether something they know is relevant to an investigation. Most people are under the mistaken belief that if they know something, there are people out there who know more and will come forward, or that there is enough physical evidence to indicate the true nature of what happened, and they really don't want to be responsible for implicating someone they aren't sure is guilty.*"[50] Alyson had experienced this over and over, so this made complete sense.

"*We see this way more than I care to mention,*" she added. "*It's amazing how most people question their own judgment about what they see, hear, or experience when it comes to potentially implicating someone in violent crime. And the worse the crime, the more likely a person is to question their own judgment about what they know. No one wants to believe that someone they knew, maybe even befriended, is capable of murder—even if they didn't like the person. It hits too close to home. So, they absolve themselves of the responsibility of speaking to investigators directly by assuming that if what they suspect is true, it will surely come out another way. Interestingly, the more they feel justified in their assessment or suspicions, the more they will vocalize it with their peers.*

So, in that sense, hearsay and gossip is helpful early in the investigation if the investigator can get an interview with the person(s) vocalizing concerns. But then you have to have the skills to interview in such a way as to garner as much information without causing anxiety in the interviewee, [or] else you won't effectively get the information you need."[50]

Kaitlyn also knew exactly what an open case meant regarding the impossibility to obtain more information from the police:

"*We will likely never know what information the case files contain unless someone is ever held responsible for Smith's death. I don't see that happening, but perhaps one day the case files will be available under the FOIA (though the chances of that, if it was ever investigated as a potential homicide, are very low).*"[50]

After reviewing the autopsy, Kaitlyn had a lot more to say: "*First, he was stabbed through his clothing. Whenever someone chooses to either shoot or stab him or herself in the heart, he or she pretty much always does it with direct skin contact to the weapon used. There is a psychological need to ensure success in the endeavor which dictates this. No one who is truly intending to kill themselves seems willing to take a chance of failure because 'clothing got in the way.' It's irrational, sure, but it's a consistent element we always see in such suicidal self-injury methods.*

"*Second, he was stabbed twice, one injury being at a depth of two inches, the second being 7 inches. I've personally never heard of this kind of thing, really, because the amount of effort, energy, and pain involved in pulling the knife back out and then doing a second self-inflicted stab is too much for someone who has sustained what is already a probable fatal injury to the heart (stab wound #1).*

"*Third, the stab wounds are very close to each other, and run in the same directions, at very similar angles. Even if one were to self-administer a second stab wound, the close proximity and similar entry direction and angle would not likely occur as it did in this case, because of the debilitating nature of wound #1. But if someone were to stab another person in rapid succession, you would be much more likely to see this type of wound pattern and presentation.*

"*Fourth, he had superficial sharp force injury on both his right forearm and the base of his left thumb. Though not characteristic of OBVIOUS defense wounds, these wounds are more likely due to a 'nicking' type of injury, created during the process of forcefully removing the knife from the chest cavity. If Smith was being stabbed and had his hand and arm in front of him, the removal of the knife from the chest would require force, and the natural 'arching' motion of such an endeavor could easily cause secondary 'nicking' wounds on the victim's arms. I've seen this before. But if the wounds were self-inflicted, I cannot come up with an explanation for what would cause them.*[50]

"*There are enough uncharacteristic elements of this 'suicide' for me to be more willing to consider this a potential homicide. Although, in order to truly ascertain what happened, I'd need to have much more information at my disposal (i.e. diagrams of the rooms, more information about Chiba—like her physical stats, where she claimed each to be during the event, Elliott's handedness, and so forth). I would definitely want to stage physical reenactments of the potential scenarios because, really, when you have unexplained injuries that is really the only way one can ascertain their nature. The absence of evidentiary information makes me hesitant to say with any certainty what happened, but I CAN tell you that, based on the information I do have at hand, my personal impression would be that suicide is highly questionable.*[50]

"*As for the logistics of using such a knife in the manner it was allegedly used, I think it wouldn't be terribly difficult for a grown man to use for suicide (since his axis of gravity and upper body strength would facilitate it) but, again, it's such an odd way of going about it.*"[50]

Alyson had read that suicide by stabbing in the chest required a lot of force, and that some of the rare people capable of doing it sometimes needed to run against a wall to force the knife to penetrate the chest. If his act had been as compulsive as it had been suggested, it was difficult to imagine Elliott could have followed through a second time.

"*Why not simply slash the wrists vertically?*" continued Kaitlyn, "*Or overdose, if (as we know he was) you are a drug user? After all, the therapeutic index of heroin is 3 (or 1:3), which means that even for the most seasoned user, it only takes three times the amount required for an AVERAGE individual of 160lbs. (which is the medical industry dosing norm) to feel the effects of the drug to kill ANYONE of a similar size. That's what makes heroin so dangerous because building up a tolerance with regular use will take a user dangerously close to the overdose threshold. In terms of intentionally killing oneself, it's the perfect method—especially for a known user because they are very keen on dosing matters.*"[50]

As a forensic behavioral psychologist, Kaitlyn also had important insight regarding the situation. Elliott had allegedly stabbed himself in front of Chiba. Although she had claimed to be in the bathroom at the moment of the stabbing, she was still there and she had allegedly seen Elliott with the knife in his chest when she exited the bathroom, a very traumatic experience for her without any doubt.

"*If I had to speculate on the choice of method,*" continued Kaitlyn, "*under the presumption that it WAS, in fact, suicide (though I'm not at all convinced), I could tell you that to kill oneself in such a manner in front of someone you purportedly care about is a very passive-aggressive act (in the most literal sense, because although the act itself is self-harming, the clear intention is to inflict maximum psychological damage on the witness). If he DID kill himself, Elliott did it intending to hurt Chiba—either psychologically, or with the understanding that such an odd event would cast suspicion on her. We generally see the former intent most often with males shooting themselves in the head with higher-caliber weapons in front of estranged love interests.*"[50]

Kaitlyn was exceptionally helpful and very precise in her vocabulary, and this last point ("*if Elliott did it intending to hurt Chiba*") had never been discussed elsewhere. This aggressive nature of an act toward a loved one sounded very out of character for Elliott.

Alyson could not have thanked Kaitlyn enough for her very precise analysis of the details of the autopsy. Kaitlyn said that she would continue the conversation if Alyson had any other concerns.

Besides Dr. Scheinin, Kaitlyn had been one of the first experts to give an informed opinion and that carried great significance. Alyson was determined to get more opinions from experts and managed to contact one of the co-authors of an article published in *Forensic Science International* ("Homicidal and suicidal sharp force fatalities: Autopsy parameters in relation to the manner of death"[51]). He simply was the perfect person to evaluate the case, as his article discussed the features that differentiate self-stabbings from homicidal stabbings. He kindly agreed to review the autopsy report and speak with Alyson, warning her that "*interpretation of the autopsy findings is difficult, as resuscitation attempts and thoracic surgery added iatrogenic injuries.*"[52] He answered in the form of an extensive list:

"*Concerning the manner of death, some findings are more in favor of homicide: 1) Sharp wound in the thorax associated with underlying bone injury. 2) Clothing defects in the chest area where are located the two lethal sharp force wounds. 3) Absence of hesitation wounds in the vicinity of the two lethal thoracic injuries. 4) Two incised wounds on the right arm and left hand, raising the possibility of defense wounds. 5) The axis of the two lethal wounds is near the vertical.*

"*Other elements may point to suicide:* 1) *All the sharp wounds found may be self-inflicted.* 2) *No clothing defect in front of the incised wound of the right arm.*"[52]

When he learned that Elliott was wearing a T-shirt, a piece of clothing with short sleeves, he dismissed this last point. He explained that someone having committed suicide this way would have probably not cut his sleeve, whereas a murderer would have probably stabbed through the sleeve of the shirt:

"*I did not take into account a short-sleeve shirt worn by the victim at the time of death. In the case of suicide, we can expect no clothing defect in front of the skin incised wound, but this finding is not constant. No clothing defect of a long-sleeve shirt would be more relevant [for a suicide].*"[52]

He also added the following regarding the small cut on Elliott's upper right arm:

"*Concerning this injury, its site is not typical for defense injuries. Moreover, the edges of the wound are surrounded by a small margin of contusion. This may raise the question about the nature of this wound. Is it a true sharp force injury? The possibility of injury secondary to blunt trauma is not excluded. So, finally, I am sharing the opinion of the forensic pathologist who carried out the autopsy. Manner of death is undetermined, although autopsy findings are more in favor of homicide.*"[52]

The co-author of the forensic article had raised a very important point, the presence of "*underlying bone injury.*" This was absolutely not stressed in other analyses, that Elliott's sternum had effectively been injured as well as his ribs and cartilage.

Alyson reached out to another expert, a renowned authority in the forensic world who had been the president of the American Academy of Forensic Science, the president of the American College of Legal Medicine, and the head of the board of trustees of the American Board of Legal Medicine. Because of his status, Alyson didn't expect an answer, but he kindly sent one. Even though he didn't go into many details like the other experts, probably because he knew he couldn't help much, his answer was nevertheless very telling:

"*I regret that I am not able to be of any assistance to you in this matter. I have no authority or means to become involved. Very suspicious case that needed to be aggressively investigated. It would be a very bizarre suicide in my experience.*"[53]

For Alyson, it was very important to realize that all these people were in agreement, and without being able to close the case because of the lack of other information—they only had the 27 pages of the autopsy report to review, whereas autopsy reports generally come with plenty of other documents that in this case were still in the police's possession—they all had agreed that the findings of the autopsy were leading to the same conclusion: it was a very suspicious case.

Fastidious but necessary work

Alyson tried to compile additional information on all the oddities of the case. It was a tedious task, but not too difficult. Suicides by stabbing were rare, but you could find data. The first thing to note was that most stabbing deaths were due to homicides,[54] and the literature affirms that they represent less than 2% of all suicides. According to an article by William A. Cox, M.D., Forensic Pathologist and Neuropathologist: "*A fundamental approach you may want to use is to consider all deaths as the result of incised and or stab wounds as homicides until proven otherwise.*"[55]

Among 700 cutting and stabbing fatalities studied in his article (and this also included death by cutting and not stabbing), 80% were due to homicide, 18% to suicide, and 2% to accident. As mentioned in previous research, the majority of them were not done in the thoracic cage but rather in the abdomen or the throat: "*One of the most common sites for self-inflicted incised wounds is the neck.*"[55]

If it was difficult to find numbers reporting how many people had committed suicide shortly after a fight, in comparison, murders following a domestic dispute were unfortunately too common, and contrary to common opinion, men were not always the perpetrators. In a 2010 study published by the CDC, it states: "*In the last 12 months more men than women were victims of intimate partner physical violence and over 40% of severe physical violence was directed at men.*"[56]

An article by B. H. Hoff established that "*Some 21.6% of the male victims in [a] 2001 survey were threatened with a knife, contrasted to 12.7% of the women.*"[57] Thus, according to this study, more women than men had been ready to use a knife in the case of domestic violence.

Then there was another thing to consider, the time and the circumstances of the incident. According to a study by R.D. Start, C.M. Milroy, and M.A. Green, "*Most of the self-inflicted stabbings (69%) occurred at night or in the early hours of the morning.*"[58] Also very few self-stabbings had been actually witnessed by someone, "*only [7% of] cases.*"[58] Elliott had allegedly stabbed himself around noon, in the presence of someone.

Then there were all the other forensic oddities and, in particular, the location and number of wounds, particularly the two deep wounds in the chest. Although several articles—for example "Suicide by self-stabbing"[58] by R.D. Start, C.M. Milroy, and M.A. Green and "Homicidal and suicidal sharp force fatalities: Autopsy parameters in relation to the manner of death"[51] by Christophe Brunel, Christophe Fermanian, Michel Durigon, and Geoffroy Lorin de la Grandmaison indicated that most suicides by stabbing had a single wound, and isolated cut wounds were predominantly observed in suicides. The possibility of several wounds was nevertheless possible since the number of cuts was generally not a good predictive factor relative to the manner of death. However, many studies[51,59] showed that the thorax was the most targeted region for homicide victims, and the upper limbs for suicide victims.[59] Many studies also indicated that, in the case of suicide, self-inflicted cut wounds were usually found in the neck or wrists.[54, 55, 60]

Another study, published in 2016 in *Trauma Monthly*,[185] attempted to assess the mortality and morbidity of self-inflicted versus assault-induced stab wounds. The authors stated that "*most self-inflicted stab wounds were non-lethal abdominal and retroperitoneal injuries.*"[185] Those researchers found an overall mortality rate for assault-induced stab wounds of 27.3%, whereas, astonishingly at least to Alyson, the mortality rate for self-inflicted stab wounds was equal to zero. The authors explained this difference by the greater numbers of wounds and organs injured in the case of assault-induced stab wounds, and also by the greater velocity of stabbing during assaults. They also commented that a significant proportion of attempted suicides by self-stabbing were "*the result of impulsive actions,*" and that often "*no mortality*"[185] was found in such cases. Additionally, in 50% of the self-inflicted-wounds, patients were drunk. Psychosis was also associated with such self-harm, the three patients with psychotic illness in the study had "*experienced mortality and morbidity no different from other self-inflicted stab wound patients.*"[185] The authors even considered a "*harakiri wound, a transverse cut of the abdomen and a traditional method of suicide in Japan.*" Because of its exclusivity to Japan, they considered it irrelevant elsewhere. Even though the study was relatively small, it was interesting to note that none of the people who presented self-inflicted wounds had wounds in the chest.[185]

The direction of the stabbing was also something to consider. In Elliott's case, both stabs were "*slightly downward.*" A vertical orientation of any chest wounds would have strongly suggested homicide, not a "*slightly downward*" one.[51]

Then there were the bone injuries, which were extremely important to consider. According to the autopsy report, stab wound #1 had "*entered the chest cavity through the 5th intercostal space,*" and stab wound #2 had "*perforated the left edge of the sternum.*"[48] According to one the largest studies conducted by Brunal et al.,[51] which included 118 sharp force fatalities, "*The presence of bone or cartilage wounds was predictive of a homicide and their absence was predictive of a suicide,*" as there was "*a higher likelihood of a homicide if bone or cartilage wounds were present and a higher likelihood of a suicide if these wounds were absent.*" The numbers could not have been more significant: "*In homicides, bone or cartilage wounds were present in 52 cases (74.3%), absent in 17 cases (24.3%) and not reported in 1 case (1.4%). In suicides, bone or cartilage wounds were present in 7 cases (14.6%) and absent in*

41 cases (85.4%). Bone or cartilage wounds were thus found to be a significant predictive factor relative to the manner of death (P < 0.0001)."[51]

In this same study the authors had written that "*in order to explain the lower frequency of bone or cartilage wounds in suicides, one can easily imagine that suicide victims avoided solid anatomical structures, such as ribs and the sternum. In contrast, the frequency of bone or cartilage wounds in homicides may be high because assailants ignore the presence of these solid structures.*"

This indicated that Elliott's perforated sternum was pointing to homicide, as previously reported by one of the experts consulted.

Another comparative study of 174 homicidal and 105 suicidal sharp force deaths conducted in the Stockholm area by Thore Karlsson and published in *Forensic Science International*[61] introduced another interesting detail: "*Of the suicide victims, 23 (22%) had suffered stab wounds that penetrated the thoracic wall. Eight stab wounds (35%) had injured ribs. In two cases (9%), the sternal bone had been transected; both these victims were males and both suffered from severe mental illness.*"[61] In other words, the suicide victims (only 2 cases) who had managed to injure their sternum had severe mental illness.

In a similar manner, another study in the *Journal of Emergencies, Trauma, and Shock* stated that the large majority (98%) of patients who had attempted suicides by stabbing themselves "*met criteria for a formal psychiatric diagnosis with 48 patients (89%) necessitating inpatient or outpatient psychiatric assistance at discharge.*"[62] This might have explained why Chiba felt it was so important to convince people that Elliott had been "*severely mentally ill,*" as she had said at her Q&A.

The severity of the wounds was another indicator of the cause of death as "*wounds caused by assailants to their victims were more severe than those inflicted by the victims of suicides to themselves.*"[51] On the autopsy report, the estimated depth of penetration of Elliott's wound #2 was between 5 and 7 inches deep (12.7-17.8 cm),[48] which was quite severe.

Another point to consider was the stabbing through the clothes which could have indicated homicide. All the studies were in agreement: In most homicides, stabbing had occurred through clothing whereas stabbing under clothing indicated suicide.[54] In most suicides with chest or abdominal wounds, the chosen area was exposed[58] and clothing damage absent.[58,60]

Numbers varied according to studies but the results were consistent: According to one study, in case of suicide, "*16 (57%) cases of stab wounds occurred after clothing had been purposely moved aside but wounds occurred through clothing in 8 (28%) cases.*"[58] Another study read: "*The stab or cut had severed the victim's clothes in five (5%) of 93 suicides.*"[61] This one also said that "*in most suicides with chest or abdominal wounds, the chosen area is exposed. Our study confirmed this observation, while noting the possibility of slashes (10% of suicide cases).*"[63] Thus, clothing damage by sharp force, although not impossible in case of suicide, is relatively rare,[64] and in Elliott's case, could have been another indication of homicide.

The lack of hesitation wounds and possible defense wounds were another concern. Often when a person stabs themself, hesitation wounds (superficial incised wounds) are made before the fatal deep wound. They indicate indecision before the final act, and also that the person has to find the right spot before plunging the knife into the flesh. One thing was certain. According to many studies, hesitation marks were a strong indicator of suicide, and were "*believed to be the most useful indication in distinguishing suicide from homicide.*"[60] According to many investigations, they were present in most cases of suicides (greater than 70%) from sharp weapon injury.[58,60,64,65,66,67,68,69]

Elliott didn't have any hesitation wounds around the large stab wounds in his chest, and his neck and wrists were intact. On the other hand, the small cuts on his palms and right upper arm could have been interpreted as possible defense wounds, although they could also have been made by mishandling the knife, according to Dr. Scheinin. They were certainly not due to self-injury, and since Elliott was right-handed, the cut on his right arm was difficult to explain.

"*Cut on inner arm, similar height of stab wound... interesting,*" had been noted by Lonnie, a nurse with a long experience in emergency rooms who had agreed to review the details of the autopsy. "*Effectively, there is no reason for Elliott to have 'tested' the knife at this location* [which was the other possibility offered by Dr. Scheinin to explain this small cut], *whereas a cut made by an attacker at the same height [causing] the fatal wound would make sense.*"[36]

Obviously, if these cuts were indeed defense wounds, they were a strong indication of homicide,[70] as defense wounds were detected in 61% of the cases in one large study,[69] and were most frequently found on hands, arms, and forearms.[69]

All these statistics were facts, not opinions. Even if statistics don't always explain everything about an isolated case, it was difficult to understand why Elliott's had accumulated all these exceptions.

Based on the statistics found in forensic literature, Alyson came up with this calculation. If suicides by stabbing only represented 2% of all suicides, and hesitation marks were observed in most cases of suicide by stabbing (>70% according to several studies), Elliott's case would belong to the 30% who did not have any hesitation marks. If the clothes were damaged in a minority of suicides by stabbing, there was no study establishing a statistic higher than 30% (most of them were actually around 10%). Finally, bone injuries were found in less than 15%[51] of suicides by stabbing (and among them, many people were under the influence of a drug or completely psychotic). If these different features were regarded as independent variables (they were indeed discussed separately in many studies), the mathematical coincidence of all these findings happening all together would be 0.02 x 0.30 x 0.30 x 0.15 = 0.0003, meaning that Elliott's case was representing only 0.03% of all cases of suicides. That would be 3 people in every 10,000.

Alyson was stunned by this very low result. It was a statistical oddity, and probably even lower knowing that it was not possible to consider other important factors, such as the fact that he was sober when he allegedly did it, and the fact he had done it at noon, in the presence of someone else. Statistics matter when determining a manner of death in cases when there are few clues to establish the circumstances involved.

This research was tedious for Alyson, going through all these details and forensic literature, and people usually don't like hard work; they want a simple explanation, the easy way out with no sweat. Alyson was accused a few times of looking too much into the details, but the truth is always in the details, and all these findings had to be considered.

To close this section, a woman from Sacramento also briefly communicated with Alyson. She claimed to have a quote from her ex-father-in-law, whose niece was married to Elliott's brother, Darren:

"So... my ex-husband's (now deceased) dad would talk to me about this case. He may have been privy somehow to insider information as he was the former Director of the Sacramento crime lab. Also, his niece is married to Elliott's bro, if they are still together. Solemnly he swore, without a doubt, that Elliott could not have self-inflicted that wound."[71]

This was just another thing to add to the pile of experts who had shared an informed opinion about Elliott's death, albeit secondhand, and this left Alyson perplexed because if somebody with such a position existed in Elliott's extended family, you had to wonder why nothing had ever been done about it.

The meds, was Elliott really sober?

The toxicology report was another important document to take into consideration, as the report gave a list of medications that Elliott had in his blood when he died. This provided confirmation that he had not ingested alcohol or street drugs that day, as no illegal drugs were found, while all of the medications that were found had been reported at therapeutic or subtherapeutic levels.[48] Even though the combination Elliott was on may have seemed excessive to some people, Alyson has been told by a medical professional[36] that Elliott was probably seeing different doctors, as it was not the same doctor who could treat a psychological condition AND a neurological one. It was highly probable that Elliott had been prescribed a psychostimulant like amphetamine, dexamphetamine, or methylphenidate to manage his ADHD by a psychiatrist, and the effectiveness of the drugs had to be monitored by this same psychiatrist. Then he was probably seeing a neurologist for other meds related to an anxiety disorder or seizures.[36]

Still, people regularly commented on his meds, blaming his "*suicide*" either on the medications he was taking or on a "*cold turkey*" rumor that he was suffering from being OFF his regular meds, despite the fact that both of these could have been easily proven false based on the toxicology report. Many people who had a personal experience with a specific drug made a connection between Elliott's death and their personal experience. With a few variations, the narration usually went like this: "*I have this experience with this drug, it's a dangerous drug, and I had suicidal thoughts....*" It is not possible to prevent people from having an opinion based on their personal life, but any personal experience always has to be considered anecdotal.

This was what was found in Elliott's system:

Amphetamine (Adderall): 0.39 μg/ml
Atomoxetine (Strattera): present
Mirtazapine (Remeron): < 0.10 μg/ml
Buprenorphine (Buprenex): None detected
Clonazepam: < 4 ng/ml
Gabapentin: < 2.0 μg/ml

All the other drugs tested (alcohol and a long list of illegal drugs) were found negative.

According to experts, there were no possible bad interactions between the drugs, except one.[74] The combination of Remeron, Clonazepam, and Gabapentin may have caused increased dizziness, drowsiness, confusion, and difficulty concentrating. But Clonazepam was found at such a low level there was not enough to have caused a psychotic crisis and made someone go crazy.

It is interesting to note that tests for some of the drugs had been done by outside laboratories, MedTox Laboratories and Quest Diagnostics, and the results had been added to the main report. The exception was Buprenorphine (Buprenex), as it only said "Done" on the main report. Buprenorphine (Buprenex), a drug used to treat opioid addiction and control chronic pain, may have been related to Elliott still suffering from his beating by the police. However, Quest Diagnostics returned a "none detected" result for the same drug, which meant that Buprenorphine should have been removed from the list of meds present in the blood when Elliott died.

During the Q&A after Gil Reyes's documentary, it was said Elliott had quit at least 10 psychiatric medications cold turkey within a few days of his suicide. In 2004, Jennifer Chiba had declared this to Liam Gowing for *SPIN* magazine:

"*In mid-September, the effects of going cold turkey were apparent. He had seven old cigarette burns on his arm. It was evidence of his pain from that heroin and crack period that was just a little too real, so he'd taken a knife to it. It was on a Friday, so we went to the doctor on Monday and found out that he'd abruptly stopped taking one of his medications [Strattera]. It's so dangerous. It throws you so off-balance. You can't just go off that. So from then on, I got a pill organizer with the days of the week, and I would administer the meds.*"[37]

Who knows if this was true. Elliott may have tried to quit Strattera at one point, but one thing was certain, he had not gone cold turkey off all medications during the days preceding his death. He had different medications in his system, and had therapeutic or subtherapeutic doses of those prescription drugs.

Since Alyson had no expertise, she consulted various websites[72] and people who had enough knowledge in the pharmaceutical field to comment.

Amphetamine (that comes from the metabolization of Adderall) and Strattera are used to treat ADHD in adults, and there were no websites saying that quitting Adderall, even cold turkey, would pose major problems. "*Most people who take it as instructed don't have any issues if they take a break from it,*"[75] webmd.com states, while some people might experience depression, irritability, tiredness, nausea, sleep deprivation.

As for Strattera, Healthline.com affirms that "*it doesn't cause withdrawal when you stop taking it,*"[76] while The RecoveryVillage.com says that "*most people who have stopped using Strattera experience very minimal withdrawal symptoms.*"[77] Plus, this was beside the point since Elliott had these medications in his system.

Knowing that amphetamines like Adderall have a short plasma life of 4-6 hours, after 48 hours only 0.02% of the original dose should have been detected, and after 72 hours the level would have been completely below detectable concentrations. Based on this, it was safe to conclude that Elliott had taken his meds very recently.

The relatively high level (0.39 µg/ml = 0.39 g/L) of amphetamines, in comparison to the normal therapeutic plasma level (pre-mortem level is around 0.1g/L), was still not a concern as studies like *Drug concentrations in post-mortem femoral blood compared with therapeutic concentrations in plasma* by Terhi Launiainen and Ilkka Ojanpera[73] show that concentrations of certain drugs increase after death. For amphetamines, there was a post-mortem increase of at least 2.8 (post-mortem blood/therapeutic plasma concentration = 2.8)[73], which made Elliott's 0.39 µg/ml not extraordinarily out of this range.

Regarding Mirtazapine (Remeron), used to treat depression, the data found online indicated therapeutic levels should be between 0.03 and 0.08 μg/ml.[73] With a post-mortem increase of 2.5,[73] Elliott's level (below 0.10 μg/ml) was in the lowest part of that range, but again there was nothing abnormal to report.

As for the two other drugs, Clonazepam and Gabapentin, used to treat seizures but also anxiety, panic, and sleep disorders, Elliott's Clonazepam level was below 4 ng/ml or 0.004 μg/ml (therapeutic doses are between 0.02-0.08 μg/ml),[73] so effectively below a therapeutic level, while Elliott's Gabapentin level was below 2.0 μg/ml, right inside the range of therapeutic doses, which are between 0.5 and 6 μg/ml.

In the end, Elliott was taking an antidepressant (Remeron), Adderall and Strattera for ADHD, a subtherapeutic dose of Clonazepam, and a therapeutic dose of Gabapentin for anxiety. Altogether, nothing out of the ordinary. He had normal doses of prescribed meds the day he died, and he had not taken Buprenex, the only med on the list that, as an opioid/painkiller, that could have attenuated the pain. He hadn't gone cold turkey and he had not been abusing his meds either. He hadn't drunk any alcohol or taken any illegal drugs. These were the facts. Plus, Alyson was confident about this information as none of the doctors and specialists she had consulted were ever alarmed by any of these doses or in that combination.

Alyson decided to contact a few forensic toxicologists, and two of them graciously agreed to comment on Elliott's toxicology report. She sent the results of the toxicology report without giving them too many details about the case, or even mentioning Elliott's name and the exact circumstances of his death. She didn't mention the presence of another person at the time of his death and their fight, in order to minimize the influence of other information on their responses. She had just told them a person had died of two stab wounds in the chest and had specified that the case had never been ruled a suicide or a homicide. Then she had asked them about the possible influence of the drugs present to commit such a suicide. The first answer came from Dwain Fuller F-ABFT, TC-NRCC, Board Certified Forensic Toxicologist:[78]

"*I will be happy to look at it, but from what you've told me, I can tell you that I wouldn't suggest the drugs influenced the person to stab themselves in the chest. That being said, while not the norm, people sometimes do stab or shoot themselves multiple times in a suicidal incident. But once again, one would be hard-pressed to suggest the drugs influenced it."* [78]

After another exchange explaining that some people would blame Elliott's alleged "*suicide*" on antidepressants, while others might blame it on the lack of antidepressants, Mr. Fuller added:

"*I would agree that from the little I know about this case, it sounds unlikely that this is a suicide unless there is extremely compelling evidence that it is. I have nothing to add on the toxicology.*"[78]

Alyson also received a response from Forensic Toxicologist Justin Brower,[79] who took the time to give a very detailed answer:

"*Here's my two cents. It does sound a little suspicious, but we've all encountered witnessed suicides with knives and other sharp instruments. If I were testifying on this case in court and an attorney asked me whether or not the presence of amphetamine could make a person do this, this would be my answer: Behavioral toxicology doesn't really exist. The presence or absence of drugs cannot be definitively linked to a person's behavior. I can tell you how drugs affect the body, and that amphetamines can cause increased anxiety, aggression, and bizarre behaviors in some people, but not necessarily in all. No one will be able to tell you 'but for the amphetamine' the person would not have stabbed themselves (lawyers love these 'but for' questions). People stab themselves every day without being under the influence of amphetamine. Likewise, there are people who routinely abuse amphetamines and don't stab themselves.*

"*This comes up a lot in suicides. As an example, a person hangs themselves. The family wants to know if they were taking their antidepressants and wondering if the antidepressants caused them to hang themselves. A different family might call and wonder if they weren't on their meds, and that's why they hung themselves. It boils down to we don't know what was going through their minds at the time of the incident, but in the example I just gave, there was obviously something else going on that they were being treated for.*

"*In your case, I'd rely more on the history surrounding the case and what the forensic pathologists think of the wounds—angles, etc. —because no one will be able to tell you with absolute certainty that the amphetamines caused him to take that action and stab himself.*

"The mirtazapine isn't really a concern either. The tip I give forensic pathologists is: if on the report you see a 'less than' we're really not concerned about it; if you see a 'greater than' we start thinking about a suicide."[79]

On Elliott's toxicology report, there was a "*less than*" for all meds, except for the amphetamines already discussed above. Thus, these two toxicologists were in agreement that "*behavioral toxicology doesn't really exist*" and drugs cannot be definitively linked to a specific behavior. Alyson thought about this a lot, especially because drug abuse and drug withdrawal had both been used as arguments for suicide in this case. But they couldn't have it both ways!

During the Q&A following the screening of *Searching for Elliott Smith*, it had been suggested that Elliott's demise was due to a combination of prescription drugs, illegal street drugs, and alcohol over a period of years, while mentioning that Elliott's doctors could have done a better job monitoring his condition.[46]

However, there was nothing in the prescriptions that could have been blamed on the doctors, and there was nothing that could have been linked to such a horrific suicide. The research confirmed this. The two forensic toxicologists confirmed this. Reyes's declaration looked more and more like an attempt to confuse people. The toxicology report was there to tell us the truth, and it was important to have confirmation from people with expertise in that area.

It was just very difficult to blame such a dramatic and painful suicide on these normal levels of prescribed meds. Wouldn't a drug user, who had used crack or opiates before, have used these drugs to, at the very least, kill some of the horrible pain?

Chapter 7: More questions about October 21

Elliott's family had been very quiet so far, but through the precious help of two allies, Alyson received some information from one of Elliott's very close family members. Despite the fact this person revealed their identity in their emails, they never got fully involved in the quest for the truth, and they certainly didn't want their name to be made public. Alyson and her allies are grateful to have the information this person sent, as well as encouragement and acknowledgment of their efforts.

One important "*detail,*" in particular, which had started as a rumor a few years after his death, was now confirmed by this family member: That fatal day, Chiba seemingly had waited for some time before calling 911, something which had never made any sense, if Elliott had been bleeding to death after the removal of the knife from the wound. Chiba had told this family member that her cell phone was busy or not working, and that was the reason why she had not called 911 immediately and why the ambulance had been delayed.[80] This was complete nonsense because Elliott had used their landline phone to call this same person just a few days before he died. This phone story was highly incriminating, and Alyson could not understand why the police hadn't jumped on this important detail. There was also a rumor (not coming from this family member) that Chiba might have made other phone calls before calling 911. Had the police checked her phone records just in case? Probably not.

A doctor's appointment

Then there was the nebulous account of the day of Elliott's death provided by Chiba. She declared to Liam Gowing, then Gil Reyes and W. T. Schultz (the author of the Elliott Smith biography *Torment Saint*) that their fight had been about a doctor's appointment she had had that day, although the exact details of the fight have never been made very clear. "*We were arguing about several things*," she declared in *Searching for Elliott Smith.*[42]

In Gowing's article, Chiba mentioned the doctor's appointment, and Elliott changing his mind about driving her to the appointment: "*We had plans to go to my doctor. He [Elliott] kept changing his mind. I got impatient. We got into a petty fight. I started crying. I went into the bathroom.*"[37]

Can you imagine killing yourself after such a trivial fight? Stabbing yourself in the heart over an argument regarding a drive to a doctor's appointment? A bigger part of the puzzle is obviously missing. Why was this appointment such a big deal? Could it be because Chiba was suddenly afraid of what the doctor had to say about their relationship? They weren't seeing the same therapist as a couple as she was individually, as far as Alyson knows.

In Schultz's book, Chiba finally admitted that she couldn't drive due to a recent DUI.[81] Alyson had found out about this DUI, thanks to Ruth,[24] a few years earlier. However, Chiba's story also included Elliott's paranoia, since it was probably very difficult to convince people Elliott could have killed himself simply because he didn't want to drive her to a doctor's appointment. This is how Schultz had summed up the tragedy of that day:

"*As they got home again, they reviewed the plan for the afternoon. Chiba had a therapist appointment; again, Elliott would need to drive her.... All this was up for discussion as Chiba laid out the day's remaining agenda. But suddenly Elliott interjected: 'Don't talk out loud in the house. You know it's bugged.' Chiba tried laughing the comment off, thinking she might neutralize it. She answered, 'I'm not paranoid like you are.' Elliott now was on the computer. He called out, 'Are you working for somebody? To sabotage this record? Are you working against me too?' Overwhelmed by the emotion of the day, feeling hyped up and anxious from the earlier medical appointment, Chiba locked herself in the bathroom.... He knocked on the bathroom door. He told Chiba he was sorry. He asked her to come out. He told her he knew he was crazy. He apologized for what he had said. But Chiba wasn't ready yet. Impulsively, as she'd said before, she told him to leave her the fuck alone. She was sick of the paranoia.*

"*For several long seconds there was quiet, only the usual sounds of the ticking house. Then came an awful noise, a scream Chiba vaguely recognized, both familiar somehow and utterly alien. A few nights prior she and Elliott had stayed up sharpening a new set of knives. As she flung herself out of the bathroom and ran to the kitchen, where the scream seemed to come from, she found Elliott at the sink. He had his back to her, but as he turned, she saw a knife in his chest.*"[82]

To Alyson, this description of the drama has always been very frustrating. It had all the characteristics of a half-told story with many holes in it. Their fight had been tamed down in Chiba's reporting of it whereas it had been described as a violent episode by the neighbors.

According to Schultz, they were having some vague argument, Elliott had shown some signs of paranoia, Chiba had locked herself in the bathroom, and suddenly he had stabbed himself twice when she refused to open the door.

It was also interesting to note an important discrepancy in the 2004 *The Guardian* article[83] by Alexis Petridis. It had been first reported that Elliott had threatened to kill himself at this moment. "*Like most of Smith's close friends, Chiba was used to him making melodramatic threats about ending his life.... Chiba ignored him and locked herself in the bathroom.*" [83] Petridis stated that Chiba had reportedly said that, less than an hour before his death, Elliott had threatened to kill himself. This was mentioned again in another article by Marty Dodge posted on Blogcritics in 2004: "*Used to melodramatic threats from her boyfriend Chiba ignored his remarks and took a shower—only to discover later he had stabbed himself.*"[84]

On a side note, Chiba's experience as a therapist should have made her react very differently. Therapists are trained to lead people who want to commit suicide out of suicide; it is basically their job. They know that all threats of suicide should be taken seriously, and that a person who is suicidal should never be left alone.

Chiba had been working with unstable kids and had experience dealing with crisis situations, but she was now saying she had ignored Elliott's threats, though she had the training and experience to respond in this type of situation.

Lois (not her real name), a lawyer who has had experience as a teenager with the type of establishments Chiba worked in, shared her opinion. Because she had been one of these kids, she was familiar with the population of children attending these establishments, which she described as "*very unstable kids, easily involved in fights, suicide attempts, attempts to awol [leave the facilities without permission] and other shenanigans.*"[85]

Lois stated that "*by the time of his death she [Chiba] really should have learned how to respond to someone in a crisis. She should have been well versed in dealing with volatile people at the time of his death. Her reaction to it was weird and maybe the only one that would come from someone IN an abusive relationship and it sounds like this guy was not like that at all. By the time of his death she probably would have learned a lot about de-escalating highly reactive people in crisis situations. This type of situation is a pretty common occurrence in the types of institutions that she worked in and I am sure she had AT LEAST a minimal personal experience dealing with a crisis, let alone someone having an emotional meltdown. She was a mental health therapist for goodness sake.*"[85]

Real life is surely not like practicing therapy, but it is still difficult to understand Chiba's reaction at that precise moment of crisis.

But was Elliott really threatening to commit suicide? When reading *Torment Saint,* the discrepancy was flagrant, as this important "*detail*" was not in Schultz's book anywhere. Instead, Schultz claimed that in the moments leading up to his death, Elliott was not threatening to commit suicide. He was paranoid, and Chiba got tired of it. To Alyson, saying "*the house is bugged*" sounds very different from saying "*I'm gonna kill myself.*" But, as had happened before, there were variations in Chiba's story.

In Schultz's newest version, paranoia had replaced the suicide threats, and was justification for what was about to come; otherwise how could such a dramatic death have occurred over such a trivial fight? Meanwhile, the injection of the sentence "*A few nights prior she and Elliott had stayed up sharpening a new set of knives.*"[82]—a sort of what-the-fuck revelation—had always been very disturbing to Alyson. What was the point of Schultz including that?

The only thing that had always been consistent in Chiba's narration is the bathroom, while different versions of what happened in the bathroom existed as far back as 2003. Deanna had told Alyson that Chiba was allegedly on the phone with her therapist in the bathroom while telling Elliott she would be "*right out.*" While this version was never officially reported anywhere, the story that circulated was that Chiba had locked herself in to escape the fight and had refused to open the bathroom door even though Elliott was crying, apologizing, and begging her to come out. This was what Chiba had more or less told Reyes and Schultz. But it was difficult to imagine Elliott begging her to come out just after a fight, since she had admitted having been in the bathroom only for 5-10 minutes, a relatively short amount of time. Why would Elliott have wanted Chiba out so badly at that exact moment? Why would this have been an emergency? If the fight was violent as had been reported by the neighbors, wouldn't Elliott have wanted to wait a bit until the anger calmed down before asking, let alone begging, her to come out?

Schultz even revealed that this had not been the first time this situation had happened:

"*It was something she'd done before. It was her way of getting some distance, a temporary respite. On other occasions like this Elliott had called [his sister] Ashley, who came by to mediate, to talk Chiba out.*"[82]

However, Schultz did not reveal why it was so important to make Chiba come out of the bathroom. What was the hurry? She would have come out of the bathroom at some point anyway. Why did she need a mediator? And why would Elliott have found the need to call his sister to try to get Chiba to come out of the bathroom? You had to wonder who really was in crisis at that moment, Elliott or Chiba? What was the danger of her staying in the bathroom? Could it have been because Chiba had threatened to do something in the bathroom? Maybe to kill herself? It is tempting to switch the roles for a moment, with Elliott now looking like the reasonable one, asking for a mediator, whereas Chiba was the capricious one, refusing to come out and displaying childish behavior despite her therapist knowledge. Chiba may have said she wanted to kill herself and Elliott may have desperately tried to prevent her from doing so. Other stories that Alyson heard later, from at least two different people, may reinforce these speculations.

In Reyes's movie, Chiba also claimed to have heard a horrible noise, while she used the term "thud" according to one family member, or "scream" as described in Schultz's *Torment Saint*, before opening the door. The fact Chiba had used all these terms at different times was also a concern for Alyson. Whatever she had heard, a noise, a thud, or a scream, had to be perceived very differently. Plus, if Elliott was still standing when she opened the door (as the police report says) what thud could she have heard?

To go back to the subject of the fight, the family member who connected with Alyson revealed a very different reason, leading Alyson to think that the argument was much more serious than Chiba had said. According to an email from the family member: "*At the memorial service, a friend of Elliott had allegedly said that Elliott had told Chiba the morning of his death that he was leaving her.*"[80] Alyson was not very surprised to read this, especially because she had heard this story from other sources.

This was effectively echoed by Alec (not his real name), a musician who talked to Alyson in 2014. He told her he was around the couple very shortly before Elliott's death. "*Yeah he was gonna bail and they fought on a regular basis,*"[86] he told Alyson.

The musician also didn't believe Elliott had killed himself, "*To stab your breast plate twice seems impossible,*"[86] he declared, and proposed some wild theories about what could have happened. He was effectively not convinced Chiba could have done it, despite his bad opinion of her. "*She could be a borderline witch, hyper calculating bitch and almost whorelike in her sexual way. Talking and what not. But killing him didn't seem like she would do that and hold it together. She would have cracked,*"[86] he explained to Alyson.

The knife, described in the police report as an 8-inch single-edge kitchen knife, was another mystery, especially because it has been kept by the police since the tragic day. Very early on, Chiba had said to Deanna that she had first thought Elliott was joking, and was even using a fake knife, which was another crazy variation of the story, as if handling such a large knife after a violent fight could have possibly been a joke.

The LAPD homicide detectives

After procrastinating for years, Alyson thought it would be a good thing to talk to the police and, around 2010, she finally contacted the East Side division of the Los Angeles Police Department and was referred to homicide detective P.J. Morris, who was in charge of the case. Over the years, Alyson would make a few phone calls to the LAPD and would save her correspondence with the different detectives in charge, first P.J. Morris then detective J. King, after Morris's retirement. The case being open, the detectives never told her very much, repeating they could not comment on an open case, but they had always welcomed her insight. "*We are not investigating this case as a suicide,*"[87] P.J. Morris had once told her on the phone.

Alyson never learned much about the knife but, in 2012, she got a confirmation from homicide detective J. King that no fingerprints had been recorded on it, neither Elliott's nor Chiba's, even though she had pulled the knife out. This may have been due to the nature of the surface of the handle, or this may have been due to something else. The detective could not say more.[88]

The knife

The removal of the knife, revealed very early on by *LA Weekly* journalist Christine Pelisek, still pointed to Chiba's guilt, but Alyson had also thought of another problem following its removal. After calling 911, Chiba had reportedly performed CPR until the arrival of the ambulance. Alyson could not imagine Chiba actually doing compressions on somebody with two open wounds in the chest. Though few details were known about what she did at this precise moment, she would have had to cover the wounds and apply strong pressure to control the bleeding. Due to a large amount of blood loss after the removal of the knife, Elliott probably went into hemorrhagic shock, and external chest compressions in cardiac arrest caused by hemorrhagic shock are damaging. In other words, CPR often worsens things.[89] Later on, the autopsy report noted that Elliott had died from exsanguination, i.e. blood loss.[48] The hospital records, obtained by the family and briefly discussed by the family member who had been in communication with Alyson, showed that the doctors had performed emergency treatment to stop the bleeding from the wounds in the heart, but had failed to notice an exit wound. Elliott had died of exsanguination before they could even try to get him to surgery.

The balcony

Almost every point in Chiba's narration was problematic for Alyson Alyson had heard many stories very early on, and things kept changing, as Chiba's story kept evolving. The balcony episode was an intriguing point because it had first been mentioned by Chiba in Reyes's documentary in 2009, but had never shown up in previous reports and articles, not even the 2003 police report. Why hadn't Chiba mentioned the balcony then? In Reyes's film, Chiba claimed that she saw Elliott running to the balcony and was even afraid he would jump off it. In Schultz's book, Elliott now had "*crashed onto the balcony, as if, she [Chiba] believed, he were trying to jump off it somehow. She tackled him there, then quickly climbed off him to call 911, seconds later performing citizen CPR.*"[82]

"*Tackled him*?" It was as if Chiba had suggested some serious physical contact during this intense moment. Plus, there was the walking throughout the house, something not entirely impossible according to Dr. Scheinin, who had told Alyson that many people continue to walk once stabbed. But wasn't this very strange in the case of a suicide? Why would a man walk from the kitchen, which according to people who had been inside the house was in the front of the unit, to the balcony, which was in the back of the unit, after stabbing himself twice in the chest? What was the purpose of walking unless this man had been afraid of something or someone? Since Chiba had declared she had first seen Elliott at the sink of the kitchen, this meant that he had walked from the front of the house to the back. And there was no reason for Elliott to jump from the balcony once he had stabbed himself twice… talk about overkill!

Blood throughout the house?

Alyson once stumbled on an interview of Robin Peringer inside an article about Band of Horses for *Filter* magazine in 2008, and in a way, Peringer confirmed a part of the story. Robin, who was playing with Band of Horses at the time, had been asked by the journalist about his friendship with Elliott:

"*I ask Robin about his friendship with Elliott Smith, and he candidly obliges. The two were close during the mid-'90s but drifted apart as Elliott began to distance himself with drugs. They rekindled their relationship just before his death, and Robin tells the harrowing story of cleaning up the blood throughout Elliott's house after the suicide. 'I get really upset when people say dumb, ignorant shit about him being murdered,' he says. 'It's just ignorant!'*"[90]...

"*Cleaning up the blood throughout Elliott's house after the suicide*" was the part that had shocked Alyson. Why was there blood throughout the house?

"*It seems odd to me that a suicide would trail blood throughout the house after stabbing himself,*"[36] nurse Lonnie (not her real name) declared during a conversation with Alyson. "*but it makes perfect sense that a man stabbed by his girlfriend would trail blood while trying to escape. Ms. Chiba could not have administered CPR while Smith was trailing blood, therefore one would hope she was busy contacting EMS.*"[36]

The blood throughout the house could only have been explained by Elliott walking around after the stabbing, maybe running away, or even fleeing something or someone. There was also another weird detail in Peringer's statement: Why were they cleaning up the blood? Or rather, when were they cleaning up the blood? Could this have been before the police's arrival? Or before the police had the chance to examine the house? It was certainly a sign that the police had never considered the place a crime scene—after all, Elliott had died at the hospital, not inside the house. Nevertheless, it sounded strange that the police would have allowed the cleaning of the blood when there were still many questions unanswered. But were they even asking questions at that time? It seems that the police had not considered the case a possible murder right away. They had declared Elliott's death a suicide immediately and had only reopened the investigation when the results of the autopsy were made public as inconclusive. Could the police have made such a big mistake?

Some answers might be found in the way Chiba handled the situation upon the police's arrival. While Elliott was dying in the ER, she had been questioned at the kitchen table, according to the police report. And it might have been the only time she had been interrogated.

"*During this questioning, she noted for the first time a Post-it note that appeared to be a suicide note left by the decedent. Jennifer [Chiba] recognized the handwriting on the note as that of the decedent and had not seen the note before that moment.*"[48]

This Post-it note was the first step toward the suicide narration, since a suicide note is proof of the act itself. Calling this Post-it note a suicide note was influential in the collective narrative although it has never been proven that the Post-it was indeed a suicide note.

A Post-it note

Alyson had actually a lot of doubts about the whole Post-it note thing. How bizarre to think that Elliott would have written a note in the middle of a fight, in the middle of the scene described by Chiba. Even Dr. Scheinin had mentioned the note was "*nebulous*"[47] because "*it didn't say anything, you had to read into it.*"[47] For Alyson, it could have been a suicide note or anything else. It was clear Dr. Scheinin didn't want to decide one way or another.

First, there was one recurrent and erroneous point that had been regularly coming back in many discussions: Had Elliott's name been misspelled on the note (with just one t)? It was confirmed several times that the note, which read "*I'm so sorry–love, Elliott, God forgive me,*"[48] was actually spelled correctly on the note, and that the mistake in Elliott's name had been made by the police officer who had written the report.

It was still important to know that the note that had been described in the police report as an "*apparent*" suicide note was conveniently discovered by Chiba during the questioning by the police after the officers arrived at the scene. Since that day, the police have kept the note and not even the family has been able to look at it. A family member once said they had tried to get information from the police through the Freedom of Information Act, even bringing in their attorney, but were still not successful.[80]

Nobody has ever reported whether some handwriting analysis or other forensic investigation has been done on the note, and this is particularly frustrating for Alyson, because one of the main arguments for suicide (especially in this case) was the idea that Elliott had indeed left a suicide note.

However, many things do not sit well in this scenario: How odd would it be to write a suicide note addressed to someone who was right there, just behind a door? And how odd would it be to write such a peaceful message asking for forgiveness, in complete contrast with the anger and despair that certainly followed if Elliott had indeed stabbed himself to death? Chiba had said many times that Elliott was pounding on the door begging her to open it just before stabbing himself twice, but she had never tried to suggest a moment in her timeline for him to write the note. In Reyes's movie, she declared she had stayed no more than 5-10 minutes in the bathroom, so how could Elliott have calmed down enough to write an apologetic note then suddenly resumed with the crazy rage and self-hatred necessary to stab himself in such a short period of time? These were two opposite states of mind, which were in blatant contrast.

Then there was the message on the note, which was very vague and impersonal, even trite in comparison with Elliott's lyrics, something that could have been written at any moment, and could have been addressed to anyone, as Chiba's name was not even on the note. But there was even another weird angle, found in W.T. Schultz's book: "*Chiba had been in the habit of sticking Post-Its* [sic] *around the house, each with [a] little encouraging message.*"[82] If this had been a habit, a thing that she or both of them were doing, would Elliott have used this same method for writing his last note ever, his suicide note? It was clear to Alyson that the note could have been written at any moment or any day, if this was a habit for the couple.

However, calling it a suicide note was a definitive way to anchor the suicide theory in people's minds. Alyson looked it up, and suicide notes are the perfect proof that suicide has indeed occurred, but they are relatively rare according to literature that reported that only one in five people (between 15% to 20%) who commit suicide leave a note. For many of them, the choice to commit suicide is impulsive, and too hastily done to find any time to compose a suicide note.

Alyson found that there was actually a lot of literature and studies done on suicide letters and notes, like that done by Daniel M. Ogilvie, Philip J. Stone, and Edwin S. Shneidman in "Some Characteristics of Genuine Versus Simulated Suicides Notes":

"*More often than was true of the simulated notes, genuine notes contained specific information, used names of people, places, and things, made frequent mention of women [they studied men's suicide notes] and gave instructions to others that were concrete enough to be actually carried out. By contrast, the simulated suicide notes contained a greater percentage of 'thinking' words, suggesting that the issue of suicide was being pondered, reasoned with, and probably rationalized.*"[91]

Ogilvie et al. also stated that, "*In general… genuine suicide notes are characterized by dichotomous logic, a greater amount of hostility and self-blame, use of very specific names and instructions to the survivor, more decisiveness, less evidence of thinking about thinking, and more use of the various meanings of the word 'love.*'"[92]

Susan Roubidoux, who wrote "Linguistic manifestations of power in suicide notes," stated:

"*By comparing both the frequencies and the context in which each type of pronoun is used, [her] study uncovered three potential indicators or predictors of genuine intent to commit suicide: subjective personal pronoun [I statements] functioning in an active context, active personal pronoun as apology and exclusive first-person plural pronouns.*"[93]… on the other hand, simulated notes used a more passive voice.

There was not much to say about Elliott's alleged suicide note. It was very simple, vague, and short, with no name included and no mention of his family. Could it have been the last writing we would get from a man who had crafted such cerebral and multi-layered lyrics? There was nothing in this short note that revealed a suicidal state of mind, nothing that showed he was about to undertake this terrible action; there was no hostility, no directive, nothing related to the consequences of his actions; only this vague and passive "*forgive me.*"

In reality, suicide notes are rarely found, and when they do they follow a pattern, which was definitively not recognizable in Elliott's trite note. It certainly did not at all reflect the complete insanity of his death that immediately followed. There was simply no intensity in the note, not even a shade of self-hatred or self-blame, and certainly no admonishment, no practical instructions, as in the case of some suicide notes. There was certainly no hopelessness, a feeling that emerges in many notes, no feeling of abandonment, no "*I just can't go on any longer*" that is often found in genuine suicide letters.

This "*I'm so sorry–love, Elliott, God forgive me*" also did not express any relief over having made the decision to die. It did not even make an allusion to the fact that Elliott was about to kill himself. It was as if Elliott was looking for a dull apology, while he was about to perform the most horrific act in front of his partner. Even if apologies are common in suicide notes, stabbing yourself in front of the person while apologizing to this same person seems very contradictory; it seemed to be two quite irreconcilable feelings. Elliott was about to do something that could have traumatized Chiba for life, something that could have made her feel terribly guilty, something that could have cast terrible suspicion over her. He should not have been in the mood for apologies.

Though Alyson had no pretension of her ability to decipher whether a suicide note is genuine or forged—some people have written entire theses about this—she wondered whether the police had ever done anything with the note, whether any expert had ever examined it. Plus, Alyson had been told by someone who knew Elliott very well that, in private, he rarely signed his full name on anything.

Once Chiba had sold the note as a suicide note, the next step was for her to convince the police Elliott had been very suicidal, and she immediately mentioned that "*Elliott had suffered from depression all of his life,*" that "*he had a history of multiple narcotics addiction (heroin and crack) and alcohol abuse,*" that he had "*engaged in self-mutilation behavior and would burn himself with cigarettes,*" that he had "*a history of one possible suicide attempt and a consistent history of verbal suicidal ideations and planning,*" and that he had "*sought treatment for this depression from several psychiatrists and was being treated with multiple prescription drugs.*"[48]

This was certainly quite a portrait to paint when the body wasn't even cold. Even though Elliott had indeed suffered from depression and had taken drugs, Chiba barely mentioned that Elliott had been through a painful detox program and she never talked about any of his current projects such as a new album, a studio, a tour, a foundation for children, a big concert coming up in November 2003, and a soundtrack for a movie. Forget about these positive points, her immediate reflex was to list his overwhelmingly depressing catalog right there on the scene, just a few minutes (or a few hours?) after Elliott's stabbing. One might regard this alarming list as a defense mechanism for Chiba.

For Alyson, this could have been an over-the-top justification of an event by someone who should have been in great distress, someone who should not have been able to function or find any justification, seated at a kitchen table, thinking about a man who was dying.

To reinforce this already shattering list, Chiba even gave the police some pages from Elliott's personal journal supporting the suicide theory. When Ruth told Alyson this,[24] she thought Chiba had been functioning a bit too well for a person who had just been through a very traumatic experience, and told Alyson something even more over the top. Chiba had allegedly said to someone that if she had read the journal entry of the day before, she would have acted differently.[24] To Alyson, this sounded like a too convenient justification of Chiba's own actions.

So, Chiba was functioning so well that she had even been able to tell the police she had seen "*two cuts*"[48] after pulling the knife out of his chest… while all the blood was coming out, and while Elliott still had his shirt on. Considering the probable panic of the moment, how had Chiba been able to see he had two cuts, two stab wounds?

The cliff episode

Chiba remained very vague regarding Elliott's history of one possible suicide attempt, but a few articles jumped on this a bit later. The story was that, on a dark night in 1997, Elliott had run and jumped off a cliff in North Carolina, landing on a tree. The cliff story seems to many people to be definitive proof that Elliott had tried to commit suicide in the past, besides the other assumptions that he had tried to overdose several times when he was working with David McConnell. This was amplified by Liam Gowing's *SPIN* article, insisting that Elliott had tried to OD by taking large amounts of prescription drugs. According to McConnell: "*So I had him on constant suicide watch. He tried OD'ing. He would say things like, 'The other day I popped 15 Klonopin, thinking it would help me die, and it didn't. It didn't work!*'"[37]

However, McConnell also declared the following in a 2011 issue of the *Under the Radar*:[26]

"*I don't think Elliott really wanted to die. There are people who I think are truly in so much pain that they want to end their lives. I don't think that was his situation. I don't think he was going to call Dr. Kevorkian to end his life because he was suffering so much. I think he was in a lot of pain, and I think he was trying to reach out to the universe somehow. And I think that he talked about ending his life a lot, and that was a byproduct of his drug use and the fact that he felt like shit. But he was such a sweetheart, and I don't think he wanted to die. I don't think that he wanted to do that to anybody. I think Elliott knew enough good times in his life and knew enough good people that he knew that there was something there to live for. I just think he was in a really dark place, and he was searching for something. He was searching for a way out. And he did talk a lot about [suicide], and he romanticized it, I think, a little bit. But it just didn't seem like he wanted to die. I think he had too much curiosity and passion for life.... It just seems more like an existential exercise than an actual desire to die.*"[26]

If overdosing is considered a passive way to commit suicide, the 1997 cliff story was something else, a very active way to want to die and apparently definitive proof that Elliott had been suicidal to the point of attempting it at least once in the past.

Elliott had talked about the cliff story in interviews, like this one published by *SPIN* in 1999, and also reported in the *The Guardian* years later:[94,95]

"*I don't like when people talk about all the bad things that have happened to them as if that makes them unique. Because I don't think I've had a harder time than other people.*

"*But, um, yeah—I, uh, jumped off a cliff. But it didn't work. It was in North Carolina or somewhere. It wasn't like I made up my mind to throw myself off a cliff. I got freaked out and started running, It was totally dark, and I ran off the edge of a cliff. I saw it coming up, and it wasn't like, 'I'm gonna throw myself off this cliff and die.' It was just, 'Ground's coming up. Who cares, whatever.' I landed on a little tree, punctured my, you know, body. It just made a really ugly wound.*"[94,95]

Liam Gowing's 2004 article in *SPIN* gave more context to the episode:

"*In 1997, Smith was recording his last indie album,* Either/Or, *an intimate, lo-fi collection. Yet the process brought him little joy. 'I recorded so many songs for it,' he later told the magazine* Under the Radar, *'and one or two of them sucked. Then three or four of them sucked. Then they all sucked and everything I did was terrible.' Instead of enjoying the buzz his new songs generated on tour, Smith ended up drinking heavily and jumping off a cliff in North Carolina, miraculously landing on a tree that broke his fall. After an unsuccessful intervention by friends at a Chicago hotel, he ended up in an Arizona psychiatric hospital.*"[37]

Finally, in his underappreciated book *Elliott Smith and the Big Nothing,*[96] Benjamin Nugent provides many more details about the cliff story:

"*Elliott was kind of in a funk, just sitting around and playing music but not much else, and it was like 'come on, we're all going to drive down to Raleigh,' says [his friend, Dorien] Garry. And I really figured out that something was wrong when he got on the turnpike and we stopped at a restaurant and he was like, 'is there any place to get alcohol here?' and it's like, 'on the New Jersey turnpike? No, you're lucky if you can get a decent cup of coffee. No. Not at all. Come on, you can make a ten-hour drive without a drink.' He just wanted to be anywhere but in his own skin at that time.*

"*On the first night of the two-night celebration, they were giving a friend a ride home from the party, and Smith had been drinking. In the North Carolina countryside, they stopped to let Garry's friend out of the car.*

"*'It was pitch black and we were in a little cul-de-sac, and [Smith] just got out and started running,' Garry remembers. The first to go after him was Tim Foljhan, a sometimes back-up musician for Cat Power who made his own music with the band Two Dollar Guitar. He and Smith had hit it off, and by the time Garry got to the spot in the darkness where they'd disappeared they were both off a cliff—Smith had run over the edge and Foljhan had followed him. '[Smith] landed on a tree and the branch went into his back,' says Garry. 'He wouldn't go to the hospital and we took him back to the hotel, and it was like "what the fuck is going on?" I felt responsible. It was my friend that I bring on this, everybody's fun happy road trip.'*

"*'At the show the next day, he was kind of, said sorry he put everybody through that, and bandaged up his back—the last thing he really wanted to do was to make a spectacle of himself and have everybody freaking out.'*"[96]

As usual, details matter, and it was important for Alyson to requote the entire story here, which looked a bit different with all the details. Elliott had been drinking, he had been running in the dark, drunk, without even knowing there was a cliff, and, with all these details, the entire incident looked like a stupid thing done under the influence of alcohol, without thinking about the consequences, not a suicide attempt.

Schultz revisited the story as a dumb act by a drunk guy in his book, despite declaring in an interview with *The Independent*, "*Being someone who had openly threatened to kill himself on numerous occasions (and had once jumped off a cliff), a verdict of suicide seemed natural.*"[97]

The facts revealed by Dorien Garry in *Torment Saint*[82] once again told us a different story:

"*As they came to a stop Elliott threw open the back door and bolted. 'He was incredibly drunk and embarrassed by the crying,' Garry says, 'And I don't think he even realized what he was doing.' The impulse was simply to run, to put some distance between himself and the car and the people in it. To be alone, in other words. Gary recalls, 'There was a drop-off at the end of the cul de sac that Elliott did not even see, no one could see it.' So, without clear intention or any true sense of what he was in for, Elliott ran off the cliff, landing on a tree that stopped his fall and punctured his back badly.... Garry's sense is that 'by no means was that a suicide attempt. He didn't know there was a cliff there, none of us did. It was just a mistake. I think he thought he was going down some kind of hill where he could be by himself and sit down and get things together.*"[82]

For Alyson it was about time to put this cliff story to rest, as it was obviously not a real suicide attempt; Elliott was drunk and upset with the people who were in the car with him. He had run away without knowing there was a cliff. He had not had the intention to kill himself. But myths are hard to overcome, and Elliott often played along in interviews, throwing in a jokingly "*It didn't work.*" The irony is that this episode continued to follow Elliott with a vengeance as an argument that he had definitively killed himself on October 21, 2003.

After going through many articles, it was becoming clear to Alyson that, psychologically, Chiba's story was not holding up. Many details of the day that Elliott died are still unclear: the time of the police arrival was still unknown and Chiba appearance at that moment was never described: "*No one has any info about how blood-stained she was when the police came,*"[24] said Ruth, who had insisted that had Chiba done CPR on Elliott she should have been soaked with blood. "*If she was soaked in Elliott's blood wouldn't they be suspicious? And if she wasn't soaked, why not?*" added Ruth. "*I think that, if she was in the bathroom, it was to wash herself.*"[24] This last part was pure speculation, but this is what people do to fill the blanks.

Meanwhile, the police report had also mentioned that a nail and hair kit had been collected at the scene but, again, no follow-up on this has ever been revealed, and Alyson and others wonder if any DNA/blood analysis had ever been conducted on any of these items. Could skin cells have been found under his fingernails? "*It is nothing like these CSI TV shows,*"[87] Detective Morris said once to Alyson. Nevertheless, he also mentioned that other reports besides the autopsy existed, although he never said anything about the nature of these reports.

Chapter 8: Abigail Russell

A starfucker

Abigail and Alyson had a very long discussion one day in December 2012. Abigail struggled with heroin addiction for almost 18 years, and in December 2012, she was still fighting it but seemed to be winning. She was a voluble woman, a flamboyant character, a little crazy at times (in a good way), and basically a kind and caring person. She had had a very difficult start in life with an abusive father and a series of bad boyfriends, but she seemed to be doing better. She had found a nice guy and was happy to be alive. She was on methadone, and she almost proudly showed Alyson her legs and arms and the holes made by the needles, as if they were battle scars. She was walking with a cane because one of her legs had been damaged so much by drug use. Her speech was a little slurred, but she could talk for hours, and she make complete sense.

Abigail had been involved in LA's East Side music scene for a long time, and had hung around a local band, the Warlocks, whose music was fueled by druggy psychedelia. In 1999, they had a popular song called "Cocaine

Blues," and had produced a very DIY video at Bobby Hecksher's house. Hecksher was the singer and main songwriter of the Warlocks and also Jennifer Chiba's boyfriend at the time. Abigail knew Chiba, although they had never been close friends. While Chiba had often tried to be friendly with her, Abigail had been very reluctant to get close. She had found Chiba volatile and too interested in dating famous people. Abigail even had a nickname for Chiba, "*starfucker*."[98]

In 2001, Chiba broke up with Bobby, and she decided to win over Elliott. Actually, in a total deluded mode, Chiba thought she was already his girlfriend.

In August 2001, Abigail and Chiba were attending the same Sunset Junction Street Fair as Alyson, and the women were watching Elliott struggling through his set, failing miserably. It was obvious that Elliott was on drugs, and Abigail was furious. She turned toward Chiba and said, "*What have you done to him?*" When they spoke in 2012, Abigail told Alyson that Chiba had asked her to score heroin several times, as Chiba apparently didn't know where to get heroin, or didn't want to do it herself. "*You are a party girl,*" she had told Abigail. "*You know where to get heroin*!" Abigail was mad at Chiba for equating heroin with partying. Didn't she know anything about drugs? Heroin was not a party drug! Didn't she know that addicts took heroin to release pain, not to party?

Abigail had scored the drug anyway, several times. She may have needed the money, or she may have not cared about Chiba's use of heroin. But Abigail knew Chiba was not really into hard drugs herself so she had to be supplying a friend of hers, one of the addicts she knew. However, Abigail realized that day that the heroin had been for another recipient, as Elliott was a complete mess despite the nurturing help of his girlfriend Valerie, who was backstage constantly trying to encourage him.

Chiba was on the defensive, "*You're wrong, I'm trying to get him clean,*" she said to Abigail that day. But Abigail was convinced that the drugs she had been scoring for Chiba had been delivered to Elliott.[98]

Elliott moved from the East Coast to the West Coast in 1999, and despite previous problems with alcohol he had not really taken hard drugs before stepping into the City of Angels (Los Angeles). As she told Alyson,

Abigail was convinced that hard drugs entered his life a few months after he met Chiba.

Although they had been in the same music circles for a while, Abigail's and Chiba's paths hadn't crossed very often, but Abigail told Alyson once that she couldn't believe her eyes when she saw Chiba sitting on Elliott's lap at one of the music parties she was attending that year. They were not in a relationship yet, but Chiba was trying very hard to get Elliott's attention. Like a few others, Chiba was thinking that Elliott would eventually be interested, and she was regularly showing up at his shows and was heard screaming "*You are hot!*"

Later on, Chiba even told people that Elliott had written many songs about her, though these songs had been written long before they had been seriously dating. At that time, before he and Chiba became official, Elliott often hung out late at night at a popular bar called the Roost on Los Feliz Boulevard, and Chiba was showing up there regularly.

Ruth told Alyson that Elliott's friends used to joke about it.[24] One night, as Elliott was about to leave for his 2000 European tour, the bar's patrons saw this scene: Chiba was intensely trying to go out with Elliott, but she was left crying, defeated. Still, things must have evolved in Chiba's favor at some point; not only was Chiba sitting on his lap at that 2001 party, but her name was even featured among the liner notes of Elliott's *Figure 8* album.

Abigail explained to Alyson that her loathing of Chiba had grown every time she had seen her, and she struggled to comprehend how Chiba had ended up living with Elliott after his rehab treatment. Although she had never pretended to have been a close friend, not even any kind of friend, Abigail had grown a bit closer to Elliott over the years since the two of them had attended the same rehab treatment, the Telesis Foundation in Van Nuys, where Elliott had first attempted to get clean before the last time in 2002. Abigail noted that Chiba never drove Elliott to the rehab center even once. Wouldn't that be the role of a girlfriend? Of someone trying to help him get clean? Abigail could not believe that Chiba had claimed she had been Elliott's girlfriend since 1999.[98]

Bobby H.

Abigail wanted to tell Alyson a story that had haunted her. One spring night of 2003, about five months before Elliott's death, Abigail was hanging out at a local bar when she saw Chiba who, under the influence of alcohol, confided in her: "*'I don't know what to do to keep Elliott,' Chiba said. 'He wants to leave me. I am ready to get knocked up by Bobby or anyone to keep him.'*"[98]

Abigail was shocked. She couldn't believe what she had just heard. How could a woman do that to someone she supposedly loved? What did Chiba expect to accomplish by this shady stratagem? At that time, Elliott had been living at Chiba's place since his rehab treatment, and Abigail concluded that things were not really working as Chiba had expected.

When Alyson heard this from Abigail, she had already learned from the family member that the romantic relationship between Elliott and Chiba had not started immediately but rather a few months after he had split with Valerie and moved into Chiba's home. Since he had alienated himself from many people, Elliott was vulnerable and in a position he had never been in before. The family member didn't believe Elliott would have ever become involved with Chiba in other circumstances and, according to this person, there were good reasons to believe she was not someone Elliott would have chosen for a relationship.[80] This fit very well with Abigail's story and added some context to what Deanna had told Alyson:

"*Jennifer [Chiba] made an earlier attempt to get with Elliott but it failed. He knew she was a crazy fan, so I don't know how he ended up with her, but drugs make sense even though she claims she got him clean.*"[4]

In the fall of that same year, Abigail was visiting her family in Michigan when she learned about Elliott's death. She was horrified and right away didn't believe it was a suicide.[98]

Abigail was determined to help solve the case, but Alyson would never know if Abigail was speculating or giving first-hand information. Abigail, who had had drug problems almost all her life, died in September 2013 of complications from drug use, just a few months after last talking to Alyson. It was heartbreaking. Alyson received a message on her phone from someone she didn't know, and didn't check it immediately. It turned out the message was from a friend of Abigail's, announcing the sad news. It was surprising to learn that, just before her death, Abigail had told this friend to call Alyson. This is how passionate Abigail had been about the cause until the end, how determined she had been to help Alyson get the facts straight.

Abigail's friend and Alyson talked for a few minutes. Alyson explained to her how she knew Abigail, and the woman right away said that she didn't want to have anything to do with this story.

Abigail had talked to Alyson a few times during the last months of her life, but her sentiments toward the events of October 21, 2003 were very straightforward. She told Alyson a few intriguing things, but since she couldn't remember where she had received the information, Alyson always had to take everything as hearsay.

Abigail told Alyson that she knew Chiba had waited some time (maybe 20 minutes?) before calling 911, and this is a story that Alyson had already heard from the family member and would hear again later from other sources. Abigail thought that an accomplice was a possibility, and she was also convinced that Chiba had taken a shower after the stabbing, as she "*had wet hair*" and was "*freshly showered*" when the police arrived.

Abigail even said that she had heard somewhere that the shower curtain was brand new. "*There was blood everywhere, on the bed, in the shower, but not on the curtain?*"[98] Abigail had said in a very angry tone. However, she died before providing a valid source for this information, and Alyson has never been able to find out anything else about it.

As a longtime member of the Los Angeles psychedelic scene, Abigail was nevertheless aware of Chiba's connections and disconnections. She mentioned to Alyson that she had talked to Bobby Hecksher a month before and had asked him about Chiba. Bobby had answered that he had not talked to Chiba for years, just like a lot of people from the good old days. "*All her friends are new ones,*" Abigail had added.[98]

After Abigail's death, Alyson decided to contact a musician, who asked to remain anonymous, that Abigail had mentioned during one of her conversations: "*It took 3 years for him to admit that Elliott's death seemed a bit eerie,*"[98] she had told Alyson. However, his answer was not the one Alyson would have hoped for; he was even surprised to have been contacted for such a thing:

"*No offense, but Abby liked to talk a lot,*" he told Alyson. "*I never knew Elliott and would never assume to know anything about him and Jenn's [Chiba's] relationship. I love/loved Abby to death but she sometimes thought she knew everything about everything. I know you're trying to write something on this, but I wouldn't necessarily take her word as law. I'm not trying to be a dick, I'm just telling you my opinion from someone who knew her pretty well. I'm not saying that she was a liar or untrustworthy, she just had a tendency to stick her nose where it didn't belong and embellish things. Sorry I can't be of much help to you, but I really have no information for you.*"[99]

Once again, Alyson was banging her head against a closed door. Abigail may have had a tendency "*to stick her nose where it didn't belong,*" but Alyson wished more people would do so! Isn't this how someone gets away with murder? People's reluctance at getting involved was once again in plain sight, and why would they get involved? They had nothing to gain and everything to lose. Alyson knew that. She knew it was a sort of lost cause, and it would require much more than an email or a request online to get anyone's assistance. Abigail was sincere in her concern for what had happened to Elliott. The problem was that most people weren't like Abigail, they did not want to risk unsettling their lives in pursuit of the truth.

Chapter 9: Isolation and domestic abuse

Quite a few women were in the race for Elliott's companionship in the last years of his life, but it was Chiba at the finish line. Like many other fans, Alyson saw her for the first time when Elliott made his comeback at the Echo, a few months after his rehab in October 2002. After that time, Chiba was a constant presence.

"*What happened to Valerie?*" Fans were asking on the message board. Since Elliott's death, Valerie has stayed very much out of the picture, and to this day she has stayed completely silent, and has not talked to anyone on the record, despite many people's attempts to contact her, including Alyson's.

According to someone close to Valerie who confided in Alyson, Elliott allegedly "*wanted to move to Scotland and marry Valerie,*" as he desired to disappear over there. Though it was unclear when Elliott allegedly had this in mind, it seemed to have been after Valerie's departure from Los Angeles, although this person wasn't sure of the timeline.

Back to early 2003. Elliott and Chiba were now inseparable, at least she was always with him at each concert. And even if the rumor of a fight between Chiba and Valerie seemed to be backed up by several sources, everyone was strangely silent about it. Chiba was seemingly taking more and more space in Elliott's life, while the aftermath of the fight was still unclear to people Alyson contacted.

Before rehab, Elliott was a Largo regular, often playing there with his friend Jon Brion. Largo, a small club owned by Mark Flanagan on Fairfax, was a very special venue. While Los Angelenos are used to noisy bars with people speaking loudly at the risk of covering the voices of the performers, there was no such thing happening at Flanagan's place, as respect and silence were the rules and the drinking was held in a separate bar, and still is.

After rehab, Elliott disappeared from this intimate scene. When Alyson and a few other women had the chance to talk to him after his show at the Echo in 2002, they asked him when he would play at Largo again. Elliott had answered with a tired voice: "*I don't go there anymore,*"[100] without giving more explanation. Then he walked away, with Chiba following close behind.

"*Chiba was banned from Mark Flanagan's place,*" Deanna said to Alyson a year later. "*She was selling drugs in the toilets and Mark does not like that at all, he is against drugs.*"[4] This may have been the reason why Elliott was not going to Largo anymore, this and his fall out with Jon Brion because of his drug use.

Despite his reticence, Elliott had distanced himself from many people while Chiba was taking over his life. "*People like Rob and Autumn were genuinely close with him. And, during that time leading up to his death, many of them were not on speaking terms with him for a while despite their love for him,*" one of the new owners of Elliott's studio told Alyson one day. "*Espinoza tried to talk to him about a few things and quickly feared that he was being put in the paranoid 'somebody that I used to know' column. He'd burned bridges with a lot of people who raised red flags of concern. Autumn couldn't watch him go down. Jon Brion tried to help but Elliott lashed out at him and lumped him in with DreamWorks as people who were trying to steal from him.*"[3]

Toward the end of his life, Elliott had definitively distanced himself from a lot of people he knew. "*I ain't gonna work on maggie's farm no more...*"[1] (h)hhelliott had jokingly written on his message board in 2002, probably alluding to the fact he was departing from his long-time manager Margaret Mittleman.

"*He did not want Chiba to be his manager*,"[98] Abigail had once said to Alyson, although Chiba's lawsuit would boldly claim the opposite. "*Elliott wanted to get rid of Chiba because she was very bossy, very controlling*,"[98] Abigail had added.

In 2003, Chiba wanted Elliott to become a client of Dr. Abigail Stanton, and it didn't matter to her that Stanton was already her personal therapist, a total no-no for a couple according to any psychologist. According to Dr. John Grohol, the founder of Psych Central, "*Unless the therapist is specifically doing family, child or couples counseling, most therapists try to avoid seeing people who know one another in a close or intimate manner. Doing so can cause all sorts of troublesome problems for both the therapist and the patient, as the therapist will hold secrets about the two parties that they may have a hard time not inadvertently divulging*,"[101]

However, this didn't stop Chiba and Stanton. "*And Stanton is a horrible doctor*,"[98] Abigail had once said. Abigail had also been treated by Stanton at one time. "*She almost killed me and gave me the wrong medication!*" This therapist had been recommended to Abigail by Chiba herself, who really liked Stanton because she was able to talk with her about "*Nietzsche, Kafka, and Kierkegaard*."[98]

With almost no old friends around and a new girlfriend, in the perspective of seeing a new doctor and the feebleness of letting his girlfriend write his set lists and book his shows, it was evident that Elliott's life had completely changed since rehab, with Chiba rapidly taking over many aspects of it. But it was difficult to entirely blame Chiba, as Elliott seemed to be willingly participating in his own isolation. He did not even try to reach out to Sam Coomes, his ex-bandmate, who was playing a show in town a few weeks before Elliott's death. Alyson heard that Sam had not been able to get hold of Elliott, who wouldn't respond to any of his calls.

After her conversations with Abigail and a few other people, Alyson was uncovering the truth little by little, but it was difficult to know what Elliott had truly decided to do with his life. Did he want to marry Chiba and start a family as some had reported? Or did he want to leave her and disappear in Scotland with Valerie? One thing was certain, his relationship with Chiba was a very rocky one, according to the numerous witnesses who had seen them together. Chiba was extremely jealous of any woman who got near him and kept him in a cage, or "*on leash*,"[29] as Elizabeth, another young woman interested in Elliott, had said.

On the other hand, Elliott was still interested in meeting other women, renewing old flames or even meeting new girls, or simply making new friends. "*I am trapped in someone's life*,"[29] he had said to Elizabeth. It was a bizarre situation, and women probably didn't want to have any problems with Chiba and didn't know what to do.

Alyson found out later that Elliott did see Valerie again, even once he had officially moved in with Chiba. To add to the confusion, just before entering rehab, Elliott may even have tried to reconnect with the French girlfriend he had in 1999. Elliott may have been confused; he may have been incapable of choosing where his life should be, and he was also changing his mind all the time. In the end, who knows if he really chose to be with Chiba as some people have said. Will we ever know?

However, to Alyson, Elliott's profile at the time of his death was growing clearer and clearer. Over the years, there had been a few other girls around, and his relationship with Chiba had nothing to do with the kind of love story told in some books and movies.

A few similar stories told before and after Elliott's death, were all pointing in the same direction: Chiba's jealous temper and a tempestuous relationship with Elliott.

Joanna

In 2003, Elliott decided to go see his ex-girlfriend, Joanna Bolme, who was playing in town. She told *Q Magazine*[102] in 2011 what happened that day:

"*The year he died Elliott came to see me play. He was excited about his studio and he hadn't been doing drugs. He wanted to show me his studio. I was going to go after the show, but (then girlfriend) Jennifer Chiba threw a fit and made him leave. That was a bummer—we hadn't hung out in years and been civil, and we were making some amends. It was the last time I saw him.*"[102]

A man wanting to sort of renew a relationship with an ex-girlfriend would have made any woman jealous, so in a way Chiba's reaction made sense. But it was difficult to understand why Elliott would have been so obedient, as if he didn't want to upset Chiba too much.

Chiba's behavior regarding Elliott's ex-girlfriends and friends may have revealed something more dramatic, and there was indeed drama at their house. It was nothing new. Alyson had already heard of Chiba's violent temper and manipulative nature. "*She made threats to all her previous boyfriends,*" said Abigail to Alyson, "*She may even have been responsible for Rivers Cuomo's depression and retreat in his black wall apartment in 1998,*"[98] she added.

Chiba and Weezer's frontman Rivers Cuomo had had a long on-and-off relationship before Chiba got involved with Elliott, although the exact duration of this relationship was questionable. Chiba had claimed a "*10-year*" relationship, while other sources were talking about a more modest timeline. According to most people, she had probably been Cuomo's on-and-off girlfriend from 1992 to 1995.[103] It was nevertheless certain that some Weezer songs from the album *Pinkerton*, and the character of Maria in Cuomo's rock opera *Songs from the Black Hole* were inspired by Chiba.[103]

"*She has threatened all her boyfriends,*" Abigail had insisted. "*She has said 'I'll kill myself if you leave me' to all of them.*"[98] Nobody would ever confirm that Chiba had said something of this nature to anyone or even to Elliott, but her litigious side probably did not encourage people to talk. However, until Abigail died, she was convinced this was the case.

Because she shared so much with him, from child abuse to depression and drug addiction, Abigail had always felt close to Elliott. She had made several suicide attempts and even had been once hospitalized at the same hospital with Chiba, who had allegedly also made a suicide attempt.

"*Well, she took heroin, but she is not a heroin addict,*" Abigail had said about Chiba. "*I bet she did it to 'impress' Elliott, to prove him 'I am like you…' to attract his attention…. Anyway she was released a day earlier than scheduled, so I think it was a BS suicide attempt.*"[98]

This sounded very bizarre, but this alleged looking-for-attention behavior echoed a few things Alyson had learned. She believed Abigail because the family member had also told her that Chiba had "*a psychiatric history and hospitalizations in mental institutions.*"[80] At least this is what this person claimed Chiba herself had said to him.

Org Records

In 2003, Chiba was trying to launch or maybe re-launch her own musical career. Elliott was helping her band *Happy Ending* with their upcoming EP, which was supposed to be released on Org Records, a UK label run by Sean Organ.[83] Sean was living in England but admitted to being tired of the stories that were coming back from LA, and after Elliott's death, he commented, "... *People described them as a Sid and Nancy couple, constantly arguing, splitting up and getting back together again. I can't really comment on it because I'm in London, they were over there in the US and I've never met them, but all I was hearing were that it was a crazed, druggy Sid and Nancy situation.*"[83]

A Silverlake musician

Alyson heard more disturbing stories, all coming from people around the music industry. First, Seth (not his real name), an aspiring musician, had been a member of the Silverlake scene at the time. He was trying to make it as a musician and had often attended parties at more famous people's houses, hanging out with local bands that had opened for Elliott a few times.

Seth told Alyson that a young front man of an upcoming band, who had grown closer to Elliott, allegedly had the misfortune to witness one of the couple's fights and Chiba's terrible behavior. "*That bitch was getting physical with him in fights. Seriously! She was like a domestic abuser!*"[104] Seth claimed the young man said at a party that he and Seth were both attending. Alyson tried to contact this person in order to confirm this story, but she unfortunately never received an answer.

Years later, Seth mentioned he had talked to people who had had a conversation with a famous singer-songwriter, known for his piano-driven songs. He admired Elliott's work very much and had even written a song about him after his death. Seth allegedly overheard at a party that this musician had talked about witnessing Chiba hit Elliott once.[104]

It's certainly difficult to have inside information about a couple's life, especially when the events occurred more than a decade earlier. Every story has the patina of shady gossip and could easily be dismissed as hearsay. However, stories coming from different sources were aiming in the same direction. Elliott Smith and Jennifer Chiba's relationship was certainly not the rosy portrait she was painting after his death. The future wedding, the garden, and the potential children were probably not their reality.

A sound engineer

In 2015, a sound-engineer named Rick (not his real name), who had been recording an album at Elliott's studio in 2002, told Alyson about strange events he had witnessed. "*Elliott had disappeared for 2 to 3 days, but when he came back, he looked horrible,*"[105] he told Alyson. "*And he gave me the worst excuse ever. He had a fight with his girlfriend who was chasing him around with a knife during an argument.*"[105] A few years later, this recollection had become a bit blurry in his mind. In any case, it was a disturbing story that he completely discounted at the time because of Elliott's serious drug problems—as this supposedly had happened before his rehab treatment. The sound engineer added: "*At the time, his girlfriend seemed to be the sane one.*"[105] However, when Elliott died, the sound engineer was shaken and troubled, and even called a friend in LA to remind him of the story, wondering what may have happened to Elliott in the end.

A fan from Florida

A few years after Elliott's death, Alyson heard several stories that once again confirmed Chiba's terrible temper. First, she heard from a Florida woman, a loyal Elliott Smith fan and frequent visitor of the message board. For this reason, Alyson had known this person for years, and even though she had only been an internet acquaintance, she was not a stranger.

This fan had befriended Chiba after Elliott's death. In a strange twist of events, Chiba had even invited a few fans to stay in her house, the same house where Elliott had violently died barely a year earlier. Since she was living in Florida, this fan accepted the invitation to spend some time in Los Angeles, especially because she had just fallen for a guy who was planning to move there.

"*Chiba took us to places where she and Elliott used to go all the time. We were up until dawn,*"[106] she told Alyson. "*I went back home, but [my boyfriend and Chiba] stayed in touch and she pretty much started taking him everywhere with her. He was a model, so I'm not surprised she wanted the arm candy. He fell on some hard times and had to move in with her. Then I found out they were sleeping together, after I already had bought a plane ticket to fly out for his birthday. It was an awkward trip. I stopped talking to her, but I was very hurt. The whole time she would call me and act like nothing was happening. While he was living with her, he would tell me stories about how she would get drunk and scream at him and throw bottles and glasses and threaten to kill herself. This was like a weekly occurrence, and he didn't realize what he'd gotten himself into. He was scared a lot of the time and she made him feel guilty like it was his fault. She was so manipulative.*"[106]

Chiba stealing this woman's boyfriend months after Elliott's tragic death was one thing, not really anyone's business to be honest, but the fact that Chiba was fighting with him was another story.

Chapter 10: Torment Saint at Skylight Books

Academia takeover

Ten years later, the investigation seemed to have stagnated at the same point, as the forensic analysis of Elliott's alleged suicide had been ignored by the media. Meanwhile, Chiba was getting another exoneration in W.T. Schultz's book *Torment Saint,* published in 2013, just in time for the 10th anniversary of Elliott's death. Alyson took the opportunity to meet the author during his tour for the release of his book at Skylight Books in Los Angeles. She was barely surprised to find herself sitting in front of Chiba (who had come with an entourage).

Schultz's talk, which he called "Elliott Smith Prehistory," covered Elliott's first years in Texas and Portland, retracing his ascension to "fame." Schultz made his sparse audience listen to very early and never-heard-before instrumental recordings (provided by Elliott's buddies from Texas), he showed pictures of Elliott when he was attending the 7th or 8th grade, and compared songs Elliott had recorded with his first band, *Stranger than Fiction*, to songs he recorded later on for *XO* and *Figure 8*.

Alyson expected Schultz to read excerpts from his book, as is often the case in this kind of event, but he had instead prepared a PowerPoint presentation to illustrate these recordings.

As expected, the Q&A started slow and dull, with the commonplace questions. Totally uninteresting for Alyson who, without having read the book yet (she had just picked it up), had been browsing through the last chapters.

People were mostly interested in Elliott's unreleased songs, and Alyson was only interested in his relationship with Chiba. After a question about the family and the difficulty in releasing unreleased material, Alyson, who really hated public attention, could not stay silent, and decided to ask a question: "*Did you talk to the Portland family?*" The question triggered some sort of convoluted answer from Schultz. "*It's a tricky question to answer. It's not true that I didn't talk to his family, but it's also a little less untrue that I did talk to his family.*"[107]

Schultz claimed he had interviewed a lot of people off the record, adding with an almost angry voice while looking straight at Alyson, "*I know that some people have said 'Schultz never talked to his family,' 'How could he write a book when he never talked to his family,'... but it's not true that I never talked to his family,*"[107] he repeated several times looking totally pissed off at that moment.

Alyson continued, asking if he had talked to a specific person, Elliott's biological father, Gary Smith. Schultz answered that Gary Smith had been the very first person he had contacted. "*We had very courteous and polite email exchanges,*"[107] Schultz said. Then he added that he still had hope that Gary, who had never talked to anyone before, would talk to him. But, according to Schultz, Gary had finally said he wasn't emotionally ready to do so, even though almost 10 years had passed. Alyson concluded that Schultz had talked to the Welches on Elliott's mother's side, and very probably to Elliott's half-sister Ashley.

"*Can you write a biography without talking to the parents?*" continued Alyson, who had decided to bother Schultz a bit more. He justified himself by saying that Elliott's parents knew him far less than his good friends, and claimed that he had compensated for not talking to the parents by the fact he had talked to so many people who really loved Elliott and were very close to him (in Portland, Texas, and LA), that it was indeed possible to write a biography without involving the family. He was, however, visibly very upset about Alyson's question. Alyson continued asking about other people, especially the ones who had been very reluctant to talk about Elliott, people like Jon Brion, Joanna Bolme, Autumn de Wilde… all the people who apparently weren't in his book.

"*It's almost a policy that they don't want to talk about him,*"[107] Schultz answered.

Alyson had actually briefly talked to Autumn in 2007, during the signing of her photography book simply called *Elliott Smith*, and although Autumn had looked a bit shocked by Alyson's question regarding Elliott's passing, she had nevertheless answered: "*Only one person knows what happened, and she is not talking.*"[108]

Similarly, in the 2010 October edition of NME,[40] devoted to Elliott with interviews of some of his close friends, Autumn had declared:

"*The circumstances surrounding his death don't sit well with me at all, but there was only one other person there, so nobody will ever know. He wasn't around the type of people where I could know for sure what would happen anymore. He was surrounded by sycophants, so who knows what could have happened? He had talked about suicide for many years, but he was always such a chicken about getting hurt! And there had been times in the past where suicide seemed more likely. He didn't have any drugs in his body that day—does that make him more or less likely to do something? I don't know. I wasn't there and we weren't talking at that time so, in a way, I felt like I had already said my goodbyes and I just hoped that maybe he would be okay someday. It's hard to mourn for a friend like Elliott Smith, because there are always 400 other people trying to prove how close they were to him, and you feel like an asshole talking about it. There are a lot of people out there who will talk about Elliott and how well they knew him in order to promote themselves, or to draw attention to their closeness to him.*"[40]

The declaration clearly refuted Schultz's claims. What kind of policy was Schultz even talking about? Not only had Autumn talked about Elliott to major media (NME), but she had shared her feelings regarding his death. Even Joana Bolme had been interviewed for the NME production.

Nevertheless, Schultz's talk brought up a few interesting points. Schultz couldn't decide if Elliott had really been abused as a child, as he was probably reluctant to say anything which could have upset the family. He said it was "*a really tough and complicated question.*"[107] He reported that Elliott's Texas friends had said they had never seen the stepfather do anything abusive to Elliott, other than witnessing verbal disputes between the two and Elliott calling Charlie an "*asshole.*" In his book, Schultz declared that Elliott had begun to recall memories of child abuse in the last years of his life, but that they could have been false memories.

"*There is no way to be certain about what happened in terms of abuse during these early years. I really don't know what happened. In the book I considered all possible sides and reported on what people had told me, and it's up to the reader to decide.*"[107]

It was more and more obvious he had talked to Ashley, Charlie's daughter, who had always denied the abuse story.

"*I don't think it is pretty clear he was abused,*" continued Schultz. "*That's true he wrote songs about it but that doesn't prove he was abused.... If you write a lot of songs and even name this person Charlie, it sounds very much like abuse, indexing something real, but on the other hand, writing a song about abuse could be a more metaphorical portrait of something that didn't happen, so this is tricky.*"[107]

Alyson thought it was really interesting that the abuse story could suddenly have become a metaphor when many of Elliott's lyrics dealing with suicide ideation had been interpreted as a proof of suicide, especially in Schultz's book *Torment Saint*: "*He had written songs declaring suicide's lure, if not its inevitability.... No one, it seems, had seriously considered a possibility other than suicide. If anything, suicide was predetermined, overdetermined, not 'undetermined.'*"[82]

In *Torment Saint*, Schultz evoked the letters the stepfather had written to Elliott to apologize, saying he had changed, and hoped for forgiveness and a restoration of their relationship, while insisting he had never sexually abused anyone. Schultz also mentioned a quote from another friend from Texas: "*There are things that I know from Texas that I will never tell anyone.*"[107]

After the Q&A, Alyson decided to continue the conversation during the book signing portion of the event. To rebound on his metaphor for the abuse part, Alyson asked Schultz if he thought it could be the same for the suicide part. Elliott talked and wrote about suicide a lot and it could be a metaphor too, right? Alyson had been somewhat disappointed that the question of Elliott's death hadn't been discussed at Schultz's talk, despite being the elephant in the room, and the subject of an entire chapter in his book.

"*Did you read my last chapter?*" Schultz replied. She hadn't had the time to read the book, but the last chapter had been the first thing she had browsed. Alyson was left unconvinced by Schultz's writings, as the last chapter(s) were obviously very impregnated by Chiba's narration.

At this time, Schultz looked even more pissed off, even offended and upset. He said he had interviewed Dr. Scheinin in depth, and she had refuted one by one all the elements that had been described as bizarre for a case of suicide. Alyson, who had also interviewed Dr. Scheinin, was surprised by this statement, but even more surprised by Schultz's uncomfortable look.

On a side note, Alyson had already had a Twitter "*encounter*" with Schultz when he was promoting his book on Amazon with a synopsis describing Elliott's violent death: "*Smith died violently... of a single fatal stab wound to the chest.*" Alyson could not let him get away with that, and she confronted him on Twitter about it. He tried to justify the synopsis by saying that "*it says 'single fatal stab wound' because that is Scheinin's restated position—only one of the stab wounds was truly fatal... based on [a] detailed interview with [the] LA coroner. Just one of the wounds perforated the heart.*"[109]

Alyson found the description misleading and she was certain that Dr. Scheinin had told her that both wounds had been fatal. The synopsis posted on Amazon has since been changed, but it was nevertheless interesting to note that a man who had claimed to have done such an in-depth interview with Dr. Scheinin had been trying to downplay the severity of the case. One stab wound looked much less dramatic than two.

While still talking directly to Schultz, Alyson decided to go back to her burning question, reiterating the rarity of suicide by stabbing in the chest. "*No, it wasn't that rare,*"[107] Schultz replied. "*What about the possible defense wounds?*" continued Alyson. Schultz claimed that Dr. Scheinin had told him that they weren't actually defense wounds—even though they had been described as "*possible defense wounds*" on the autopsy report in 2003—and that if there had been defense wounds they would have been found in larger numbers.

"*And the stabbing through the shirt?*" continued Alyson. Again, Schultz said it was not rare, and much easier to do when people are wearing a T-shirt instead of a buttoned shirt. He was determined to refute any of her arguments, whereas Alyson had done plenty of research on these points. Since, in the book, he had dismissed this last point (the stabbing through the clothing) based on a quote from recording engineer Fritz Michaud stating that "*Elliott would have never been caught with his shirt off,*"[82] Alyson took the occasion to point out that there was a very well-known photo of Elliott posing shirtless. Schultz took this as an attack and grew angry. He said that Dr. Scheinin actually had wanted to rule it a suicide, but had been careful in order to spare the family. Alyson had a hard time believing him. If Dr. Scheinin's purpose had been to spare the family, she had also been casting suspicion on someone else at the same time, and wouldn't it have been even worse, in a sense, to imply it was a homicide, to imply someone else had done it? And in this specific case, to imply that Chiba, the only person present, had done it?

Plus, this had not been Alyson's impression from Dr. Scheinin at all, as she had never tipped the scale in favor of suicide or murder during Alyson's interview with Dr. Scheinin. "*Dr. Scheinin was neutral as to the manner of death as I would expect any clinician in her position to be when handling a post-mortem with compelling evidence both for and against suicide,*" nurse Lonnie had commented. "*I have not read Mr. Schultz's entire account but it maybe he was very selective about which of her remarks, or which parts, he chose to use.*"[36]

But Schultz wanted to have the last word, the last argument. "*There is not a friend that I have interviewed who doesn't think it was a suicide!*"[107] he said as if he wanted to close this debate once and for all. But Alyson remembered an old segment on NPR from the time when *From a Basement on the Hill* was released in 2004, during which Largo owner Mark Flanagan had declared on the air "*I don't believe he killed himself.*"[110] Could this have been more direct? This was at least one friend who had expressed an opinion opposite to suicide in a very public manner.

Then there was a long article published by *Pitchfork* ("Keep the Things You Forgot: An Elliott Smith Oral History")[111] to commemorate the 10th anniversary of his death, with plenty of people talking about Elliott, ironically many who had not talked to Schultz. Among it all, there was a declaration by recording engineer Rob Schnapf, who had participated in the final touches of Elliott's posthumous album:

"*It's a cool, beautiful record. He wrote it when he was alive. He didn't write it when he was dead, he didn't write it after a suicide, or after a murder, or whatever the fuck happened. When he was writing it, he still wanted to live his life… after a suicide, or after a murder, or whatever the fuck happened.*"[111] In this quote, Rob didn't sound like someone having no doubt it was a suicide.

There was also the Flaming Lips concert in Los Angeles that Alyson had attended, during which Wayne Coyne and bandmate Steven Drozd had dedicated a song to Elliott and declared: "*We were on tour, I forget it has been a few years now, we were on tour when we heard the news that our friend Elliott Smith had died. And I don't think we will ever really know if he took his own life or whatever the actual circumstances were.*"[112]

These are only a few examples that come to mind. Years later, after the screening of *Heaven Adores You,* [113] a documentary made about Elliott's life that totally excluded Chiba from the picture, Alyson had a short conversation with someone involved in the movie, and he candidly told her that Elliott's friends were divided on the question, with half of them believing he had killed himself and the other half being suspicious or considering that he was murdered. Any way you look at it, we were far from "*there is not a friend who doesn't think it was a suicide!*" claimed by Schultz.[107]

Alyson ultimately replied that she had talked to people who didn't believe it was suicide, and were, at least, suspicious. Schultz could not have been more upset. He was particularly angry at the fact that Alyson had not been impressed by his interview with Dr. Scheinin and his interpretation of her analysis.

Reyes and Chiba are back on the scene

But the day wasn't done. Shortly after her confrontation with Schultz, Gil Reyes, who was still there, called Alyson over, probably recognizing her from her bold questions during the infamous *Searching for Elliott Smith*

Q&A. He was committed to being friendly; he even wanted to make peace, asking Alyson if she would agree to have a coffee with him, and even a talk with Chiba. "*What? Would she accept an interview?*" replied Alyson. "*Maybe,*" Reyes replied. "*There is no need for all this,*"[114] he added, referring to Alyson's internet writing about the suspicious circumstances surrounding Elliott's death. He still wanted to convince Alyson that Chiba was totally innocent, saying he had talked to someone from the police (of course he couldn't reveal who this person was) who had informed him they thought it was a suicide. The problem was that Alyson had talked to detectives J. King and P.J. Morris over the years and they had always told her they couldn't say anything because the case was still open. Why would the police have acted differently with Reyes, especially when the family couldn't obtain any information, even through the Freedom of Information Act?

Suddenly, Reyes started talking about the cuts, especially the one on Elliott's right arm, the possible defensive wound that was at the center of much speculation, and he came up with this story: "*Elliott could have done this to himself when falling on the balcony.*"[114] Alyson was surprised. How many explanations did he want to manifest about these cuts? First, there was the sneaky insinuation they were due to self-cutting that he claimed during the Q&A after the screening of *Searching for Elliott Smith*, and now Elliott's falling on the balcony was the reason for the cuts?

A few years ago, a friend sent Alyson an old interview of Reyes published by the Cardinal Times, Lincoln High's school paper,[115] in 2005. Lincoln High was a Portland high school that Elliott had attended, and the school paper had interviewed Reyes because of his desire to do a documentary about one of their indie-rock heroes. At the time (2005), Reyes hadn't met Chiba yet and had a totally different perspective for his movie, as was demonstrated by this excerpt of the article:

"*Reyes has veered away from Smith's death in his documentary, saying he 'didn't want to deal with that part [of his life]'.... No accusations have been made, but investigations are still in progress. Reyes feels the authorities 'jumped the gun in calling his death a suicide,' which led the press to 'come down on the fact that he was depressed.' Reyes's documentary looks upon Smith in a different light, encompassing the entirety of his career in music, not simply his death.*"[115]

For Alyson it was clear that, if in 2005, Reyes thought that the authorities had "*jumped the gun in calling his death a suicide,*" something had happened between 2005 and 2010, as a large part of his movie was actually spent demonstrating Chiba's innocence in Elliott's suicide.

Since Reyes was there at the screening, talking about this horrible day, Alyson decided to confront him about this old interview. His answer was very evasive. First, he couldn't remember what she was talking about, then he said in a tone of mockery, "*You are quoting a high school paper?*"[114] as if he wanted to dismiss the whole thing. Lincoln High was a respected school, the interview was valid, and the article was actually well written. At that time, Reyes was filming the Portland part of his documentary and was interviewing Elliott Smith's former teachers at Lincoln High.

It is very interesting to note that Reyes was very unwilling to recognize he had felt that way just a few years ago. It looked like everything changed when Chiba approached him a few years later, asking if she could participate in the movie.

But that day of the screening, Reyes looked like a guy who wanted to play the mediator between Alyson and Chiba, and he made the introduction. Alyson had already briefly talked with Chiba, at the Getty Museum during a homage to Elliott in 2005, but Chiba had given her the cold shoulder at the time. Now, six years later, Chiba remembered Alyson. "*You asked me those questions at the Q&A,*"[116] she said in a mellow tone. Alyson asked her immediately if she would do an interview with her, and a young guy who was standing there took Chiba by the shoulders, glared at Alyson, and said in a borderline menacing tone, "*She will think about it.*"[116] That night, Alyson gave Chiba her phone number, fully aware she would never hear from her.

Chapter 11: A few old friends

Over the years, Alyson had managed to speak with many people who knew Elliott, but one of the main problems had always been this was still a small number of people, and the number of people willing to go on the record even slimmer.

As a matter of fact, many of Elliott's friends and colleagues had always been reluctant to talk publicly, and some of them like Jon Brion and Sam Coomes had never spoken out about their late friend. Alyson had a brief exchange with Sam, but each time she tried to approach one of Elliott's close friends like him, two things were obvious: They hadn't been in contact with Elliott recent to his death, and they were certainly not present at the moment of his death, so they were very reluctant to comment on it. Plus, the subject was still extremely painful for them because of unresolved issues at the time of his shocking death.

"*The chances of you getting the truth out of one of Elliott's crowd is very slim*," Alyson had been told a variation of this by several people, and it was true. Elliott's crowd hadn't been very cooperative, and even if some of them had suspicions, they probably didn't want to point the finger at someone without concrete evidence, or they may have been afraid of a potential lawsuit from Chiba. After all, she had already sued a handful of people.

However, Alyson was surprised to encounter many people willing to talk to her off the record, engaging in a conversation without even asking about her intentions. With a few exceptions, the information she got through these conversations has never been contradictory, and that is an important point. Consistency is a good sign in pursuit of the truth. Alyson decided to listen to anyone eager to talk to her, whether this person wanted to stay anonymous or not. She was well aware that any anonymous reporting would be dismissed and criticized as "*hearsay,*" but it was not very different from what other journalists had done for similar cases, and what W. T. Schultz had done at times for his book *Torment Saint,* as he had not always named his sources. Alyson had actually spoken with people who verified they did not talk to Schultz, and she was prepared to prove her own conversations had genuinely taken place, if needed.

An old friend from Hampshire College

There were a few people who had no problem going on the record, including Serena Williams. Serena had attended Hampshire College in Amherst, Massachusetts with Elliott in the '80s. When she exchanged a few emails with Alyson in 2013-2014, she was especially eager to talk about the last time she had seen Elliott. She had known him for sixteen years and had been suspicious of his alleged suicide since the day he died, while vehemently saying to Alyson that more should have been done to uncover the facts surrounding Elliott's death. Right away, Alyson liked Serena, who told her she wasn't interested "*in remaining anonymous,*"[117] having "*nothing to hide.*"[117]

During the last months of his life, several concerts had been booked, and Elliott played three gigs in New York in June 2003. Eager to say hello to her old friend, Serena had decided to go to one of the shows. Before the concert, she had met Valerie Deerin without suspecting that she was one of Elliott's old flames. Both women were determined to see Elliott after the show. Serena told Alyson:

"It was just too much of a coincidence that in that small window of time she was in town and that I met her, and we both happened to know Elliott, and I just happened to be going to his show... and just happened to have a plus one. She was so excited to go, just giddy with happiness. I had never met her before... it just seemed so unlikely that she actually had been in this serious relationship with him as well. But I never understood why there was such an explosion once we got to the venue either. From my own experience, Valerie was very personable and kind, and she was not capable of hurting a fly, so the fact that Jennifer [Chiba] accused her of 'assault' was just really bizarre and seemed entirely out of context. Now it makes a lot more sense to me."[117]

Despite the fact that Elliott had moved in with Chiba, Valerie had apparently not given up. Serena did not expect Chiba's reception, though Valerie probably did, but didn't care. When Chiba recognized Valerie, she threw a tantrum, began to scream and made a scene. Serena, who witnessed the incident, told Alyson:

"I was with Valerie Deerin. A terrible row took place between her and Jennifer Chiba, Jennifer accused Valerie of attacking her. Later, Jennifer would not let her come backstage with me and my other friend. Jennifer loudly and falsely accused Valerie of attacking her (it was patently untrue as I'd been with her the entire time and nothing of the sort took place). Elliott gave me his number to give to Valerie so he could talk to her privately later, and then we all spent the night at my friend's loft together."[117]

Serena told Alyson what happened when she met with Elliott:

"When I spent time with him alone that last night, Jennifer Chiba was not there for most of it but he never talked about her as a serious girlfriend to me; rather he seemed to be weary of her and he apologized profusely for her behavior. She basically yanked him away from me in the middle of a conversation and brought him into another room next to the one we were hanging out in backstage (or downstairs in this case). We could actually hear her screaming, she was so loud, and she was insisting that Valerie had assaulted her. It was crazy. And if that were really the case, then why is it not in the new book that is out? Being assaulted is far worse than being called 'a whore'... but she won't say it now because it never happened."[117]

Serena was alluding to Schultz's book, who had mentioned a clash between Chiba and [Valerie] Deerin in it: "*Once, according to Chiba, Deerin called her a 'fucking whore,' and accused her of addicting Elliott to heroin.*"[82]

Serena was right. If Valerie had effectively assaulted Chiba, why hadn't she said so to Schultz?

"*She made us all leave,*" continued Serena, "*breaking up the party because she was so angry, and she seemed to think I was responsible for having brought Valerie knowingly. She told my friend 'if he sees her he'll kill himself' which also seemed psychotic of her. And yes… Elliott was happy to see Valerie, but Jennifer [Chiba] wouldn't let them near each other. That's why he gave me his phone number—so she could get in touch with him later.*"[117]

Since she was his girlfriend, it was somewhat comprehensible to see Chiba react this way when she saw Valerie; after all, what would any woman do if an ex showed up at your boyfriend's gig? But it was a strange scene, denoting a lot of insecurity in their relationship, and a very uncomfortable love triangle, especially because Serena was suggesting that Elliott did not consider Chiba a real girlfriend.

According to Serena, Elliott stayed calm, looking very embarrassed by Chiba's behavior, but he was happy to see Valerie. She was happy too, despite what had happened between them. Hadn't Valerie screamed "*Get a backbone!*"[118] at one of Elliott's shows at the Music Box back in January? If that was really the case, how could she have yelled that somewhat aggressive remark but now be eager and happy to see him just a few months later? There are still many questions, but something still existed between Elliott and Valerie.

Chiba's scene made Elliott and Valerie's reunion very difficult, although Elliott didn't seem to care too much about Chiba's anger and jealousy, according to Serena. Did he give his number to Serena in a desperate attempt to talk to Valerie again? To date her again? To leave Chiba and go back with her? It's possible that Elliott didn't even know what he was doing at that moment.

Alyson was stunned by the story but this echoed another episode told by Nelly Reifler on her website, The Weeklings.[119] Nelly was an old friend of Elliott's (she often called him Steven in her narration), and just like Serena she had visited Elliott backstage after a show in June 2003 at the Knitting Factory:

"*I went back inside. The set was almost over. I found Noah. We made our way to the green room door. A gigantic bouncer blocked the way. He asked my name, I told him, and he slid through the door. Moments later he returned and informed me that I was not allowed to visit Elliott.*

"*I remember beginning to shake. Was it true that Elliott had decided to dump his old friends? Had I imagined, all those years, our good conversations? Then I reminded myself about the spectacle I'd just witnessed. Elliott was not in his right mind, and apparently the rumors whispered by mopey white undergrads were true. Then the door opened again, and a young woman was standing there. She was one of the singers who had been on stage with him. Pretty in an unremarkable way, wearing a T-shirt and jeans. She was smiling at me, reaching out her hand. She apologized. 'I'm so sorry!' she said. 'I'm Jennifer [Chiba]. Come in. I didn't realize you were that author.' At first, I didn't know what she was talking about. And then—oh, yes—I was an author, sort of, almost. But what did that matter? If I hadn't written a book, I wouldn't have been allowed to see Elliott? And she was a gatekeeper, deciding who could greet Elliott? This was worse than if he'd simply not wanted to see me himself. Right then, I didn't like her. She still refused to allow Noah entry.*" [119]

This perfectly echoed the already mentioned story told by Joanna Bolme in *Q magazine*.[102] Chiba was, indeed, quite the gatekeeper.

How many stories did people need to hear to understand Chiba was filtering who could approach Elliott? Serena had said, "*Other friends of mine had similar experiences with Jennifer [Chiba] though. She seemed very intent on keeping Elliott away from his old friends.*"[117]

On the other hand, Serena had described Valerie as "*a very mild-mannered, easy-going person and not at all a control freak,*" while she hadn't been very impressed by Chiba's personality: "*She was not wholly successful at controlling Elliott as he still gave me his number to give to Valerie to get in touch with him after Jennifer [Chiba] screamed and yelled and accused her of assault. Still, Jennifer was the type to cause a huge fuss if things were not going her way whereas Valerie was not like that.*"[117]

After that loud and unpleasant encounter with Chiba, Serena had been suspicious of what had happened:

"It seems that this Jennifer [Chiba] character has got away with a lot and this has all gone unchecked. She seemed to be a dreadful type of person, but I really only had that one experience with her. I just happen to think that certain things don't seem to add up, and she also proved she was capable of being a very cold liar and a huge drama queen. The other thing that struck me was that Elliott did not seem that into her. He did not seem invested enough in her to kill himself over anything she would say or do.[117]

"He did not seem to take her that seriously. She did not seem to be able to control him when it came to him doing what he wanted to do, though she certainly did try. I also will mention that Valerie was not 'on drugs,' and Elliott was more sober than I'd seen him in years… he was on many antidepressants which he showed me. There were several… literally a whole backpack of them. But he was in very good form. I'm not sure what happened in the next few months."[117]

According to Serena, Valerie had told her that "*she had to break up with Elliott because she couldn't deal with his drug issues*" and, to Serena, it was logical that Valerie would have wanted to reconnect because he seemed to be doing better. Serena said:

"Elliott was not as hopeless and helpless as she's [Chiba] made him out to be. She also asserted that he was terribly unstable because he had gone off all of his medications, yet antidepressants were still found in his system, so that can't be entirely true either. He was working on an unfinished project (and it's unlikely he would have just said 'fuck it' for that alone). He seemed hopeful and positive when I last saw him. (It may have been June but somehow I thought it was later than that—more like August or early September.)

"It's so convenient to use his past bouts of depression coupled with his music as evidence of his suicidal tendencies. That's the trouble. He has the image of a gloomy, sad guy (which he was only part of the time, whereas most of the time he was a lot of fun). It was so easy to make his death out to be a suicide from the legacy he created. I have a strong hunch that Jennifer Chiba knew this and continues to use this to her advantage and it's exactly how she has been able to manipulate the story in her favor. They weren't together for that long, but I knew him well for sixteen years, and I feel strongly that more should be done to uncover the facts."[117]

Serena made a lot of sense, and since she had known Elliott for a long time, Alyson also wanted to ask her what she knew about the child abuse he had allegedly endured. The abuse story had apparently aggressively resurfaced in Elliott's memory towards the end of his life and had been used in the narration that he had killed himself. Serena had this to say:

"*This whole thing about the sexual abuse of his stepfather, for some reason, does not ring true to me. I know he hated his stepfather. We talked about it a lot as I also have a stepfather that I had a terrible time with. It's very possible that Elliott had some repressed memories surface regarding abuse, but I doubt the validity of how much they played a part in his depression.... Why this would become intensified at the end of his life is dubious. I mean, he always felt like that. So that he suddenly became upset about repressed memories of sexual abuse seems possible, but not to the extent where it would have made him suicidal.... These memories did not drive him to kill himself and seem to be exaggerated for effect. Basically, I think that ANYTHING that Jennifer Chiba has to say is not to be trusted. Unfortunately, it seems as though she has been able to leak a lot of inaccurate information to the press to make Elliott look worse off than he was, so she will look better. As I mentioned before, she did not seem to be able to totally control him. He was going to do what he was going to do regardless of what she wanted.*"[117]

Alyson was really pleased to hear someone talking at length about Elliott. Serena had nothing to gain by trashing Chiba; this was a genuine and informed opinion. Serena was also very perceptive when talking about Elliott's personality and apparently complicated love life:

"*I don't think that Elliott had any ONE true love. He was too complex to be simplified in that manner. He could love a lot of people, but he tended to drive away the people who he truly cared about who also cared for him, in the end, which is pretty common with most people who indulge in drugs. It's basically standard self-destructive behavior. He wasn't this doom and gloom kind of guy most of the time. He was very smart (he studied philosophy in college and was an excellent student); he also liked to joke around. He was really sympathetic, and you could talk to him about anything, but he wasn't so overly depressed that he would have taken his own life unless things were really, really, really bad. The last time I saw him he was so excited to be sober, and he was ready to embark on some new things. The only thing in his life that seemed to be a problem at that time was that horrible girlfriend of his and yet she's the one saying he was going off the rails."*[117]

Beside Valerie, Serena also knew a lot of Elliott's "*famous*" friends such as Marc Swanson and E.V. Day, and she was aware of their resignation and lack of involvement in a possible search for the truth:

"*I guess people are just too exhausted, sad and confused to know how to proceed and they have accepted there is not really anything more that anybody can do to get the criminal justice system to investigate this on a grander scale. There is a sense of helplessness that pervades over the whole situation. Everyone I know who knew Elliott is protective of him to some extent, but most of us didn't see him very much near the end of his life, and I think nobody knows what to really think.*[117]

"*When he died it was very difficult for me to accept that he had killed himself. It just didn't seem to add up, and had he decided to take that route, I didn't think he would have stabbed himself in the heart. I immediately got in touch with Neil Gust [from Heatmiser] because I thought Neil would know. But Neil was very bitter and angry. He told me that Elliott was beyond repair, and that it was entirely plausible that he had killed himself. Since I thought that Neil knew Elliott better than anyone, I had no choice but to believe him. (Neil is a great friend of mine, and I hung out with both Neil and Elliott throughout my college years and saw them a few times after they had moved to Portland.) However, in retrospect, I don't think that Neil had been in touch with Elliott right before he died, and he may have based his perceptions on things that had occurred before. He was also still very pissed off at him for several personal reasons. But at the time I supposed that if Neil affirmed that suicide was probable, then his words were not to be taken lightly, as he knew Elliott much better than I did."*[117]

This long conversation with Serena was another confirmation that many of his old friends, who had not been in contact with him during his last years, were not questioning the suicide story because of Elliott's past and many unresolved issues.

"*Frankly, most of Elliott's old friends were not a big part of his life shortly before he died,*" confirmed Serena. "*Accounts vary, but it's common knowledge that he was not doing very well. A few of my friends staged an intervention with him at one point, and he never really forgave them. But he still was accessible, and he still would see us whenever there was an opportunity to do so. I never felt completely cut off from him, and I don't think anybody ever was unless they decided to cut themselves off as in the case of Neil.*"[117]

It is important to sum up three essential points from this:

1) Serena was very angry at how botched the police investigation had been, she was convinced that there was more to the story than what Chiba had stated, and she could not comprehend why there had not been more dissent.

2) She thought Chiba needed to be questioned and interrogated, as people who lie also change their stories, so there would likely be inconsistencies. Alyson told Serena she had already noticed many of them by comparing Chiba's previous statements.

3) Most people were taking the simplest route, as it was a lot easier to shrug their shoulders and go with "*there is nothing I can do, and Elliott might have done it,*" than truly getting involved. In a way, it was also less painful to think that he had willingly killed himself than to think that he had been murdered and that his murderer had gotten away with it. Alyson had been wondering about this last point for a long time, and she was very grateful to have had this long exchange with the very courageous and outspoken Serena.

Jerry

A few months after that long conversation with Serena, Alyson had the chance to talk to another outspoken character, Jerry Schoenkopf, who had been Elliott Smith's drug counselor as the program administrator for Malibu Ranch Residential Treatment Center. Both men had stayed friends over the years, and they had been so close that they had started the Elliott Smith Foundation to benefit abused children together.[120] Valerie Deerin, Elliott's girlfriend at the time, had helped found it—she had even made a deposit to start the funding—and, according to Jerry, Elliott had signed some papers to create the foundation just 20 days before he died.

"*The foundation has been dormant for the last year, while Smith dealt with his drug problem, but now it's his number one priority,*"[26] Alyson had read in one of Elliott's last interviews, the one he had given to *Under the Radar* in March 2003.

Unfortunately, the foundation was never finalized because the project basically died with Elliott. Alyson managed to talk to Jerry on the phone in 2014 and he had some interesting things to say.

On the phone, Jerry couldn't have been more direct. During the first minutes of their first conversation, he told Alyson that he thought Elliott had been murdered. Usually, people take some detours before making a statement such as this. They often say they are suspicious of what happened, but that was not Jerry's case. He was even going on the record with his name, as he didn't care about sounding controversial.

This was very unusual, but Alyson could tell Jerry's old friend Elliott still really mattered to him: "*Having been his counselor for years... people get to know one another... he was a heroin addict and if he had decided to kill himself he would have done it with an overdose, that's what heroin addicts do, they don't take a knife to puncture their heart.*"[121] Jerry also told Alyson that he had found the way Elliott had died absolutely "*unbelievable and incredible.*" In particular, he thought it really implausible that "*a very peaceful, quiet, serene human being would stab himself in the chest twice... once is already incredible enough, but twice?*"[121] Jerry was not buying it at all, and he knew Elliott and, in particular, he knew Elliott's problems.

The best part was that Jerry said he had said the same thing to W.T. Schultz, who apparently never really took into consideration what Jerry had to say. In *Torment Saint,* Schultz had written, "*Jerry and Elliott never went more than a month without talking,*"[82] which certainly demonstrated what a close relationship they had formed, even continuing with a quote from Jerry: "*Elliott was interested in the dark side, but I don't remember any obsession with death, I don't know that he had a death wish.*"[121] However, Schultz had relegated another important part of Jerry's statements to the notes at the end of the book, in tiny print: "*Jerry told me that, if Elliott had wanted to commit suicide, he would have done it by heroin overdose not stabbing!!*"[82] Jerry confirmed to Alyson that he had said the same thing to Schultz, that he had told him he thought it was murder. It is clear that this part of the conversation had been edited out because it did not fit the theory presented by the book, the theory that Elliott had undoubtedly committed suicide.

During her conversation with Jerry, Alyson learned that the police had even talked to Jerry, and he had told them exactly the same thing, but apparently this hadn't been enough to move the investigation forward. Over the years, a lot of people seemed too eager to accept it was a suicide, mostly on the basis of Elliott's depressive nature and his song lyrics, whereas nobody had paid any attention to someone like Jerry who knew Elliott very well and was saying that stabbing himself in the chest was totally out of character.

Alyson asked Jerry about Jennifer Chiba, whom he had met a couple of times. He admitted not knowing her very well. He had just met her briefly and he had never had a real conversation with her. This point was very interesting to Alyson as Chiba had always pretended to be such a big part of Elliott's life. Jerry summed it up: Chiba had started as Elliott's drug dealer in an effort to ignite a relationship. She had been providing (maybe selling) Elliott heroin, and he had ended up living with her and then they had become boyfriend and girlfriend.

"*Usually it is the women who move in with their drug dealers,*" Jerry added, "*but in his case he was a man moving in with his female heroin dealer.*"[121] We were very far from the romantic encounter at Spaceland described in *Torment Saint.*

Jerry also mentioned Valerie Deerin, who he liked a lot, describing her as an "*extremely nice person,*"[121] who did everything she could for Elliott, and someone who didn't want to have anything to do with drugs. Jerry added:

"*But when he moved in with his drug dealer, he continued using drugs which she was buying and supplying, and then you had the fight…*"[121] referring again to the fight between the two women.

"*This is totally psychotic,*" Jerry said about the self-stabbing. "*Elliott was unbalanced and depressed but he was not psychotic; it would require a psychotic person to do that type of action.… Plus this is not Japan, this is the United States, this is not culturally known or accepted in any way, that would not have been in his consciousness.*"[121]

Jerry also said he had no doubt Elliott was clean at the time of his death, but he didn't think he had been clean for as long as it had been reported—about a year, as Chiba had told the police.

"*I don't believe he had been clean for that long,*" Jerry said, "*but whether he was clean or loaded, that's not something he would have done, as it is not something I or you would do, no matter how sad we got!*"[121]

Jerry had seen Elliott just a few days [maybe two days] before he died, and Alyson didn't hesitate to ask him about Elliott's state of mind. "*He came to see me before he died, he was okay, he had been depressed for years so there was an underlying depression even when he seemed to be alright, there were times when he was better or worse but there wasn't anything unusual when he came to see me just a few days before he died.*"[121]

Deanna, the devoted fan who had talked to Alyson very early on, had also mentioned she had seen Elliott at the Roost, a bar on Los Feliz Boulevard, just "*two weeks before his death.... He looked great. Last time I saw him. I could tell he was clean. He was happy. We spoke for a while as Chiba waited impatiently and [was] obviously annoyed that he was talking to me.*"[4] This was in total contradiction to what Chiba had said during the Q&A after *Searching for Elliott Smith*, describing Elliott as someone who was paranoid at the time of his death, and "*suffering from a serious mental illness.*"[46]

Musicians from the past

Then there was Sybil (not her real name), a female musician based in New Orleans, who had known Elliott and Chiba when she was part of the California music scene. Since that time, she had moved to another state, but she had the chance to know Elliott in their early music career, when both of them were living in Portland. Sybil was not convinced that Chiba was ready to quit partying and give up on drugs when Elliott was ready to change his life after the painful treatment at the Beverly Hills clinic, the Neurotransmitter Restoration Center. When she talked to Alyson, Sybil mentioned Chiba's restless behavior, and said she was still abusing alcohol and drugs. "*Booze and speed,*" as she put it. And that's why she was not really surprised to learn that Chiba had received at least one DUI, on August 30, 2003.[81]

"*Jennifer Chiba has a long history of volatile relationships, and excess partying,*"[122] Sybil told Alyson, "*We all used to party together back in the day and she was known for excess.*" Sybil even went on to suggest that Chiba may have been drunk or high on October 21. "*I was told she was in a bad way before he died. I can't prove she was high but that was the general opinion back then.*"[122]

This was pure hearsay and speculation, and Alyson was not convinced of this, because if it had been the case, how could the police have missed that? Nobody knew if they had tested Chiba for anything, but there was nothing in the police report saying she looked or acted drunk or high.

There was still this solid rumor (confirmed to Alyson by a family member) that Chiba had waited some time before calling 911. Could she have done that to let the effect of her high dissipate a bit? Some websites[84] reported Chiba had been taking a shower at the precise moment of Elliott's death. Could she have done that to give herself time to come down from her high? Anything was possible. Alyson didn't like to speculate; she greatly preferred facts.

Sybil was so convinced she was right that she had even reported Chiba's party behavior and history of volatile relationships to the police, while telling them to do more investigation. "*I saw her a few years ago in Los Angeles,*" Sybil added, "*and all she could do was talk about how she was being interviewed about him and such. It was all self-glorification and she had no real grief about him being gone. It was like she was basking in the limelight. It made me sick to my stomach. I knew Elliott from when I lived in Portland, Alyson, there was something just so off about her. Elliott had been doing much better before he died, he was really trying to turn things around. There is no way he put a knife though his own chest.*"[122]

Sybil had even a bit more to say: "*I ended up buying her [Chiba] heaps of booze one night trying to get her to talk and I came very close to breaking her down. I asked her what really happened, and she almost told me, but we were interrupted by a friend. She teared up and seemed like she wanted to get something off her chest and then a mutual friend popped up and she totally changed demeanor.*"[122]

This was just Sybil's impression, and it could have been easy to dismiss one story coming from one person, but the problem was that this musician was the umpteenth person talking about Chiba's erratic behavior and violent temper. There had been Sean Organ's Sid and Nancy situation mentioned in the *The Guardian* article,[83] the sound-engineer's knife story,[105] the Silverlake musician's possible domestic abuse stories,[104] and the story of the Florida fan's boyfriend and a dating experience with Chiba that had turned into a drunken nightmare.[106] It was difficult to ignore all these people.

"*I don't know how serious it was,*" the Silverlake musician had said to Alyson. "*I just overheard it at a party and logged it mentally.*"[104] And that was always the problem, dramatic hearsay overheard somewhere, which unfortunately would not have much weight in court, even given the extraordinary condition that all these people would agree to testify. At best, all these stories could all have been accepted as circumstantial evidence but then all dismissed.

Of course, Alyson had not forgotten the story told by Caroline,[12] who was working in the recording studio next to Elliott's. She had been visibly terrified of Chiba and had felt compelled to write long posts to tell about her encounter with the woman who she had been calling "*the dark force.*" Even though Caroline had never witnessed any violence, her melodramatic description of Chiba has always been interesting: "*There was a dark force in Elliott's life and it wasn't him, drugs or depression, as far as I could tell. But this is only my perspective so I could be wrong. It even had a name, but I won't say it and I won't even give it a sex because that's not the point. The point is the dark force did exist for whatever reason and it did have a huge part or hold on Elliott's life.... The force had black hair and dark squinting eyes and the whitest of skin, beautiful in a haunting scary kind of way. The force seemed arrogant and entitled and that made me uncomfortable.*"[12]

Finally, there was the late Abigail Russell, who had been suspicious of Chiba from the get-go and had told Alyson she believed Chiba could have done almost anything to keep Elliott as she was even "*ready to get knocked up by Bobby or anyone to keep him.*"[98] Abigail had also told Alyson that Chiba had threatened all her boyfriends with statements like "*I am going to kill myself,*"[98] which amazingly was echoed in some of the previous stories.

There was still another thing to add to this impressive list. Alyson had also been troubled by the words she had heard from different people when talking about Chiba, as several people had used the term "*knife freak.*" Although they are anonymous here, these were very reliable sources; one of them was a member of Elliott's close family, another was a record producer who had worked with Elliott, and yet another was a musician from a band that has been associated with Elliott. There was no coming back from that. Alyson managed to talk to B., one of the musicians from that band:

"*She had a fascination with knives,*"[123] said the musician who also expressed his surprise that nobody had kept the investigation going. "*Jenn [Chiba] was definitely crazy. She dated our keyboard player before Elliott. She had issues. Some fascination with knives. I have my doubts about suicide. The thing is that he sang about suicide, so everyone assumes. Last time I saw him at the health food store he was doing great.*[123]

"*She was not necessarily violent, but she was that girl you didn't want your friends to be with,*" the musician continued. "*It was like what the fuck is she doing to Elliott for him to stay with her? She's a fucking psychiatrist for fuck sake. She had him under her thumb. I had my worries when she dated a guy in our band [before Elliott]. It came as no surprise she fucked with Elliott's brain.*"[123]

It was a long list of troubling stories, all coming from different sources, even if anonymous sources may sound suspicious or unreliable, was it possible to dismiss all these similar stories?

Alyson knew her research was turning into a character assassination. However, The Cedars-Sinai therapist, who had also attended the *Searching for Elliott Smith* Q&A, had given a mini-report to Alyson after observing Chiba answering questions for an hour:

"*If it is always possible to panic, the way Chiba behaved afterward is not consistent with someone who has remorse about what she has done. In everything she said and did, she dissociated herself from the situation, she distanced herself from what had happened, just like when she locked herself in the bathroom. That was a dramatic event, something people build symptoms of, but I did not see any symptoms in Chiba, even at the Q&A; she always distanced herself from the event, she withdrew herself from the crime scene, which is typical of Borderline Personality Disorder.*"[17]

This therapist had been working at Cedars-Sinai for 20 years, and she had seen a lot of people in the ER who had committed suicide. She said she had never seen a self-inflicted stabbing in the chest; in the stomach yes, but never between the ribs.

"*What killed Elliott is the removal of the knife, because he lost his blood. But during the Q&A Chiba said the coroner had told her the wounds would have been fatal anyway, so it was as if she was not feeling guilty at all, he would have died anyway, I am not responsible for his death!*"[17] the therapist added.

Chapter 12: A tale of two lawsuits

The first lawsuit

If Chiba had been eager to vindicate herself with the media, barely a year after Elliott's death, she went in a new radical direction on July 30th, 2004. She came back from London or wherever she was at the time and sued Elliott's estate.[23] At the time, the estate was run by Marta Greenwald, Elliott's stepmother.

Before the lawsuit even happened, the always well-informed Deanna had warned Alyson that Chiba was about to sue Elliott's stepmother simply because she didn't like her. According to what she had heard, Chiba had tried to contact Elliott's stepmother for money and her request had been rejected.

Ruth, the Northwest coast fan who was constantly posting on the message board and had some unknown but real connections with the Portland family, was convinced that Chiba would try to pull out every negative and slimy thing she could to hurt the family and, eventually, if the lawsuit reached a trial, get the jury's sympathy. Ruth sounded very concerned as she knew

Chiba's ability to manipulate opinions, something Alyson had fully realized during her numerous conversations with people about her.

In her lawsuit, Chiba was claiming to have started a romantic relationship with Elliott in 1999, and to have moved in with him on August 26, 2002, and lived with him until his death on October 21, 2003. She was suing "*for breach of oral contract, quantum meruit, declaratory relief, and constructive trust,*"[23] claiming she and Elliott had entered into an oral agreement in August 2002 to "*live together, cohabitate and combine their efforts and earnings... share equally any and all property accumulated as a result of their efforts whether individual or combined... and hold themselves out to the public as husband and wife.*"[23] The complaint was also claiming that Elliott had promised to provide for Chiba's "*financial needs and support for the rest of her life*" *in exchange for her domestic services as his* "*homemaker, housekeeper, cook, secretary, bookkeeper, and financial counselor... forgo[ing] any independent career opportunities.*"[23]

A separate paragraph also stated that Chiba had agreed to be Elliott's "*manager and agent for the purposes of arranging [his] booking and scheduling [his] appearances for musical performances*" and to carry out "*the preparation and production of [his] album*" *in exchange for* "*15% of the proceeds earned and received.*"[23]

Chiba was claiming Greenwald had breached the agreement by refusing to pay her for performing her contracted services. She had attached to her complaint a creditor's claim in excess of $1 million for the contracted services she had rendered to Smith and for the proceeds from his compositions, performances, and albums.

It was seen as such a bold and insensitive move to many, although Chiba managed to find plenty of supporters among fans.

A few years later, Alyson was able to connect some dots. First, the complaint said that Chiba and Elliott had entered into an oral agreement in August 2002. But this did not add up. The *SPIN* article had clearly stated that Elliott had moved into her place during the fall of 2002, and that he was still in "*tremendous psychic pain*"[37] at that time.It is stated in Schultz's book: "*In August 2002 he latched on to a biological remedy, a decidedly fringe medical solution called Neurotransmitter Restoration, developed initially by William Hitt.*"[82]

If Elliott had started his treatment in August 2002, would he have even been able to make such an oral agreement at that time? While he was not even done with his detoxification treatment? While he was still hallucinating, thinking about white cars following him? How could Chiba have trusted an agreement made by a man who was still in "tremendous psychic pain" and basically not himself? It seemed that her narration contradicted itself, as in her lawsuit Chiba was presenting a healthy Elliott, rational enough to make a life-engaging agreement, while she also talked about a paranoid Elliott with a serious mental illness at that same time period. She could not have it both ways.

Then there was her claim that she and Elliott had started a romantic relationship in 1999,[23] in contradiction with plenty of other facts. First, it was clear to many that Elliott had no romantic relationship with Chiba[80] before he moved in with her that fall 2002. As a matter of fact, Elliott had been in a relationship with Valerie Deerin around 2001 and 2002, and had other girlfriends before that. Then, when he finally moved in with Chiba, he was more in need of care than a relationship, and Ruth, the fan with mysterious connections with Elliott's family, had told Alyson that they had not been romantically involved during the first months. After Elliott's death, the family member Alyson had communicated with said that the family even had access to the records from Elliott's psychiatrist, Dr. Schloss, and that the records had revealed that Elliott had been very reluctant at first to get involved with Chiba "*because she lied a lot*."[80] Dr. Schloss had even suggested that Valerie's fears of Chiba had not been realistic because she would not have been someone Elliott would have taken seriously for a relationship.[80] He was wrong, of course.

There was still another remarkable thing. This "*breach of oral contract*" had suddenly turned into something completely different during one of the Q&As Chiba did after the screening of *Searching for Elliott Smith* in May 2011. At that time, Chiba had come up with a new explanation for her lawsuit: Elliott had "*told her that if something happened to him, he didn't want his family to have control over his music because they would censor it, change it, and destroy the integrity of it*."[46] This was confirmed by Liam Gowing, who was also present at the Q&A—this was a different night than the one attended by Alyson a few days earlier, but she had managed to talk to a few people who had been there. In other words, the lawsuit was now taking on a very noble aspect, since Chiba was suing to preserve the integrity of Elliott's music, to prevent censorship.

This was well received by some fans as, the posthumous release had not included all the songs, and in particular, some songs like "Abused" and "Suicide Machine" may have been censored, since they were not included on the album. If the exclusion of "Abused" was not really excusable, and it was a laughable idea that "Suicide Machine" could have been censored. Despite the stigma attached to the title, the song was exactly the opposite of a suicide wish, with cynical lyrics that were in fact mocking people who had always wanted to see him as this doom tortured artist, this sad sack with suicidal ideation. In that song, he was revolting against this cartoon character of him that had been constantly popping up in the media.

On the other hand, plenty of other song lyrics included on the album may have suggested suicide, for example "King's Crossing," "A Fond Farewell," or even "Strung Out Again." There were enough references to death, self-destruction, and suicide in that album to play into the suicide narration.

Ashley, Elliott's half-sister, had left long comments on the message board to explain her point of view:

"*... Is not including a song on a particular record censorship? If so, Elliott is guilty of censoring all of his past records too. Sure, there are reasons, (sometimes technical, sometimes opinion-based) that some songs aren't on there, but Elliott would have had to make these tough decisions too, and whether or not he had a 'finished' track listing in his mind is up to interpretation. Ask anyone who's ever worked on a record with him. He goes back and forth up until it's finalized. I can say that I personally didn't strongly object to any songs that were his own compositions making it. There just wasn't enough room to include all the songs, so choices were made.*

"*Abused is one of those songs that everyone says was censored. Well, I can tell you that that song was recorded well before* Figure 8 *came out, and Elliott actively chose not to include it on that record. We have proof of that. Did I want it included on this one? I think it's a beautiful song, and I do hope someday that it gets released, but others in [our] family may have a different idea. I don't know, and I can't speak for them....*

"Other songs, like True Love, were really meant to be on there, but his vocals were so raw and unclean on the version we had intact that we weren't sure Elliott would have put it out. We did find out the whereabouts, later, of a cleaner version, and hopefully, that can make it out eventually. We'll see. It literally was found about three days late to make the cut.... Basically what I'm saying is that decisions HAD to be made, and so songs got chosen over others. None of us are conspiring to hide anything, at least I can speak for myself, and as for not wanting to put depressing songs on there, listen to the music. If we were really censoring the songs, pretty much NONE of them would have made it. There wouldn't have been a record. Elliott's songs are beautiful, and sad, and touching, and heartfelt, and sometimes very autobiographical, and sometimes more metaphorical. But there's no doubt that this is a dark record. He was in a dark time for most of the last 4 years. And those dark songs still made it. Because we felt that that's how he wanted it."[124]

At the time of the Q&As, Chiba had already lost her lawsuit, after amending her claim twice, but, obviously, she hadn't lost her animosity toward the family. This new declaration that "*he didn't want his family to have control over his music because they would censor it and change it*"[46] was pointing the finger at the family as the bad guy, and Chiba was trying very hard to present them as a censorship agent.

There are many examples to prove her wrong. Johan Wohlert, of Danish indie band Mew, had said in an interview that, on September 18, 2001, he had helped Elliott in the recording of the Beatles' "Hey Jude," a song which was supposed to be on the soundtrack of Wes Anderson's *The Royal Tenenbaums* but was never released for some reason. But Johan had revealed something important: Elliott's father, Gary Smith, had been with him [Elliott] during the recording, even participating in the vocals of the songs.[125] If Elliott had been recording with his father, how could he have been on bad terms with him? How could this scene of Elliott sharing such a moment with his father (both men loved the Beatles) even fit with an alleged fear of his family taking control of his music?

Furthermore, a close family member had told Alyson he had talked to Elliott on the phone just two days before his death. Elliott may have had some fear directed against his label but there was no way he was fearing a threat coming from Gary or Marta, who became the people responsible for making music decisions for the estate. This fear story could have been completely made up by Chiba, and Alyson was certain that censorship had not been the reason why Chiba had sued the family. It was a Marvin lawsuit, a term mentioned in the lawsuit.[23]

When Chiba had first claimed she was Elliott's "*manager*" and "*booking agent,*" and therefore was entitled to 15% of the proceeds earned and received on all of Elliott's "*performances and album sales,*" she had asked money for work she wasn't licensed to do.[23] After dropping the entire paragraph about her "*manager and agent*" role in November 2004, since she was revealed not to be a licensed talent agency, she amended the lawsuit in 2006, pursuing her claim under the cohabitation agreement. The court found inconsistencies in the pleadings of the complaint and its amended versions, and Chiba eventually lost her lawsuit after a series of very aggressive attempts, which stretched over more than three years.

Thus, pretending she had sued the family for another reason a few years later was only done to gain people's sympathy and make Elliott's family look like the wrongdoers in the story: that they were the censors and she was the victim.

The second lawsuit

The story of Chiba's legal battles does not end there. In her lawsuit, Chiba had been represented by Ronald Gold and Justin B. Gold of Oldman, Colley, Sallus, Gold, Birnberg & Coleman. In September 2008, she attempted a second lawsuit, this time against these same lawyers.

In the new complaint,[126] Chiba reiterated her role in Elliott's life, saying that they had been long-time romantic partners—although this time, she had omitted the year 1999 mentioned in her first lawsuit—and that she had been living with him at the time of his suicide as husband and wife. The key to this lawsuit was an aggressive attack against Elliott's stepmother Marta Greenwald, "*from whom Elliott was long estranged,*"[126] as the lawsuit stipulated. Once again, Chiba was trying to make a family member look bad and was stating that Marta had become "*the personal representative of his estate because Elliott had left no instructions to the contrary.*" Chiba's lawsuit claimed that Marta Greenwald had "*opportunistically sought to assert total control over Elliott's assets and affairs.*"[126]

"*It became clear to Jennifer [Chiba] that Greenwald wanted to take control of Elliott's intellectual property and master tapes (including unreleased work) and maximize their commercial appeal for monetary gain.*"[126]

As Alyson knew, the family was not exploiting Elliott's work; otherwise, many more releases and reissues would have been done. They were more concerned about honoring Elliott's memory than cashing in, since they had funneled some of the money to several charities, such as Outside In, a Portland social service agency which helps homeless youth and marginalized people.

In short, Chiba was suing her lawyers because she had lost her first lawsuit against the estate, and she was accusing them of "*egregious professional negligence* [and] *malpractice*" by "*adding superfluous and untrue allegations to the lawsuit that effectively left it no chance of reaching a jury.*"[126]

The lawsuit also claimed that "*defendants stubbornly stuck by their imprudent allegations even though they knew the allegations were not true and [were] fatal to Jennifer's [Chiba's] claims,*" whereas it was Chiba herself who had been providing the misinformation (she had never been accredited as Elliott's manager) and allegations. She even claimed that her case may have had some chance to be reviewed by the Supreme Court, but "*defendants missed the filing deadline for the petition, solely because they made a counting mistake when they calendared the deadline. The Supreme Court thus neglected to review Jennifer's Petition, and the case was over.*"[126]

However, the most important point of the lawsuit was in paragraph 3:

"*Blindly blaming Jennifer for the tragedy, Greenwald undertook a vindictive campaign to rewrite Elliott's history with Jennifer excised. Part of this effort involved denying the certain legal rights that she would otherwise hold as a result of her relationship with Elliott. Because Greenwald was obviously adamant about cutting Jennifer completely out of the picture, Jennifer was forced to sue Greenwald. The lawsuit sought monetary damages, as it must have, but also involved deeply emotional matters for Jennifer. For one, she felt responsible for protecting the artistic integrity of Elliott's work. In addition, the lawsuit would have essentially been a referendum on the truth and significance of her relationship with Elliott, especially in light of Greenwald's efforts to publicly denigrate it and even accuse Jennifer of his murder.*"[126]

To Alyson, it was very clear that this was the real motive of the lawsuit, or certainly one important point that had motivated Chiba to launch this second lawsuit: she could not stand to have been excluded from the picture by the family and, especially, could not swallow the fact that the family, at least Marta, was extremely suspicious, or even convinced, that she had killed Elliott. To Alyson, this was proof that the family, despite their silence, had been highly suspicious about what might have happened. According to this document, Elliott Smith's stepmother had accused Chiba of murder.

Once again, the law was not on Chiba's side, as the case was dismissed at the end of 2009.[23]

Interestingly, none of the lawsuits were mentioned in Schultz's book. There was not even an allusion to the first one against the estate. When questioned by Alyson, Schultz justified his choice by saying that he had written an Elliott Smith biography and that a subsequent lawsuit would have been irrelevant because it had happened after his death. However, Schultz had nevertheless mentioned several other posthumous details and events. As for Reyes, the first time Alyson saw his film *Searching for Elliott Smith*, she had noted a sentence at the end of the movie mentioning the lawsuit, while in the version released online at the end of 2019, this had been edited out.

Chapter 13: Building the myth

Torment Saint was in fact the second Elliott Smith biography. The Ben Nugent book *Elliott Smith and the Big Nothing*, published in 2004, just a year after Elliott's passing, was first, but it hadn't made a big impression among fans. There was a general feeling that Nugent's book had been a rushed experiment and nobody very close to Elliott had been involved. At least, Nugent hadn't tried to close an open case. At least he hadn't let Chiba direct the narration and he had left the mystery of Elliott's death an open question.

After Schultz's and Reyes's respective book and movie, Chiba took control of the narrative. She was the only survivor of the event, she had only talked publicly three times (including Gowing's 2004 interview), and nothing else was supposed to follow. In a very Charles Kinbote move, Schultz had declared that he had written the definitive Elliott Smith biography, and with quotes like "*Elliott was in love with depression*"[82] he had set the tone in stone, or at least he thought he had.

Schultz had gone much further, though, defending Chiba on any occasion and, of course, never missing the opportunity to make the comparison with another violent rock n' roll suicide, Kurt Cobain's death.

"*The conspiracy theories against Chiba also echo those against Courtney Love after Kurt Cobain's suicide,*"[97] he had declared to *The Independent.* "*I think part of it is misogyny, hating on the evil harpy who supposedly destroyed the hero.*"[97] This argument bothered Alyson. To refute valid concerns by evoking misogyny seemed lazy and misplaced. Suspecting something else than a suicide had nothing to do with misogyny; it was the result of long and tedious research. And what about Schultz's own preconceived opinion about Elliott's personality? There were enough discrepancies and inconsistencies in his story to be suspicious. To Alyson, it was bizarre that Schultz would be defending the suicide story with such passion and stubbornness.

Schultz had named his book after misheard lyrics, *Torn Mainsail/Torment Saint,* and had kept this title despite being told by numerous fans that he was making a mistake. Then he wanted to have the last word on Elliott's fate, even though the coroner and the police hadn't concluded anything.

"*I'm convinced that he committed suicide,*"[97] Schultz had declared in his same interview with *The Independent.* "*Everybody I interviewed for the book who would talk about that agreed, with maybe one exception—and that was someone who didn't know Elliott all that well. We're talking about a person who had overdosed numerous times in the last couple of years of his life, had cut himself, had always been depressed, was going through the difficult process of getting off the drugs that he was addicted to—and who was still feeling deeply paranoid because of all the crap he had used. He was suspicious of people spying on him, of trying to kill him. He was not in his right mind for the last two years of his life.*"[97]

Schultz was talking with assurance, even though he had never met Elliott and, to document these last two years, had mostly talked to Chiba, the unreliable narrator. With this portrait and the constant comparisons with Kurt Cobain in the book—his name is mentioned 40 times—there was no argument left, despite Alyson having spent so much time and energy fighting this caricature.

As Reyes had attempted before, Schultz had tried to dismiss every forensic point one by one, and in *Torment Saint*, he declared that Scheinin had even suggested that hesitation marks could have been erased by the actual stabbing (or by the subsequent medical intervention).

For Alyson, it was quite strange that there was suddenly this new explanation when she had herself asked Scheinin about this precise point several times. Not only had Scheinin not even made an allusion to this possible explanation for the absence of hesitation marks, but she had repeated several times that their absence was unusual.

Alyson had been particularly furious that Schultz had tried to discredit her in his book. Without naming her, he had called her a "*completely dishonest*" fan, claiming Alyson was "*clearing things up for a friend… in effect misrepresenting herself*."[82] But Alyson knew she had not lied to Scheinin at all, as she had effectively corresponded with someone who knew Elliott and a very close family member.

Plus, Alyson had taken extensive notes during the interview, when Scheinin had refused to be recorded, and Alyson was certain she had not misquoted her. Where could the misquotes have been when Scheinin had kept such a neutral tone?

But how could Scheinin's tone and statement have been so different? How could she have mentioned a gut feeling toward suicide with Gowing, but not with Alyson? How could she have almost completely dismissed the importance of the absence of hesitation marks with Schultz, whereas she had not done so with Alyson?

Fortunately, another interview with Scheinin, done by French journalist Ana Benabs and published by *France 24* in 2018,[127] seemed to be in accordance with Alyson's impression: "*She [Scheinin] explains to France 24 that the absence of hesitation marks on the singer's body is another important point to consider,*"[127] which does not suggest that the hesitation marks could have been destroyed by subsequent action as Schultz had claimed in his book that Scheinin had told him.

Dr. Scheinin had even declared to *France 24* that the "*majority of the persons who attempt to commit suicide with a knife open their veins or slice their throat,*" and she had even said that "*it is unusual to stab oneself through the clothing.… I don't remember another case of a person stabbing himself in the torso.*"[127] But she carefully added that it was difficult to remember every case during a 23-year career.

Since Dr. Scheinin had communicated with Ana Benabdelkarim (Ana Benabs),[128] the author of the *France 24* article, Alyson was very confident with these declarations, and they validated her own conclusions: the forensic points of the autopsy could not be dismissed very easily to prove it was a suicide.

At this point, Alyson was ready to believe that Gowing and Schultz had edited quite a lot of what Dr. Scheinin had told them. There was a strange tendency for neither Gowing, Reyes, or Schultz to question Chiba's actions and behavior. If Gowing had explained at great length that he had checked everything Chiba had told him, it was difficult to understand why he had not questioned her raid at the studio or her removal of the knife, for example. In contrast, after just talking to a few people, it had not taken long for Alyson to realize that there were many discrepancies in her narration.

A wedding proposal?

Chiba was introduced as Elliott's fiancée in Reyes's 2009 documentary. Just after Elliott's death, there was a story circulating that Elliott had allegedly proposed to Chiba a few days before the tragedy. The new owner of Elliott's studio had even said this to Alyson: "*Chiba told me the 'because I love you!' story from the tracking of King's Crossing. She told me that after she nervously did the take, Elliott came into the tracking room and proposed. I believe it to be true, but the source was of course Chiba.*"[13]

One thing was certain, late at night on October 13, 2003, Chiba had sent an email to a fan she was corresponding with, saying: "*He finished King's Crossing tonight (and I'm on it!).*"[129]

Alyson had also read on the fan message board that Chiba was in possession of this final version of the song, whereas another version, without the "*because I love you*" part, was supposed to be included in the posthumous album. Chiba had allegedly given her version to Ashley, Elliott's half-sister, at the last minute because she wanted that version to be on the album.[25]

The rumor that Elliott had proposed on the day of the recording of "King's Crossing" never reappeared anywhere, except during a conversation with Gowing, who told Alyson what he had been told by Robin Peringer:

"*He and Jennifer [Chiba] were planning on being married and he was excited about having a child with Jennifer. I know one hundred percent Elliott wanted to marry Jennifer.*"[38]

After Elliott's death, Chiba had registered on the fan message board under the name "*BrideTomorrow*,"[25] and even if very few people knew it was her, this screen name was very telling.

Whether they were about to get married or not, as a therapist, Chiba should have known that starting a relationship with someone who has just been through rehab is strongly discouraged. She had even attempted to start their relationship immediately after his treatment, when he was still very vulnerable and probably unprepared. On the website AlcoholRehab.com,[130] the following is stated on this subject: "*One of the worst things that an individual can do in early recovery is jump headfirst into romance. It is strongly advised that they remain focused on themselves until their sobriety is strong. Once they are settled in their new life, they can then begin to consider sharing it with somebody else.... It is recommended that people who are still within the first year of their recovery should avoid beginning romantic relationships. This is because their priority needs to be staying sober. The first few months of recovery are often described as an emotional rollercoaster because there is so much going on. The last thing that an individual will want to do will be to add the stress of a new relationship to the mix. It is going to take all their attention to make it through this early part of recovery.*"[130]

How come Chiba, a licensed marriage and family therapist/art therapist[15] with many years of experience—she had received her license in 1995[131]—could not have even applied this elementary rule?

In his book, Schultz had curiously kept this idea very low-key and he hadn't even mentioned a marriage proposal. Why had this important part of the story suddenly vanished from the narration? Could it be because the date of the alleged proposal had changed several times?

Whether Elliott had proposed to Chiba or not, a marriage proposal clashed with the information sent to Alyson by one of Elliott's family members that Chiba had told a friend that Elliott was about to leave her. Relationships can change rapidly, things happen, but now that Elliott was gone, Chiba could claim to be his eternal fiancée.

A pregnancy?

This same family member Alyson spoke with had also commented that, a week or two before Elliott's death, Chiba had informed Elliott's father she may be pregnant. Elliott had said over the phone he had "*good news*" to tell but couldn't say anything yet because Chiba hadn't given him permission to tell anyone. After he died, Chiba informed the family that she might have been pregnant and that she would tell them when she knew for sure, but after a couple of weeks, she told them she wasn't.[80] It was actually the second time Alyson had heard this story, as Deanna had already told her something very similar years ago, outraged by Chiba's manipulative stratagem. With an over-the-counter pregnancy test, it would have been simple for Chiba to know in a few minutes if she had really been pregnant. And if she didn't want to tell the family before being sure a baby was successfully on his or her way, why had she been teasing the family with a "*I might be pregnant*"?

Strange Parallel director Steve Hanft, in an exchange with Alyson, confirmed that the couple was trying to have a baby, and Steve even said that Chiba had a miscarriage weeks after Elliott's death. It was difficult to know for sure whether Chiba had really told him this or if Steve was not remembering correctly, but for Alyson, there are big differences between "*might have been pregnant*" and having a miscarriage.[132]

The Disney Cottages neighbor engaged in some communication with Chiba after Elliott's death. Chiba had told her that she and Elliott had been trying to have a baby, and for some reason, the lady neighbor had found this difficult to believe. After spending some time around Elliott as a friendly and nurturing neighbor, she had come to the strong impression he was against the idea of having a baby of his own, possibly because of his own story. "*This story of getting married and having a baby, it was so not like him, plus it never came up with Valerie,*" she had declared to Alyson.[39] There was so much variation in the wording around Chiba's supposed pregnancy that it was impossible to know the truth. How could Chiba have wanted to form a family in that climate of constant fighting? How could she have wanted to form a family with a man she later deemed paranoid and mentally ill?

Mythmaking

Some media had been slowly building the myth of Elliott and Chiba's relationship. Some people dismissed their fights with a casual "*every couple fights*" excuse, whereas it certainly looked like something much more serious to others. In Gil Reyes's movie, Chiba had been the tearful victim, the caring person who had basically devoted her life to saving Elliott's. "*It was a lot of work,*"[42] she had even said during her monologue in the movie, erasing the other girlfriend(s) from the picture, and in particular, Valerie, who had supported Elliott during the peak of his drug addiction.

Alyson was also outraged by the treatment Valerie had received in Schultz's book. In *Torment Saint*, she had been described as "*a little young*," "*the merch girl*," "*no more than a tour hook-up at first*," "*not artistically inclined*," someone who "*may have been drawn to drug takers*," and finally the girlfriend Elliott "*had sent home*"[82] Basically, there was nothing very good said about her, while Chiba had been painted with a much more flattering brush, probably because she had been the main source of information.

On the other hand, the Disney Cottages neighbor, who had had the time to get to know Valerie, had described Valerie to Alyson as "*protective of him*," "*very sweet and caring*," and "*the adult in the relationship, though still very young*."

An introduction?

Chiba had told Schultz that she had met Elliott at Spaceland, a Silverlake intimate club venue. This story almost sounded too good to be true: "*At Spaceland, he first met Jennifer Chiba. He had wandered in just as she'd finished a gig—Chiba played bass in a band called The Warlocks. Mutual friend Steve Hanft was there too, and Elliott asked for an introduction. He and Jennifer talked some, about compassion and Russian literature, about the Ferdinand story, one of Chiba's favorites from childhood too, both staring at their shoes, both smiling shyly. To Chiba, Elliott seemed 'really uncomfortable,' his usual transient awkwardness showing. He had just moved to LA [Elliott moved to LA in 1999]—he didn't even know his phone number—so he asked for hers, then gave her the number of [Elliott's manager] Mittleman's assistant.*"[82]

One of Alyson's friends had nevertheless found this slightly different version from Chiba in The French Magazine *VoxPop*,[133] in an article about Elliott published in 2010:

"*We briefly met at Rockfest, but later, when he had moved to Los Angeles, I asked my friend Steve [Hanft] to introduce me to him. We were both shy and were smiling while looking at our feet. He offered me a drink and we talked about Russian literature. We were both fans, especially Dostoevsky. This led us to a discussion about compassion, depression and hospitalization. A rather deep conversation to have with someone you've just met! But it was natural. He said he would come to see my band, The Warlocks, later in the week. And he came!*"[133]

Based on this, it was difficult to decide if Elliott had asked for an introduction or if Chiba had. Nevertheless, this small variation in the narration had some importance, and all this talk about Dostoevsky and Ferdinand the Bull (one of Elliott's tattoos, as any fan knew) seemed a bit too much, as all this sounded like a sort of soul-mate-make-believe.

After talking to many people, Alyson developed a different version of the meeting between Elliott and Chiba. At the exception of Jerry Schoenkopf, all wanted to stay anonymous, but the stories were more or less similar:

"*Chiba got Elliott drugs early on, then stopped as I understand it. That was her way into his life. But being with him probably meant you were scoring for him/with him anyways,*"[134] said someone who had worked very closely with Elliott for a long time.

This echoed what Elliott's drug counselor, Jerry Schoenkopf, had said to Alyson about the way Chiba had entered Elliott's life. Their relationship started with her providing drugs for him, then Elliott ended up living with her and she became his girlfriend.

Even Liam Gowing, in his "Mr. Misery" article published by *SPIN* in 2004, had acknowledged that there were plenty of people saying that same thing, that Chiba had provided drugs to Elliott:

"*But in some way is she responsible for his death? Possibly, according to Elliott's friends who lost touch with him after he began using heroin and crack heavily in Los Angeles, and to those who knew Chiba from her bleakest days, when she played bass with the notoriously drugged-out psychedelic rockers the Warlocks. These people blame her for enabling Elliott's romance with heroin.*"[37]

Then there was Abigail, who had told Alyson more or less the same story and had herself scored heroin for Chiba, who at the time was trying very hard to get Elliott's attention.[98]

The neighbor of the Disney Cottages had also acknowledged that Valerie had to travel to Scotland quite often because of her passport situation. At one point, she did notice that Chiba had entered the picture, "*It happened very quickly, and Valerie was gone for a while,*" she said. "*But he never appeared to me like a womanizer, so Chiba did the work!*"[39]

The neighbor had also noticed there were some shady people hanging around the house when Chiba was there. "*People who were with Chiba scared me, some looked like drug dealers. Valerie did say that Jennifer Chiba was giving drugs to Elliott.*"[39]

The romantic meeting at Spaceland had supposedly happened in 1999 (as noted in Chiba's lawsuit), and Chiba had been using this first meeting as the beginning of a romantic relationship she was trying to sell. However, the rest of the story may have been slightly different from her fantasy, as Alyson was convinced that drugs may have played a much more important role in Chiba and Elliott's relationship than, let's say, Dostoevsky or Ferdinand the Bull.

Chapter 14: Chiba's best friends

Karrie

If Alyson talked to plenty of people who had assassinated Chiba's character, there were also some people who had plenty of good things to say about her. Some of them had clearly gone to great length to defend her.

One of them was a recent friend, who had been Chiba's roommate for a while before she got married. This person had kindly answered, but Alyson had been quite stunned by her lack of knowledge about the events of October 21, 2003, and the simplistic arguments she had come up with:

"*Chiba shares a passion for educating underprivileged youth. Also like me, she has a very corny sense of humor and loves silly puns. Chiba fervently wanted to become a mother. Jen [Chiba] shares her Elliott stories with friends because it helps her heal. As you've discovered, everyone close to her knows she is entirely innocent without asking for evidence, because she is simply incapable of harming anyone. I understand your inquiry and appreciate your love for Elliott.*"[135]

Could a corny sense of humor get you out of any trouble and prevent any questioning? This answer seemed quite laughable to Alyson, who could not understand why so few people had an inquiring mind. "*Without asking for evidence?*" The case was still open, for God's sake!

Barlow

A few years after her conversation with Karrie, Alyson also received some information from two other people who knew Chiba. One of them was musician Lou Barlow, who first replied the following when asked about Elliott's death:

"*His bio-dad contacted me and we had coffee and he asked me the same question… my answer, I do think he'd be capable of stabbing himself because he seemed deeply self-destructive and angry… he also went cold-turkey after years of hardcore drug abuse... if u are bent on going after Jenn [Chiba] suffice to say she gained nothing from his death and has suffered greatly already.*"[136]

Again, the cold turkey argument was not a satisfying answer, since everyone should have known that normal doses of different legal meds had been found in his system and should have controlled his mood. Why didn't Barlow know that or why did he refuse to admit that? After explaining a few more things to him, such as the opinion of the different forensic experts Alyson had talked to, Elliott's sternum injuries and other forensic oddities very rare in cases of suicide by stabbing, Chiba's removal of the knife, her refusal to talk to the police, and her lawsuit against the family, Barlow took an angrier tone:

"*If the cops dropped it then I'm not sure what pursuing it further on the behalf of Elliott does... his father was looking for closure and had a tremendously painful relationship with his son... I don't know what you want to achieve … justice for a guy who pretty much spent most of his life trying to hurt himself or, let's be honest, kill himself… openly… I dunno... it's very sad and if u are mounting a campaign to drag Jen [Chiba] to jail I would suggest there might be better things to do with your time.*"[136]

This tone was a surprise to Alyson; How could she be "*mounting a campaign*" to drag Chiba to jail? She was just gathering facts. And was "*Elliott talked about killing himself*" the only argument these people could provide? It was not true that Elliott had "*spent most of his life trying to hurt himself.*" He had also released five beautiful albums, played numerous concerts, and had a life filled with friendship. Strangely, Barlow's words had on Elliott-got-what-he-deserved tone, whereas he had not addressed any of Alyson's points. The tone was also too aggressive to not be interpreted as jealous or defensive. Years ago, Ruth had told Alyson that Lou Barlow's wife had been Chiba's best friend for years, and Chiba had even done some babysitting for them. Perhaps that explains why he was so quick to defend her.

Peringer

Robin Peringer was another failed attempt at gathering information, but a necessary one. Alyson probably knew it before talking to him, but she had to try anyway. After all, Robin had been all over the place during these last years. He had been Elliott's constant companion on stage, then one of the first people to speak to Gowing, Reyes, and Schultz, and finally he was this strange character who had been seen at the wall with Chiba just after their raid of the studio, two nights after Elliott's death. Interestingly, Peringer was not interviewed for the 2014 documentary *Heaven Adores You*, despite the fact that he had played with Elliott in every 2003 show.

Back in 2003, Robin had been heard saying that Elliott had been "*very happy, always laughing, very upbeat, cracking jokes all of the time,*" and that "*there was no sign, what-so-ever of anything like this happening.*" Then, a year later, that same Robin had said to Liam Gowing that Elliott had hurt himself with knife cuts on his arm on other occasions prior to his death. In another interview, he had also declared he had helped Chiba "*clean up the blood throughout the house.*"[90]

Since he had also moved in with Chiba as her roommate for a little while just after Elliott's death, Robin has stayed very close to the scene during all these years. He was at first very reluctant to talk, declaring he would answer just one or two questions:

"*I sorta learned to not talk too much about Elliott as everyone has their minds made up on him and his end. But we can try,*"[137] he wrote to Alyson.

When she asked Robin about his last encounter with Elliott, he answered:

"*I'm not sure of my last encounter. He was on some days and off others. The talk of moving was more in hopes of staying clean away from LA. He had a studio in North Hollywood but literally, it could have been moved anywhere.*

I'll never know if he was truly off drugs, I found drugs in his studio but had no idea when they entered, they could have been forgotten or purchased that day. He was being given prescription drugs by his therapist, I remember him taking something like 25 Adderalls when we played New York, I don't know if he slept at all on that trip. I can say he seemed good while we were rehearsing for ATP, but there were both good and bad days."[137]

This was slightly different from his declaration at the wall just after Elliott's death, about his upbeat mood, the idea of a garden, and the plan for a recording à la Beatles, but discrepancies were to be expected. However, as soon as Alyson mentioned the nonconclusive results of the autopsy report, the extreme rarity of suicide by stabbing, that the case had been left open by the police, and the cloud of suspicion still hanging over Chiba, he replied "*We're done.*"[137]

Alyson knew that would happen. She didn't know what to think about those "*25 Adderalls,*" since this was the same guy who had declared that Elliott had cut himself in a very serious manner a few weeks before his death, had done three "*really tremendous knife wounds*" on his left arm using "*the sharpest, biggest knife,*" when no such wounds had ever shown up in the autopsy report.

If it's highly probable that Elliott was harming himself, it was nevertheless interesting to note the likely exaggerations of Peringer's description, in comparison to when Chiba had talked about "*superficial ones, at various points on his body.*"

At this point, it was difficult to know anything about the current state of Robin Peringer's relationship with Chiba, but he was certainly still defending her in the most unhelpful way. Why wouldn't he have helped clear her name if he was convinced of her innocence? Why wouldn't he have tried to present to Alyson some compelling facts proving Chiba's innocence and shut down her suspicious inquiry? His angry reaction was that of a man with no argument to bring to the table. He had had the same angry reaction when he had been interviewed by the *Filter* magazine journalist eight years prior, and had declared, "*I get really upset when people say dumb, ignorant shit about him being murdered.*"[90]

A defensive reaction once again? It was impossible to ignore.

Although she never had the chance to talk to him, Alyson had also heard that recording engineer Fritz Michaud had defended Chiba in front of other people, even claiming she was "*harmless.*" She certainly had many allies besides Reyes and Schultz.

Chapter 15: The party girl is gone in the limelight

To Alyson, there was still some confusion about exactly what Chiba had been up to in the days following Elliott's death. A female musician who had known her very well during the glorious days of the band Brian Jonestown Massacre (late '90s-early '00s) had told Alyson that Chiba had left the country just a few days after the tragic event, and Abigail had told Alyson more or less the same story. After talking to a lawyer about 24 hours after the tragedy, Chiba quickly left the country.

"*I haven't heard anything about her at all since Elliott Smith died, she seems to have disappeared completely, not saying anything at all about what happened that last day at their place,*"[138] a neighbor had commented.

There had been one questioning with the police on the scene, but Chiba had declined a second one because her lawyer had told her to stop cooperating, and she may have already been out of the country not too long after this. Abigail said that Chiba had even thrown a going away party before leaving.

Hong Kong

Mark, an independent journalist who had also been doing some research on the case, had told Alyson that Weezer's frontman Rivers Cuomo—Chiba's former boyfriend—had bought her a one-way ticket to Hong Kong immediately following Elliott's death. Mark had confirmed that he had obtained this information from reliable sources and he had told Alyson that Chiba had flown as far as Boston, but after seeing there was no indictment, she had decided to return to Los Angeles.[139] She had not really been ready to leave at that time.

Chiba was present at the tribute show at the Fonda on November 3, and Alyson saw her on stage at the other tribute at All Tomorrow's Parties on November 8. Therefore, Chiba had stayed in Los Angeles for a little while and had conveniently shown up at the tribute shows. According to Ruth, Chiba had left about a week after Elliott's death, then had come back for the tribute shows, then had left again. She had then stayed in New York, then London (Deanna had received emails from London[4]), and she had even visited her father in South Africa, as some photos had been posted online as evidence.

Vice Magazine

It was well documented that, almost immediately after Elliott's death, Chiba tried to reconnect with Rivers Cuomo, who even wrote a song ("The Other Way") about the episode: "*I wrote that song for Jennifer Chiba after Elliott died, and I wanted to console her, but I was confused and skeptical about my own motives for wanting to do so, so I wrote that song about that,*"[143] Cuomo had declared publicly. The song was demoed acoustically on November 8, 2003, exactly 18 days after Elliott's death, which demonstrated how fast things had been going between Rivers and Chiba.

It was difficult to know what Chiba was doing when she was overseas. Over the years, Alyson got a few pieces of information from many independent sources, in particular from someone who had been helping set up *Vice* magazine in England and had been traveling a lot for this reason. He told Alyson he saw Chiba several times at parties, either in New York or London—he couldn't remember as he was going back and forth. He described Chiba as a heavy partygoer, doing a lot of drugs (cocaine) at the time—and since he had right away admitted he was also doing a lot of drugs himself at the time, he was not judging Chiba for being a drug-user.[140] These parties happened during the first few months following Elliott's death, and after reading about the case, he remembers being stunned by the scene: "*It is so strange, everybody is so friendly with her, there is absolutely no skepticism, no stigma! She is so awesome, and this is so odd.*"[140]

At the time, Chiba was already dating another musician. "*She went straight from Elliott to the drummer of the Pixies,*"[140] the man said. The fact she was dating another musician just after Elliott's tragic passing didn't make her look very good, and he even used the pejorative "*starfucker*" to refer to her, a term that Alyson had strangely heard many times from Abigail Russell.

Besides the Pixies' drummer, Alyson had also heard that Chiba had allegedly dated comedian David Cross when she was in New York. The fan from Florida had said, "*She dated some other musicians after Rivers, before Elliott, and then after Elliott died, she was dating some American Apparel model (who was also a waiter, she took me there to eat once and I met him). All of the parties we went to and all of the dinners out, everyone there was 'someone' and they all liked to surround themselves with other industry, famous, interesting people.*"[106]

There was another guy who spoke to Alyson, a host of a podcast about murders in the music world. He was briefly interested in the Elliott-Chiba story and said to Alyson, "*One of my good friends went on a date with her [Chiba] shortly after and he was freaked the fuck out… he was matched up. He said she was sketchy as fuck and he is convinced she did it.*"[141]

This was also echoed by another woman named Susie, who had told Alyson that she had been loosely associated in the same circle: "*I remember seeing her with a lot of dudes.*"[142]

Every time Alyson talked to someone, another guy showed up in the picture. Though Chiba's dating life had nothing to do with her potential guilt or involvement in Elliott's death, Alyson could not comprehend the immunity she seemed to have everywhere, this "*no skepticism, no stigma*"[140] surrounding Chiba. Yes, Alyson had talked to many people who had expressed their skepticism, but no one had demonstrated anything close to public outrage.

After this list of potential new and ex-boyfriends combined with accumulated research pointing towards her guilt, it was difficult for Alyson to give Chiba the benefit of the doubt. It is true that everybody reacts differently to trauma, but it was really difficult to reconcile the woman crying non-stop at Elliott's funeral (according to a witness) with this partygoer, this indie-musician-serial-dater she had become just a few weeks later.

Follow the money part 1

Alyson had been able to look up Chiba's marriage and family therapist license, a license which has to be renewed every 5-6 years, but Chiba had not renewed hers from June 2001 to October 2005.[131] She had been living in Los Angeles during that time, then abroad for a while after Elliott's death, but she was most likely back in LA at the moment of the first lawsuit, in July 2004. What was Chiba's source of income between 2001 and 2005, when we know that rents are no cheap commodity in Los Angeles? Chiba may have received (and probably had) money from Elliott when he was living with her, but this most likely barely covered a year.

There was also a persistent rumor that Alyson had heard from different sources, that Chiba had been financially supported by Rivers Cuomo.

"*It's not a rumor, she told me herself,*" the female fan from Florida had said. "*She [Chiba] said she dated Rivers for like 10 years and after they broke up, Rivers took care of her financially, even when we [Chiba and the fan] were friends. She [Chiba] said he [Rivers] never really got over her and continued to call her and try to get her to come over. I think maybe he was just worried about her.*"[106]

Alyson had heard a similar story from at least three other people besides this Florida woman: Deanna, Abigail, and one of the new owners of Elliott's studio had all said Chiba had claimed that her ex-boyfriend was financially supporting her. The studio owner had even said that Chiba had told her that she would get Cuomo's money to sue the family.[13]

Alyson had no idea how to interpret this. She knew the 10-year relationship that Chiba had with Cuomo was greatly exaggerated, as it had actually been an on-and-off affair between 1992-1995, according to Weezerpedia.[103] And the fact she had dated so many other guys during that time was also more evidence. Among these men were Bobby Hecksher from the Warlocks, the keyboardist of an indie band, and probably director Steve Hanft—just to cite the ones Alyson had heard about—so there was simply no time for a 10-year relationship with Cuomo, unless Chiba and Alyson didn't share the same definition of "*relationship*."

There were two possibilities regarding the recurrent claim that Rivers Cuomo was supporting Chiba financially. If it wasn't true, then Chiba had another source of income, but if it was true, you had to wonder why Cuomo was still sending money to an ex-girlfriend many years later. Interestingly, Cuomo had described their relationship in the liner notes of *Alone II*:[144]

"*Since late '92, through many of the difficult days of playing the clubs in LA with Weezer, Jennifer Chiba had been my kind-of-girlfriend. I had benefited greatly from her care and yet I had always kept my heart hard to her, believing that if Weezer did make it, I would want to be free for the many superior options I imagined would be available to me. Now in the summer of '94, as Weezer was indeed starting to make it, Chiba said she would resist me because of my refusal to commit. But whenever Weezer came through town I called her up looking for a place to stay (because I was no longer renting an apartment) and she gave in, letting me into her heart and home. In mid-July, when Weezer came to LA to record some B-sides, I stayed with her. We had an argument. She wanted more commitment and I wanted freedom. At the end of the work period, I flew back to my mom's house in Connecticut and on July 14 wrote a song called 'I'll Think About You' that I hope captured the pain and conflict of my situation with Chiba…*"[144] Cuomo came across as an asshole in this commentary, and it was clear he had no intention of committing to her.

Several songs on the album *Pinkerton* were rumored to have been written about a half-Japanese girl, i.e., Chiba. "El Scorcho" and "No Other One" were probably inspired by Chiba, as well as "Walt Disney," "Hot Tub," and "I'll Think About You."[103] Undoubtedly, there has been a lot of Chiba in the life of Rivers Cuomo, who has always been an open book for his fans, since he even used to post blog entries about his personal life on MySpace or LiveJournal, and used to post on the Weezer board as "*Ace*." And with "The

Pinkerton Diaries," a long journal entry and an invitation into his private life and intimate thoughts, fans have always known many details about his inner world.

There was also the unfinished space rock opera *Songs from the Black Hole,* recorded by Cuomo at the end of 1994, telling the story of Jonas (Rivers Cuomo himself), a man involved in a love triangle with a "*good girl*" (Laurel) and a "*bad girl*" (Maria), the ship's cook, with whom he would eventually father a child. As Cuomo explained in the liner notes of *Alone II,* the character of Maria had specifically been written with Chiba in mind:[145]

"*I started planning and writing out sketches, music, and songs. To stand for my relationship with Chiba, I imagined a character named Maria (a role which I hoped to be sung by Joan Wasserman* [sic] *of the Dambuilders, though I abandoned the project before asking her). In the liner notes to Alone I, I quoted the opening scene of The Black Hole in which Maria lets the guys know how she feels about being called a 'b***h.'*"[145]

In the rock opera, Jonas had a history with Maria, but views her as "*too crazy,*" whereas he feels he could settle down with Laurel, who doesn't love him back. The songs of the rock opera were a sort of insight into Chiba and Cuomo's relationship. Maria/Chiba wanting to hook up with Jonas/Cuomo, whereas he only wanted to be her friend. Interestingly, this also strangely resembled Chiba's story with Elliott, as she consistently desired a relationship with a successful singer-songwriter. If she had failed to achieve this with Cuomo, it had finally happened with Elliott at the end of 2002.

According to Cuomo's songs, Chiba always wanted him to commit, whereas at the time, he was living the rock star life, sleeping around with groupies. It's quite possible that, years later, Cuomo may have felt guilty after all, and this might have been the reason why he was still supporting Chiba several years later. To Alyson, it was a strange arrangement, but somehow explainable. The fact that Cuomo had even written the song "The Other Way" to console Chiba after Elliott's death fit with the idea of this strange arrangement.

Elliott Smith's foundation

At the time of Elliott's death, his foundation for abused children was far from being finalized, as it generally takes about a year for all the paperwork to be filed and a foundation to be established as a legal and recognized charity. Just before his death, Elliott had started the process with Valerie Deerin and Jerry Schoenkopf, but the Elliott Smith Foundation (ESF) never made it to an official status. It turns out that the papers had been signed on October 1, 2003, exactly twenty days before Elliott died.

There was no money in the foundation, and Jerry had actually told Alyson that he still owed some money to Valerie that he had never had the chance to return. When Elliott was still alive, there had been some intention to raise money and, the last time Elliott had played in Portland, money from T-shirt sales had reportedly been advertised for the foundation.

Elliott's sister started the Elliott Smith Memorial Fund (ESMF)[146] a few days after his passing in an attempt to continue his work despite his departure. This created some confusion, as there were now two burgeoning foundations (the ESMF and the ESF), although neither of them was finalized. According to Ruth, Chiba may have possibly been involved with the ESMF.

The ESMF became the official one used for several tribute shows, although the proceeds of the tribute at the Henry Fonda Theatre on November 3, 2003 supposedly went to *The Elliott Smith Foundation* as was indicated on the ticket.[147] The ESMF, which would have needed another year to be fully established, was funneling donations into already settled official charities such as Free Arts for Abused Children in Los Angeles. Donations were sent to a PO Box at a small Postal Works place—very probably the same PO Box used by Elliott for his future charity—and the checks were passed along to Free Arts for Abused Children.[146]

However, the Portland family, who was running the estate, decided to go with another Portland charity called Outside In, so at this point there were two official charities linked with the ESMF. Money was raised this way during the first year (or two) after Elliott's death, then, after a few announcements on Elliott's official website, fans were asked to send checks directly to the two charities. At least, this is what the official story stated.

Follow the money part 2

Per usual, there were some rumors around the money situation. Deanna, very early on, had asked the question: "*Where does Chiba's money come from*?"[4] And then there was Abigail, who had said to Alyson that Chiba had stolen money from the foundation before leaving for abroad,[98] something Alyson has never been able to verify. However, Alyson heard the same thing from Mark, the freelance journalist,[139] who, without ever meeting or communicating with Abigail, had done his own research and was convinced that Chiba had stolen money from the foundation. According to his sources, Chiba had allegedly been apprehended by federal postal inspectors for accessing and cashing checks earmarked for Elliott Smith's charity. He had apparently heard this from two people. For Alyson, it was just hearsay, but this was the story he had told her: Two sources had revealed to him that Chiba had apparently posed as Valerie Deerin to pick up the checks at a PO Box. Valerie and Elliott had started the foundation together with this same PO Box, which authorized two key holders. Since Valerie had been involved with the foundation very early on, it was probable she was still in possession of one of the keys, whereas the other one was held by Elliott. The key may have landed in Chiba's hands after his death. Chiba allegedly used the key to pick up the mail while posing as Valerie but was apprehended when she tried to cash the checks. According to Mark, Valerie had found the box empty, asked about the mail, and had been told that it had already been picked up by "Valerie."[139]

Without being able to verify the information, Alyson knew she had to take it with a grain of salt. But in case it was actually Valerie who had picked up the mail, it must have happened very shortly after Elliott's death. In that case, it would have meant that Valerie had stuck around a bit longer than had been reported by Schultz. "*As Chiba put it 'he [Elliott] sent her back to Scotland.'*"[82] Schultz had written in *Torment Saint*. However, Schultz had also written that Valerie had "*stayed around LA for at least a matter of weeks, if not months.*"[82]

The reality is that Valerie had been in and out of Los Angeles for a while. If this post office story was accurate, this meant that Valerie had stayed in LA after Elliott's death, without being officially involved in these tribute shows. Even though the entire thing was still strange, it was not impossible, and almost comprehensible. Valerie had been replaced by another woman (she obviously did not like) and her ex-boyfriend had died in a violent way.

Why wouldn't she have wanted to know more about what had happened to Elliott? Valerie might even have suspected Chiba had something to do with Elliott's violent death.

There was another intriguing thing, a strange coincidence that Alyson had noticed. Jennifer Chiba had her own PO Box (Chiba Jennifer Rie: 2658 Griffith Park Blvd #151) at this same Postal Works place as The Elliott Smith Foundation (2658 Griffith Park Blvd, #195). This didn't mean it was proof that Chiba had stolen the money from the foundation, but the two PO Boxes were conveniently located at the same place.

Since Valerie had never agreed to any interview—except her off the record conversation with Gowing—and since she would have been the only one who could have cleared up the uncertainties of this story, Alyson could not do much more with this.

One thing was certain. Without a license, Chiba could not have been working as a therapist from June 2001 to October 2005. However, she was traveling the world after Elliott's death, had been seen at parties in London and/or New York, had stayed a few months in London, and had been living in Los Angeles the rest of the time. Where was the money coming from?

Chapter 16: Meet the neighbors

The first approaches

For a long time, Alyson had tried to contact the various neighbors who were living on Lemoyne Street when Elliott died, but she had never been successful at getting any valuable information. One response she did get was from the Steffens, who were living next door in a blue house. They had once answered a timid email she had sent in the hopes of starting a conversation. But whoever had answered, either Roger or Mary, they had shown right away they had no intention of continuing the discussion. Alyson had simply received a very brief note saying, "*Elliott Smith killed himself and left a suicide note. We have nothing more to say.*"[148]

It was a dry declaration lacking further possibility, a mindset to discourage any inquiry, especially when Alyson had stayed very vague in her email, just mentioning she was doing some research about Elliott Smith, who was their neighbor at the moment of his tragic death in 2003. It was as if they had guessed her real intention right away, or they may have done some research on their own. But why were they so certain when the coroner and the police were not? Maybe because Chiba had been a close friend of Mary Steffens, as Alyson discovered a bit later? They had a mother-daughter kind of relationship, she had heard.

Then there was Richard Cromelin who was living across the street, and despite being a writer for the LA Times, could not provide any information "*beyond what is out there,*" he told Alyson. "*I didn't have any contact with him when he lived on Lemoyne. any info and insights I got were in the obituary.*"[149] Ironically, Richard had written Elliott's obituary for the LA Times, before realizing he was living on the same street.

Rosa

Finally, there was Rosa, an ex-neighbor who was not living on Lemoyne Street anymore but remembered the horrific details of that tragic day. She said she saw the paramedics wheeling Elliott up the driveway, with the blood-soaked gauzes on his chest.

"*He looked lifeless. The last image that I have of him will forever haunt me,*" [150] she told Alyson. Rosa had contacted Alyson and, despite being quite reticent to talk, she had surprising details to reveal. Rosa was sick the day Elliott died. She was stuck at home and was awoken by the sirens of the ambulance.[150]

"*I had initially thought that he had overdosed,*"[150] she told Alyson, adding that it didn't take her long to realize that something completely different had happened because of all the blood on Elliott's chest.

"*I remember seeing her [Chiba] come out after they took him,*" said Rosa. "*Supposedly she was outside of the restroom when the cops first arrived but then barricaded herself in their [Elliott and Chiba's] restroom.*"[150]

That was something Alyson had never heard. "*She had a blanket wrapped around her, so unfortunately I couldn't see anything,*" added Rosa. "*All I really remember is that Chiba was in there for what seemed like forever. Firemen and cops were knocking on the neighbors' doors to see if anyone knew her and could get her out of the restroom. Then one neighbor agreed and eventually convinced her to come out of the house. And when they all walked out, she had a blanket draped over her shoulders. But she played the victim from the get go.*"[150]

Could it be possible? Would the police have not included this important part of the story in their report? Alyson kept thinking about the conversation she had had with detective Morris and him telling her there were other files and reports not made public. Could this important detail be in those secret files?

Rosa finally commented that she thought the neighbor who had convinced Chiba to come out of the house was Mary Steffens, as the two women had developed a very close friendship. This could explain why the Steffens were undoubtedly convinced of Chiba's innocence.

"*Her daughter told me that Mary challenges anyone trying to convince her otherwise*," said Rosa. "*She says that she'll shut everyone down*."[150]

"*But everyone knew Chiba as a crazy chick*," continued Rosa. "*We called her the hipster Courtney Love. I don't know why she had anything on her or why it took her so long to exit the restroom. The way that most people see it is that she is innocent and has buried the past, so to speak*."[150]

Rosa tried to help Alyson, as after all, she had lived there and she knew the people who were still living there, but she found closed doors everywhere. "*I spoke to a few people who still live on the hill and for the most part, they all defend her*," she told Alyson. Rosa even warned Alyson against another family living on the same street. "*They didn't like Elliott for very stupid reasons… because he used to park in front of their house*."[150]

It appeared there were a lot of problems with the neighbors and with Lemoyne Street being a narrow street running up the Echo Park hills. It was not an easy place to find a parking spot. But covering up a potential murder because the victim used to have some unruly parking habits seemed outrageous to Alyson.

"*Yeah, they were assholes to him*," said Rosa. "*The night before everything happened, I had to wait until he got home to apologize because they [my uncle] slashed his tires*."[150] You would end up with a flat tire for parking in the wrong spot? Unbelievable.

"*No one wants to talk,*" added Rosa. "*Shoot, I'm even regretting it. I was just a kid when it happened, and no one ever believed me. The way that I see it is, I waited too long to say anything so people may say that my credibility isn't valid*."[150]

Rosa said later she didn't witness the barricade episode, but it is what she heard. However, she did remember the cops being there for a few hours.

"*It was a crime scene.... I was home and heard yelling the night before,*"[150] she added. The night before? If true, they had argued for a long time.

"*She's an awful woman. I've seen her throw so many temper tantrums at parties,*"[150] continued Rosa, who again insisted she was still very young at the time, around 18 years old.

She was also certain of one thing. Chiba, while living with Elliott, was stalking another man named Danny, who was living a few houses down the same street. "*She used to call him, wait outside and show up to his parties uninvited,*" explained Rosa. "*I heard of her pulling out a knife on Danny. That's what my dad said, that Danny and his dad told him.*"[150]

Rosa also remembered that when she saw Elliott just the day before he died. "*He was as sweet as usual to me. He was very much coherent.... He was just tired and stressed out but he was all smiles. She did this to him because he was leaving her,*"[150] added Rosa. How many times had Alyson heard this before?

Rosa mentioned her cousin Joey who was also living next door to Elliott and Chiba's. "*Joey was the one who hid from the cops because of the fact that he was growing a lot of weed and was in possession of narcotics,*" explained Rosa. "*But he's the one who heard everything that day.*"[150]

Joey

It took two years for Alyson to find Joey, not that she was trying every day, of course, but it was something in the back of her mind. Joey had to be somewhere, but she didn't even know his last name and couldn't ask Rosa because she had suddenly disappeared from social media. She had not even left a phone number or an email address, and was seemingly nowhere to be found. One day, while tracking down people who had lived in the neighborhood, Alyson sent a few brief messages to what seemed to be random phone numbers. She was trying to reach people, explaining in a few words the purpose of her inquiry, the event that had occurred 18 years ago on Lemoyne Street. "*Would you be open to talking with me?*" Alyson asked in a simple message. Some messages went undelivered, other ones never returned an answer, but one came back with the simple "*Sure.*"[151] It was Joey and he was willing to talk.

After a brief text exchange, Alyson met with Joey on a Saturday afternoon at a small coffee shop in Echo Park, and he offered to continue the conversation inside his car, parked just a few yards away. Alyson immediately thought it would be a good idea for the confidentiality of this type of discussion, and Joey, a very friendly guy, told her he had been living in the neighborhood for a long time. The year Elliott died, Joey was living at 1853 Lemoyne Street, the house just next to Elliott and Chiba's, and on October 21, 2003, Joey was in his backyard with a friend and their Akita dogs. Elliott and Chiba had been fighting all morning long but, Joey said, that was happening on an almost daily basis.

"*I never used to pay attention because it was every day… they were never not fighting.*"[151]

Alyson believed him, as this is what she had heard before multiple times, and she had once heard from another neighbor, who had requested anonymity, the following statement: "*She and Elliott have had this emotional, dramatic table-turning, door slamming, screaming 'I hate you' type of relationship, typical for a manic and a depressed individual right? My wife has witnessed it herself in a bar one night. Well, they were having one of those episodes.*"[151]

According to Joey, the couple had a strong love-hate relationship, constantly screaming at each other followed by peacemaking.

Joey was in the backyard the morning of Elliott's death when he heard them scream very loudly. They were "*right there,*" said Joey, referring to the living room located in the back of their unit, even mentioning that their sliding glass door was open. It is probably very difficult to recall an event that occurred such a long time ago, but Joey said that Elliott and Chiba were fighting well before noon, when he heard Chiba scream, "*I don't give a shit, fucking die!*"[151]

This terrible declaration was immediately followed by a long silence. "*They were arguing at the top of their lungs and then it got quiet,*"[151] said Joey to Alyson. But according to Joey, it was "*loud and clear*" and there was no way this scream could have emitted from behind a closed door. This point is very important when we have heard so many times that Chiba had said she had locked herself in the bathroom. The silence made Joey and his friend very anxious, and Joey said he didn't hear Elliott scream at all, or if he did scream, it was not loud enough for Joey to hear anything. He looked at his friend and asked him, "*Did someone get killed?*" They decided to leave the house. "*We got spooked,*" he said. "*You hear something you should not be hearing.*"[151]

They left the house, had lunch out, and came back around 1 pm, just when the paramedics were carrying Elliott away. Since we know that Elliott died at 1:18 pm at the hospital, Joey's timeline may have been a bit off, but not by very much.

After talking to his friend, Joey estimated that probably several hours had passed since the time he had heard Chiba scream that terrible sentence. Once again, it was very difficult for him to remember the exact time, but he was certain that a long period had passed between the fight and the paramedics' arrival.

"*I was there outside when he was taken away,*" Joey said. "*I remember, and nobody ever asked me anything.... I don't remember seeing the police because probably if I had seen them, I would have approached them.*"[151]

To Alyson, these allegations were very compelling, and in complete contradiction with Chiba's story that she had locked herself in the bathroom and came out when she heard a terrible scream or noise. But Joey was claiming that, if the stabbing had effectively occurred just after Chiba's loud "*fucking die*" scream—as the silence that had followed may have suggested—Elliott and Chiba had been fighting in the living room, so Chiba was not locked inside the bathroom.

The fact that Joey remembered the fight had occurred earlier in the morning than we would have thought was also disconcerting, when we know for sure that the 911 call had been placed at 12:18 pm.

Since we know that Elliott was admitted to the hospital at 1:10 pm, the ambulance was probably there shortly before 1 pm. There are barely 5 miles between the house and the hospital, so the ambulance should not have taken longer than 10 minutes.

Since Joey was gone for a few hours, he had no idea what happened between Chiba's scream and the ambulance arrival, but for him, the two events had been separated by an awfully long time, something that could have even been several hours. One thing was certain, he had enough time to go out for lunch with his friend and come back. For Alyson, even one hour sounded unbelievably dramatic. Could Joey's testimony confirm that Chiba had waited a long time before calling the ambulance?

Joey told Alyson he wouldn't mind talking on the record, and that was a big surprise, as she had never experienced such a willingness to get involved in this now 18-year-old sordid story. Most people she had talked to hadn't been very eager to do so for a bunch of reasons, mostly because they thought it wouldn't change anything, or because they simply didn't want to be bothered. Over the years, Alyson became convinced she would get more information from people like Joey rather than Elliott's friends or fellow musicians, but whatever motivated Joey to talk to her, either the fact that he considered Elliott almost a friend—"*We could have been friends*," he said—or just because of his naturally amiable nature, Alyson couldn't have been more grateful that he did.

Joey had described Chiba as a very intense person with a strong will who had often been mean to him. She had even tried to sue him years before. Although he had never seen her do drugs, he said she was a heavy drinker. She had lived at this place for a very long time and had often received free rent from the owner, Andre, because the house was in bad condition.

"*She got so much free rent, she complained about the conditions of the house*,"[151] Joey said. Once again, Joey had met Elliott over a parking argument, since Elliott used to park in front of 1853 Lemoyne and the owner was not too happy about it. They had a fight, but it was not very serious, as Joey explained. "*What I liked about him is that he was forgiving*,"[151] as Elliott had forgotten about the fight over the parking space the next day.

Joey had lived at 1853 Lemoyne Street for a while, then moved to 1857 Lemoyne after Elliott's death, just below Chiba's unit, a few days before the house was sold to a new owner, Adam Gerstein. He told Alyson that drummer Robin Peringer was now living with Chiba, and they made a lot of noise. "*They would come home at 4 am, very drunk, and would make a lot of noise, throw things down, even start drumming*!"[151] Joey, who had a newborn at the time, was quite furious and would knock on their door without any success of quieting them down. Joey then added a very pertinent detail. He knew without a doubt that Chiba and Peringer had a sexual relationship very shortly after Elliott's death.

"*These two had no shame!*" Joey told Alyson, who asked him how he knew for sure. "*She was very loud,*"[151] he added, with a grin on his face.

When the new owner Adam Gerstein took over in 2004, he managed to evict everybody that year, first Chiba,[152] then Joey, who hadn't seen her since.

For Alyson, Joey's testimony was a huge part of the puzzle, although she was well aware that memory can distort a lot of details after so many years. Joey didn't seem to have forgotten the words Chiba had screamed that day, and he had been quite consistent when repeating the story and after having been asked more questions. It was clear that this extremely uneasy feeling (of potentially being a witness to murder) had stayed with him. For Joey, it was very straightforward. Elliott and Chiba had had a crazy relationship and it was most likely a crime of passion without any premeditation.

Joey was the closest person who could have been considered a witness to the events of October 21 but, unfortunately, the police had not spoken to him at the time. Yet he kept his promise to Alyson and talked to detective J. King a few weeks after talking to her. Caroline, the studio owner who had witnessed Chiba's restless behavior just after Elliott's death, had never spoken to the police either. In the end, very few people had contacted the police, and the police had not contacted them, certainly not the neighbors, according to what Alyson had found out.

Chapter 17: Conspiracy theory

Despite all of Alyson's research, the myth of Elliott—i.e. the tortured soul, the tormented artist capable of committing suicide by stabbing himself in the heart twice—was still very much alive, for two reasons: first, people had never looked closely into the details of the story; and second, people always prefer to believe the easiest explanation, the most comfortable one. A self-loathing artist with suicide ideation, a depressed ex-junkie with low self-esteem, had to have committed suicide; there was not even a window for the murder theory. Alyson knew she was fighting against the world, or almost, despite a few signs here and there that many of Elliott's friends were, at the very least, suspicious.

For example, there was the comment left by Larry Crane, the recording engineer turned Elliott Smith archivist. Late in March 2010, after a post on a music blog discussing and criticizing Larry Crane's remastering (or not) of Elliott Smith's albums (*Roman Candle* and *From a Basement on the Hill*), Crane had written: "*Speaking of cleaning up, your facts on Elliott's passing are incorrect.*"[153]

That music blog mentioned Elliott's suicide, like an impressive number of other articles posted on the internet. Yet it was interesting to see Crane correcting the article with a "*your facts on Elliott's passing are incorrect,*" apparently questioning the suicide theory.

After the screening of the documentary *Heaven Adores You* at the Regent in 2015, a movie that had consciously ignored the controversy around Elliott's death and even completely omitted Jennifer Chiba in the narration, Alyson noticed Autumn de Wilde's strong reaction to one of the audience's questions. The famous photographer, who had a part in the movie, was participating in a Q&A, and she had literally jumped from her seat when someone had asked the people on the panel if they thought that fame had contributed to Elliott's suicide. "*First, we don't know what happened to Elliott that day!*"[113] Autumn had said, looking upset.

Just after the screening Alyson had a short conversation with someone involved in the documentary, it didn't take long for him to admit that people were very split on the death question. Apparently, half of Elliott's friends thought he had probably committed suicide, whereas the other half thought he had been murdered.[113] One thing was sure, we were far from W.T. Schultz's declaration in the *Seattle Weekly*: "*No one, not a one, strongly believed or even suspected he'd been murdered.*"[154]

Schultz's main argument was the Occam's razor principle that did not make any sense to Alyson. How could stabbing yourself twice, through the thoracic cage, without any hesitation wounds and through clothes be the simplest explanation? The combination of all these features was the opposite of Occam's razor, because if a case presents one oddity, the occurrence of many of them at the same time could not be explained easily. But if many people were suspicious, why had these people been so reticent to get involved or be more vocal on the subject, at the very least? Why was Alyson constantly told things such as "*focus on the music,*" "*we will never know,*" "*the case is forever unsolved.*" As if this story had been one of the biggest mysteries of the universe. People tend to forget this is not just a mystery but a crime, an open case that deserves closure.

Detective King

Alyson was not a conspiracy theorist. She despised most conspiracy theories and thought of herself as having a rational mind. She disliked it when people called any alternative to suicide "*a conspiracy theory.*" It was indeed incorrect to call it a conspiracy when the LAPD had never closed the case, when the coroner had never decided between suicide or homicide. It was a misrepresentation of the situation.

Alyson didn't even like when people started their sentences with "*I believe that....*" Alyson liked evidence and had never presumed to know exactly what had happened, but she certainly didn't "*believe*" anything. Alyson had also managed to have real contact with the LAPD over the years. She had talked on the phone with homicide detective P.J. Morris then J. King and had had an ongoing correspondence with Detective King, sending him information when she had found something she judged to be of interest. He had always been grateful, at least he appeared to be in their email correspondence.

"*It's always good to hear from you, and I welcome your input. The information you forwarded is certainly very interesting, and I'm grateful for you sending it. Should anything develop, I will let you know. Take care, and thanks again.*"[88] was the type of emails Alyson had received from Detective King. He had even clarified a few things for her, in particular the fact that several people had told her that the case was now closed because they had seen on the coroner website that the case was marked "*closed.*" Detective King immediately cleared up this confusion: "*I looked at the Coroner link you sent. As far as the Coroner case being 'closed,' that has nothing to do with the police investigation. The police case remains open.*"[88]

Bad journalism had often repeated this same error, confusing the coroner case (basically closed after the autopsy was done) with the police investigation, which is still open. Nevertheless, there were plenty of people calling Alyson a conspiracy theorist, or even a misogynist for daring to suspect a poor woman who had already suffered so much since the death of her fiancé. These kinds of accusations have been persistent since the beginning, and Alyson decided to try asking the question directly to Detective King, "*Do you consider me a conspiracy theorist?*" To that he had answered:

"I do NOT consider you a conspiracy theorist. By compiling peoples' recollections in an effort to clarify an event, you're merely doing what police do every day. Additionally, you seem to have a very good grasp on what is interpretation, opinion or speculation, and what is a provable fact. Please know that I'm always grateful for the information you provide, so do not be deterred."[88]

This had been a great validation that Alyson could use as a counter-argument when someone questioned her credibility. Since Detective King was so eager to clarify ambiguities, she had even gotten the chance to ask him about the difference between a cold case and an open case. Once again, his answer had been very helpful:

"This case is not technically a 'cold case' because that term (as we use it at RHD [Robbery Homicide Department]) refers to an unsolved murder in which all leads have been exhausted. Elliott's case is an 'undetermined' death investigation that will remain open until [such] time as a definitive conclusion (i.e. homicide, suicide, accident etc.) is reached by the police."[88]

It was an interesting statement, since he was clearly saying that the case was still open because they had not exhausted all leads. He was even hopeful in the last part of his email: "*Lastly, I, like you, have not forgotten this event, and as is the case with all unsolved investigations that I have undertaken, I retain hope that someday someone will provide first-hand information that will enable us to reach an unequivocal conclusion.*" [88]

Detective P.J. Morris

After learning that Detective P.J. Morris had retired, Alyson thought it could be a good idea to contact him once again. When they had talked on the phone in 2010, he had repeatedly stated he could not say anything about an open case, but Alyson hoped his willingness to talk about Elliott Smith's case may have changed now that he had retired. She remembered him saying at one point in their first conversation: "*But you know we are not considering this case as a suicide!*"[87] Although she knew that any death scene had to be conducted as a homicide investigation until the facts proved differently,[155] she still thought it had been a good indication of his approach to the case.

Detective P.J. Morris had also mentioned additional reports beside the files Alyson had acquired from the coroner, and he had confirmed that the suicide note and the knife had been in the police's possession since that day.

After many unsuccessful attempts, Alyson managed to contact P.J. Morris, who didn't seem to remember much about the case: "*I vaguely remember that case. I've been retired over 10 years now,*"[87] wrote P.J. Morris. After Alyson refreshed his memory with a brief summary of the case, he added: "*The only thing I remember is that the case needed additional investigations and evidence to move the case forward.*"[87] But he also made this important acknowledgment: "*I only remember that it was a very suspicious incident.*"[87] "*Very suspicious*" deeply mattered to Alyson, even if it was an opinion, because it was something new that Morris had not shared before.

Alyson remembered having had a discussion with Gil Reyes regarding the sentence posted at the end of his movie, which read "*An LAPD detective reviewing the case says off-camera he believes it was a suicide.*"[42] While Reyes had always refused to give Alyson the name of this LAPD detective, that statement was in complete opposition to Morris's. When she had asked Reyes in person, he had simply dodged by saying it was confidential information.[114] Confidential? Why? Did Reyes have a special status with the police, or did he want to intimidate her, or did he simply lie? Alyson, on the other hand, had spoken with both Detective J. King and Detective P.J. Morris, who were in charge of the investigation, while Reyes had nothing to provide.

To progress, the case needed more evidence, and Alyson knew Joey, the next-door neighbor, was not the only one who could have provided information about this tragic day, as he had told her he was with a friend in his backyard. However, this friend was really not interested in sharing anything. After talking to Alyson, Joey had even tried to contact a few musicians who knew Elliott and were living in the neighborhood, though their reactions had almost made him regret talking to Alyson. He told her that they grew angry and defensive. "*Why do you want to open this can of worms?*"[151] the front man of a local band had said to him.

This was sort of surprising in a way. What did he mean exactly? Did he mean that speaking to the police would cause more problems? Or would bring something more unpleasant than expected? Alyson already heard something similar from a recording engineer when she had talked to him about her research: "*Well, be warned, it's not gonna turn out how you think and it's not going to make you feel any better about anything.*"[134]

Well, Alyson had not been conducting intense research as a form of therapy, or in pursuit of self-satisfaction. She desired the truth, simply the truth, and Elliott's disappointing relationships with some people was not going to keep her from it.

Alyson had considered several scenarios, although she didn't like speculations because they were just that: speculations. She was hesitant to eliminate any possibility, even the prospect that Elliott had effectively threatened to take his life that day. That was certainly a possible hypothesis, in the light of Joey's revelations and Chiba's scream, "*I don't give a shit, fucking die!*" But a threat could have just been a threat and the real question had always been: Who had been holding the knife when it entered his chest?

If Joey did remember the events correctly, Chiba's voice was not coming from behind a door; the couple had been fighting in the living room, which could have explained the balcony story she had mentioned twice, in Reyes's documentary and Schultz's book.

When Alyson had the chance to talk to a fan[129] who had spent a few days at Chiba's place after Elliott's death, she once again discovered some discrepancies with Chiba's story. At the time, several fans and moderators of the message board had become friendly with Chiba, and many of the threads that had attempted to discuss Elliott's death had been censored or sent to another board, in an attempt to protect Chiba and her reputation. In exchange for their protection, some of these people had sleepovers at Chiba's house.

Many years later, one of them had shared with Alyson his surprise after watching Reyes's documentary. He told her he had never heard of this balcony story before. He had been told by Chiba that she had found Elliott standing outside the bathroom door with his back turned to her when she opened it. Then Elliott had turned around, struggled back to the kitchen, and collapsed on the floor.

"*That's why to me it was a big deal being in the kitchen because that was the place where he had died,*"[129] he had told Alyson. The couple arguing in the living room, located on the other side of the house, and Elliott falling on the balcony dramatically changed the story.

Chapter 18: Can we sum up the events of October 21 once and for all?

It was not an easy task to compile an accurate timeline of the events surrounding Elliott's death, with an unreliable narrator and missing pieces of the puzzle. There were still uncertainties and rumors but, at this point, Alyson thought it would be a good achievement to gather all these events in order, including the discrepancies, in a sort of timeline starting on October 21, 2003. This is what Alyson put together:

On Tuesday, October 21, according to their next-door neighbor Joey, Elliott Smith and Jennifer Chiba had been fighting in the morning. At one point, Chiba had screamed "*I don't give a shit, fucking die!*"[151] a terrible declaration that had been followed by a long silence. Joey had not heard Elliott scream, whereas Chiba had reportedly said that she had heard him scream (or make an awful noise). The long silence had been interpreted by Joey as the moment of the stabbing, because their fight had abruptly stopped just after that. Because Chiba's voice sounded clear and loud, Joey hadn't had the impression that her scream had come from behind a closed door, whereas she had stated she had locked herself in the bathroom at this tragic moment.

Knowing that Elliott had been stabbed twice (with a 2-inch-deep wound and a 5/7-inch-deep wound that had even reached the heart), it might have been difficult for him to scream. Alyson had read that when air finds its way into the chest wall with an open injury, the pressure that keeps the lungs inflated is disrupted and a pneumothorax occurs. The air pushes on the outside of the lungs and makes them collapse. Whether Elliott's lungs had partially collapsed or not, a loud scream at this point may have been difficult, although it states in *Torment Saint* that Chiba claimed Elliott had made "*an awful noise, a scream Chiba vaguely recognized, both familiar somehow and utterly alien.*"[82]

Chiba had then removed the knife from Elliott's chest, and followed him until he crashed onto the balcony, located in the back of the house.

For Alyson, it was always really important to focus on the removal of the knife from Elliott's chest when he was still standing, a scene which somehow sounded more gruesome than the removal of a knife from the chest of someone lying down. Chiba, a licensed marriage and family therapist since 1995, had worked as an art therapist for 15 years in several community mental health organizations, including Five Acres,[16] a school for abused and damaged children. Though panic could not be ruled out, it was almost certain that Chiba had been trained in CPR and first aid, and knew better than to remove the knife.

It was also important to note that, with this scenario, there was no time for Elliott to write the alleged suicide note, and no psychological opportunity for an apologetic note. If Elliott had effectively committed suicide, it had been an impulsive act during a violent fight, and something that could only have been interpreted as aggressive and out of character. Killing himself in front of his girlfriend who, on top of this, was allegedly pregnant, sounded sadistic. Everything in Chiba's narration sounded out of place, especially her claim to have locked herself in the bathroom while he allegedly had been threatening to commit suicide (?), or had acted paranoid (?), depending on the different versions of Chiba's story. Either way, Chiba's detached behavior toward Elliott, with her years of experience as a therapist, was surprising.

At 12:18 pm, Chiba had finally called 911, and the call was immediately referred to the Los Angeles Fire Department. However, there was a persistent rumor that she may have made other phone call(s) before calling 911, and neighbor Joey insisted that Chiba's scream had occurred "*way before noon*,"[151] leaving the possibility that a lot of time passed between the stabbing and the 911 call. Chiba also later admitted to one of Elliott's close family members that her call for an ambulance had been delayed because her cell phone wasn't working properly. A strange excuse to make because this same family member assured that Elliott and Chiba's landline had been working fine just a few days before. One thing was certain, the possible lapse of time between the stabbing/removal of the knife and the 911 call could have explained Elliott's immediate cause of death: exsanguination, i.e. blood loss.

Chiba performed CPR—strangely on two open wounds since she had removed the knife from his chest—until the paramedics' arrival. A few minutes later, they took Elliott away, unconscious but still alive at the time. This was most likely between 12:30 and 1 pm.

According to another neighbor, Chiba had been seen outside with a blanket wrapped around her[150]—although it was a very hot day—around 1 pm, just after Elliott had been carried away. Of note, Chiba had not traveled to the hospital in the ambulance with Elliott.

Since it was stated in the police report that police officers had arrived "*once the decedent was taken to the hospital*,"[48] Chiba couldn't have been interrogated by the police when the paramedics were at the scene. Unless the paramedics didn't want her to ride in the ambulance with Elliott, Chiba had not been prevented from jumping in the ambulance by police officers because they were not there yet.

Later—although the exact time has not been clearly established—police officers arrived. Detective J. King said that police officers were present at the scene before his arrival and, according to the police report, Chiba was interrogated at the kitchen table.

Although there was no trace of it in the police report, a neighbor told Alyson that Chiba may have barricaded herself in the bathroom[150] at one point and that a mediator may have come to convince her to come out. However, Detective King said later that that was not an accurate description of the event.

Elliott was admitted at the hospital at 1:10 pm and died at 1:36 pm.

According to one of the neighbors, the police remained at the residence for many hours, and during the police interrogation, Chiba conveniently pointed to a "suicide note" written on a Post-it that she had not seen before. She also told them Elliott had been struggling with depression his entire life, and had a history of multiple narcotics addiction (heroin and crack) and alcohol abuse. She also added he had been clean for a year, while still taking multiple prescription drugs. She told the police officers that Elliott had been engaging in self-mutilating behavior and had suicidal ideation, with a history of one possible suicide attempt, and she gave the police officers some pages of his personal journal.

Chiba also admitted to having removed the knife when Elliott was still standing, adding that she had seen two cuts before Elliott had collapsed. Elliott had possibly walked from the kitchen area in the front of the house to the balcony located on the back of the house, although mention of the balcony came much later in Chiba's narrations.

The police officers contacted Felice Ecker, Elliott's publicist, a contact possibly provided by Chiba herself, whereas she would later pretend to have played Ecker's role—i.e. arranging the booking and scheduling appearances for his musical performances—barely a year later in her lawsuit against the estate.

Chiba arrived at the hospital one hour after Elliott had passed away, so probably around 2:40 pm, according to Schultz.[82]

Two nights later, Chiba drove to Elliott's studio in the valley with two guys in a jeep—one of them most likely being Robin Peringer. They packed boxes and boxes in the trunk of the car around midnight,[12] and just after, the trio stopped by the memorial wall on Sunset Boulevard to give away copies of Elliott's last single to the fans who had gathered there to pay homage.[11]

According to information that Alyson received from an independent journalist, Chiba may have left LA in the following days, as she allegedly had a one-way ticket for Hong Kong paid for by Rivers Cuomo.[139] However, after a stop in Boston and seeing that the police were not prosecuting her, she had returned to LA.

Chiba next attended several tribute shows, one at the Music Box on November 3 and another one (All Tomorrow's Parties) on November 9 in

Long Beach, where Lou Barlow and friends had taken the time slot reserved for Elliott and his band.

If people cope in different ways with tragedy, Chiba certainly moved on with her life very quickly, and the alleged flight to Hong Kong does not make her look good. Someone even told Alyson that they had seen Chiba with ex-boyfriend David Cross, having a good time and laughing at the bar the Roost, just one or two days after Elliott's death. Several people commented that they would have been unable to physically move for weeks after witnessing such a tragic and gruesome death.

The proceeds from the November 3 show benefited the Elliott Smith Foundation, the charity for abused children that Elliott had intended to establish just before his death, but was not operative yet. According to the independent journalist, Chiba may have been apprehended by federal postal inspectors for accessing and cashing checks earmarked for the foundation, while posing as Elliott's ex-girlfriend Valerie Deerin. It was still a rumor Alyson had not been able to confirm, but it is important to take everything into consideration.

In the following months, Chiba left LA for longer periods, and she stayed in New York City, London, and even South Africa where her father, Hiroyasu Chiba, lived.

When the results of the coroner's report were made public in early January 2004, it revealed that the results of the autopsy were not conclusive and the coroner did not eliminate the possibility of homicide. Chiba almost immediately made a declaration via MTV,[19] saying she had nothing to hide and was not a suspect, even claiming she was confident that Elliott's sister and parents and everyone close to him knew the truth.

Five days later, the family did not respond as Chiba had expected,[20] but rather asserted their confidence in the police investigation to determine the actual circumstances of Elliott's death, while declaring no one could claim to know "*the truth.*"

During that time, Chiba had probably been going back and forth between England and the U.S., yet she was back in Los Angeles when she sued Elliott's estate (represented by Elliott's stepmother Marta Greenwald) in July 2004.

At that time, she was living with drummer Robin Peringer at the same place of Elliott's tragic passing, and Joey the neighbor, who had moved into the unit below her bungalow, confirmed that the two were lovers during the year following Elliott's death.

According to people Alyson spoke to, Peringer had not been the only guy she had hooked up with following Elliott's tragic passing. At the very least, she had gone on a date with a friend of a podcaster shortly after Elliott's death, and one of the co-founders of *Vice* magazine[140] had seen Chiba dating the Pixies' drummer during some parties, also shortly after Elliott's death.

Around that time, a fan, who had been invited for a stay over at Chiba's house, also mentioned Chiba having a relationship with several other men, including this fan's new boyfriend.

In June 2004, the apartment building where Chiba was renting had been sold and bought by Adam Gerstein, and in September 2004, Chiba was evicted by the new owner. She was then forced to move into a new place in Echo Park, and some of the same fans still visited her in the following years. Since her therapist license[131] had not been renewed from June 2001 to October 2005, she could not have been working as a therapist during these years, and so she had no known source of income to pay rent while still living in Los Angeles. She had told several people that Rivers Cuomo was supporting her financially.

Around that time, Liam Gowing interviewed Chiba for his article that was published by *SPIN* magazine in December 2004. The article supported the suicide theory, largely blaming depression, drugs, and child abuse for Elliott's strange suicide.

Chiba amended her case against the estate twice, but finally lost in October 2007.[156]

During all those years, Chiba certainly did not act like someone in mourning or carrying a guilty conscience. In contrast, she had been in both full protective and aggressive mode. She had aggressively sued Elliott's family, amending her case twice; she had tried to intimidate the owners of New Monkey studio, claiming it should be hers; and, in September 2008, she sued her own lawyer Ron Gold for malpractice, professional negligence, breach of fiduciary duty, and infliction of emotional distress.[126]

If she had been keeping a low profile on social media, Chiba was very active in major media. After her interview with Liam Gowing in 2004,[37] she participated in Gil Reyes's movie *Searching for Elliott Smith,*[42] released in 2009. In a filmed interview, she narrated the events of October 21, 2003, once again claiming her innocence. In the first version of the movie, Gil Reyes and Chiba even went to the Los Angeles Police Department, camera in hand, in order to contradict the police report and prove that Chiba had talked to the police. This problematic stunt-like scene had already been edited out by Reyes when Alyson saw the movie.

In the movie, Chiba mentioned the balcony for the first time, declaring she had been afraid that Elliott would jump from it after the stabbing. In her first narration to the police, she had mentioned that Elliott had walked away, while she stated to other people that Elliott had collapsed in the kitchen. With the new balcony story, she was forced to acknowledge that Elliott had walked through the entire house once stabbed, since the kitchen was located in the front of the house, and the balcony in the back.

In 2013, Chiba was prominently featured in W.T. Schultz's biography *Torment Saint,*[82] as her name could be found 43 times from pages 7 to 223. She claimed her complete innocence once again during the last chapters of the book, with Schultz's help. In his version, Elliott had "*crashed onto the balcony,*" and she had "*tackled him there, then quickly climbed off him to call 911,*"[82] a detail that was a significant departure from the police report, which previously stated she had "*followed him to where he collapsed.*"[82]

Many years later, the case remains open, and Detective J. King confirmed he had finally talked to Joey the neighbor.[88] Meanwhile, Chiba is now living in Wales with her husband, an English man named Alex Whomsley.

Chapter 19: Suicides by stabbing are highly unusual, but not unheard of

Strange Parallels

Suicides by stabbing are often qualified as highly unusual, although not unheard of. While researching this, Alyson had mostly been stumbling on homicide cases, because suicides by stabbing were so rare. Interestingly, many other stories she found presented some parallels.

For example, there was the case of Yekaterina Pusepa[157] that appeared remarkably close to Elliott Smith's tragic case. In May 2013, Pusepa, 22, was found by the police on a Manhattan sidewalk, while her boyfriend Alec Katsnelson was lying in the street with a knife wound to the chest. She lied to the police, reporting Alec had taken the knife from her hand and plunged it into his own chest during a heated argument. While trying to mask her crime as a suicide, she had changed her story under questioning and was subsequently found guilty of having stabbed her boyfriend. At this point, the narration diverged from Elliott's sad story, because the boyfriend had survived and had been able to tell the police she had stabbed him. Not unlike Elliott and Chiba, Pusepa and Katsnelson were having a relatively short and tumultuous relationship, with previously reported fights, and the neighbors had heard them screaming and making threats.[157] Hadn't Joey the neighbor said Elliott and Chiba were fighting on a regular basis? Hadn't Sean Organ, the owner of Org Records, compared their relationship to a Sid Vicious and Nancy Spungen situation?

In a very eerie parallel, it was mentioned that Pusepa had a DUI, just like Chiba, and had screamed for someone to call 911 while she was helping her boyfriend before the police's arrival. When the police arrived, Pusepa was "*drenched in blood, blotchy handprints covering her arms and T-shirt,*"[157] and we can imagine it was probably the same case for Chiba, although nothing had ever been noted about her appearance in the police report. Similar situations tend to bring about similar developments.

There was also the case of Eline Melters,[158] a 23-year-old Dutch woman who had allegedly committed suicide on December 8, 2009 by stabbing herself three times in the chest in the presence of her boyfriend, according to the police. Eline's brother, Daniël Melters, a post-doctoral student at NIH/NCI, researched his sister's death meticulously, since he had been very suspicious of the police's conclusion. Once again, the parallels with Elliott's story were incredible. Eline supposedly stabbed herself in the chest after becoming agitated, while Mart, her boyfriend, had fled into the bathroom. Based on the boyfriend's testimony, she had then run out of the house and tried to enter a church but failed, collapsed on the ground, and died before making it 200 yards further.

The Dutch police had declared Eline's death a suicide only two hours after discovering the body, which shows how a fast investigation can be butchered in the Netherlands as in the U.S.[158] Daniël's research only reinforced Alyson's conclusion, as he investigated the same points that she had, because, just like Elliott, Eline had no hesitation marks or possible defense wounds, and the stabbing had occurred in the presence of her boyfriend. The statistics found for Eline were once again skewed toward murder just like for Elliott. The Dutch police simply stated that Eline was "*psychotic,*" though she had never been diagnosed with any psychiatric disorder. The major difference with Elliott's case was that Eline's had been closed and ruled a suicide. Due to Daniël's persistency, he managed to have Eline's dossier reviewed again by the DA in Maastricht a few years ago,[158] and the investigation was reopened. It takes a diligent family member eager to engage in a persistent fight to obtain such results.

There was no shortage of examples of domestic fights ending with a stabbing. There was a Colorado couple, Brandon Watkins and Jacqueline Souza,[159] who were about to get married in 2018. Souza told the police that they were fighting because Watkins had wanted to invite an ex-girlfriend to the wedding, and Souza suspected the two were having an affair. Souza told the police that she had found Watkins with a knife sticking out of his chest when she had come out of the bathroom... a very familiar story. Why is it always the bathroom? Souza said Watkins might have stabbed himself over the argument; she also suggested an intruder had attacked him; and she finally claimed that Watkins had grabbed her by the throat and pushed her up against the wall of the garage. She also said that he had fallen on top of the knife... changing her story many times just like Chiba, who had called 911 and performed CPR until the police's arrival.[159] After an investigation, Souza was arrested on suspicion of second-degree murder, but a few months later, no charges were filed by the Deputy District Attorney.[160] The family continues to fight for justice for Brandon.

Millionaire Phillip Vasyli was a similar case, a man found with a single stab wound in a luxury Bahamas mansion in 2015.[161] Because he was left-handed, the position of the wound had been found to be problematic, and since there had not been any evidence of intrusion and the security system had been turned off, his wife Donna was arrested and charged with his murder. However, she was freed two years later, with a retrial still pending today.[162]

There was even the very recent case of Chaniqua Boyd in Fort Knox, Kentucky, charged with the stabbing of her husband, an Army sergeant first class, following a domestic dispute.[163] Chaniqua Boyd said she didn't intend to stab her husband identified as "V.G." and that he instead "*lunged into the knife*" during their argument and that he was the one who "*came at her.*" However, V.G., who survived the stabbing, told law enforcement that his wife followed him to the kitchen where the two continued to argue, punched him in the face twice, and then stabbed him in the chest.

All these cases displayed the ordinariness of this type of situation: a couple arguing and ending with one or several knife wounds in the chest of the man. But if it was not difficult to find cases of domestic disputes ending in stabbing, it was certainly difficult to prove beyond a reasonable doubt that the women were guilty. One thing was nevertheless certain, none of these men were small guys. Brandon Watkins looked like a bodybuilder, while Phillip Vasyli, who was not a small person either, didn't even have any defensive injuries. Therefore, the argument that a man would have more defense injuries, based off the assumption that a man under attack would fight a woman, is invalid in these cases since even these larger men displayed no such defense wounds.

The frequency of such domestic events contrasted with the rarity of suicide by stabbing. There was nevertheless the case of André 'Dédé' Fortin, who had died of stab wounds in 2020. Since he was also a musician, the front man of a very popular Quebecois band Les Colocs, this was a strange coincidence. Fortin had been found dead at 38 in his Montréal apartment in 2000, with a knife still in his body. According to TVA Nouvelles,[164] his death was considered suspicious by the police, who had not been able to declare at first whether it was a suicide or a homicide. Though certain wounds on his body had been considered suspicious, some notes left by Fortin indicated that the singer may have been depressed, and because of the absence of evidence of a break-in, the coroner finally established it had been a suicide. The coroner declared: "*The victim has not elected a simple and quick way to end his life. He must have suffered greatly before dying.*" An important detail of the story was the apparent wound, located in his stomach. According to *Guitar Noise*, "*He had a knife in his stomach and odd bruises*" and "*two autopsies had to be performed to conclude that it was, in fact, a suicide.*"[165]

Two autopsies? At least, people had tried a bit more for Fortin than for Elliott's, but if Elliott's case was indeed a suicide, Alyson could not have emphasized enough the different location of his wound... the abdomen. Self-inflicted stab wounds in the thorax/chest are actually so unusual that a few specific cases have been the subject of medical research papers, like a case in Nepal,[166] or the case of a man with one stab wound in the chest but a psychiatric history of paranoid schizophrenia. [167]

It is also interesting to note that, while being an extremely rare form of suicide, very few people who had attempted to commit suicide by stabbing actually died: only 7% according to a 2012 study.[168]

Drug mafia?

There always had been another possibility, and Alyson once listened to a podcast and heard a disturbing story told by Largo owner Mark Flanagan. Mark was the guy who had declared on NPR in 2004: "*I don't believe he killed himself, that's all I'll say about that, but I really don't, but, having said that I wasn't surprised because he had been through a really rough time, you know, and I would see him from time to time and it was not getting any better, it was rather than surprise just really gut wrenchingly sad.*"[110]

This declaration had always intrigued Alyson, for if Mark didn't think Elliott had killed himself, while insisting on Elliott's rough time with drugs, how did he think Elliott had died? Who had killed Elliott, according to Mark?

During the 2015 podcast *You Make it Weird with Pete Holmes,*[169] Mark, who rarely agrees to interviews, talked about his club Largo and Elliott at great length. He revealed a surprising story that had happened three or four years before Elliott's death. That day, Mark was at Largo, looking out the window from his office upstairs, and saw in the parking lot underneath:

"*It was really unfunny, it was a drug deal that went bad at MacArthur Park. He [Elliott] had bought some heroin that was bad heroin, and he went back to challenge the guy on the content of his purchase and the guy stabbed him… and he showed up at Largo and there was blood everywhere in his car.*"[169]

Mark wanted Elliott to go to the hospital, while Elliott didn't want to go because he was afraid of getting arrested on a drug charge. Mark finally took him to Cedars Sinai where they gave false names so Elliott could be treated.

"*He had been using drugs so it was a really tough time and that was the final straw for me, after that I just went to the head of his record label, I went to his manager, went to his A&R guy and everyone that was in his life, including Jon Brion, who was producing him at the time,*"[169] said Mark, who added that after his attempts at an intervention Elliott never spoke to him again. To which, Mark said:

"*So it was kind of a rough ending, but it's fine because I feel like he was on a horrible path at that point and at least I have tried.*"[169]

After such a traumatic episode, it was not difficult to imagine what Mark could have thought about Elliott's death. Maybe there had been another dangerous drug deal, and maybe Elliott had been stabbed again during another drug deal turned bad?

This sort of echoed what Alec (not his real name), a musician and friend of Elliott had told Alyson. He was one of those friends who didn't believe that Elliott had committed suicide, and he had alluded to the possibility that Elliott had been murdered following a drug deal gone nasty.

"*I don't know that I'm a believer of the suicide theory and not sure of the Chiba murdering him theory either but there are some things leading up to his demise that were suspect but [I'm] not sure really about any of it,*" Alec had declared. "*I'm aware that his system tested clean by the time an autopsy was done but yeah there was some stuff in the weeks leading up to his death that sounded like he may have been hiding from some people that he used to buy drugs from in large quantities and they're not the kind of people you want knowing where you live.*"[86]

However, Alyson had never thought the theory of an intrusion in the house was even possible. With Chiba in the bathroom for only 5-10 minutes—as she claimed—how could a drug dealer have even found the time to enter the house, murder Elliott and disappear without being noticed? And if Chiba had seen or heard them, why hadn't she said anything? Why had she told everyone it was suicide?

"*If the Mexican mafia came into your house and murdered your dude and said you're next unless you keep your mouth shut and there wouldn't be evidence of intrusion,*" Alec had replied. "*They would've just come in like any other time. I saw the quantities he dealt in. If you just stop one day those people are gonna think you're a narc. That's how they think. There is nowhere you'd be safe from the Mexican mafia. He [Elliott] had asked a friend of ours to hide him just two weeks before saying they were after him and wanted to hurt him. I know Chiba and don't think she did it. That's my spider sense. He would buy 20k at a time.*

And often. You are dealing with scary people at that level. She left to NYC and stayed at friends for months afterward. everyone can believe what they will."[86]

The fact that Chiba left Los Angeles a few weeks after Elliott's death was well documented, but this was not proof she had been hiding from the Mexican mafia. To Alyson, this theory never made sense. What were the odds that the Mexican mafia had shown up just at the moment the couple was fighting? Plus, wouldn't Joey or another neighbor have seen or heard something? It was a very bright and sunny day, and an intruder would have had a lot of trouble going unnoticed. Plus, despite the disappointing investigation, the police report had mentioned a nail and hair kit collected at the scene,[48] very probably for DNA analysis; otherwise, what was the point of doing so? If Elliott had been murdered by an intruder, couldn't we have expected the police to have found someone else's DNA?

Despite the fact Mark hadn't had any recent contact with Elliott—they hadn't spoken since early 2001—he was aware that Elliott had no illegal drugs in his system when he died, as he said in the same podcast:

"*I also thought with him, that I'd read enough about David Bowie and Keith Richards and all these people that have been through like horrible drug addictions and then came through it, and I just always thought that for some reason it was very naive to think, oh you know he will pull through, and he almost did so, because I mean, according to autopsy he didn't have these illegal [drugs] like he was doing when I was with him.*"[169]

Since he knew Elliott had cleaned up, it's difficult to imagine that Mark was still thinking about the McArthur Park drug deal, but it was nevertheless what he said in a 2004 Blender article as well:[170] "*I don't believe that guy stabbed himself in the chest. It just doesn't add up. I wouldn't be surprised if someone else did this. He was doing drugs with lowlife scum. He was around a lot of creepy people—some very negative, dangerous people.*"[170]

People often discredited Mark's statement under the pretext that he hadn't been in Elliott's life since 2001, but for Alyson that was not a valid argument. Mark had seen Elliott at the peak of his drug addiction and still didn't think Elliott killed himself.

Nevertheless, there was the troubling statement of musician and friend Alec: "*There was some stuff in the weeks leading up to his death that sounded like he may have been hiding from some people that he used to buy drugs from in large quantities...*"[86] and another strange declaration by Caroline, the studio owner, had also alluded to something scary in her long posts: "*What I do know for sure is that Elliott was afraid of someone in the last two weeks, I know he changed the locks, I know it wasn't the person I described to you [Chiba] he seemed to have complete faith in this person.*"[12]

All these declarations were troubling, but if an intruder had managed to kill Elliott at noon on October 21, 2003, he may have been the most light-footed and efficient individual, and he may have committed the perfect crime.

Chapter 20: What is left to do?

Eighteen years later, not much is left to do if the people who have information are still determined to stay quiet and if Chiba herself is never going to say more… and why would she? She had talked to Gowing, Reyes, and Schultz. She was done.

Jakob (not his real name), a criminal defense attorney who had reviewed all the official documents and Alyson's information, wrote: "*From the perspective of a criminal defense attorney, if Elliott was murdered by Jennifer Chiba, there is no way there would be a prosecution or conviction without some sort of confession. First, let me tell you that I think you've done a very thorough job and your reporting on all of the elements is very well done. All of my comments come from the perspective as a criminal defense attorney and what I've learned over the years judging people. But I have no first-hand knowledge of any of this. Anything I say must also be cloaked in the fact that I am a massive fan of Elliott's music,*"[171] he added, as if he wanted to apologize.

"*There could be 'breaks' in the case based on evidence (the 'suicide note' comes to mind) or the timeline (the [neighbor's potential] testimony comes to mind), but the fact is that so much time has passed and recollections from a 17-year-old case are going to be spotty at best. Any criminal defense attorney worth his/her weight would just have too much to work with to create a reasonable doubt [that he didn't kill himself] assuming that she [Chiba] did it. The police/prosecutors know this. The police also know that they kind of bungled the investigation from the start, so yeah, absent a confession, I just can't see any progress on that end.*"[171]

Alyson always valued the opinion of experts, and Jakob was one. Whatever he had to say, bad or good news, she had to take his perspective into account.

"*Now I have no medical training,*" he continued, "*so take this for what it's worth, but I have interacted with many people over the course of my career. Ms. Chiba seems to me to be a pretty serious narcissist and quite possibly a sociopath. I believe many narcissists are sociopaths. This does not mean she killed Elliott, but to me, it means that most everything she did/does regarding Elliott must be seen through her eyes and her self-interest. Again, I don't know her but based on what's available, I know the type of person she probably is. I would suspect that she cared very little for Elliott ever and that he was simply another attempt by her to satisfy herself through his fame and importance. Again, I must reiterate that I've never met her, don't know her, and that my comments are made based on suspicions of her based on what's reported. But my experience with many narcissists is that they are generally charming in person and very manipulative. I suspect Ms. Chiba is very intelligent, very charming, and extremely manipulative in person. She generally gets what she wants in relationships because of this. I bring this up because, whether or not she killed Elliott, she clearly manipulated the timeline and the evidence suggests that she manipulated the evidence. This could be the result of her thinking 'holy shit what just happened' and automatically going into self-preservation mode recognizing that she was going to be a suspect even if he did commit suicide. Regardless of what happened, I can say it's my belief that in the immediate aftermath, Elliott's condition and potential survival was not on her mind. Her own well-being and self-preservation were.*[171]

"*I also have a sneaking suspicion that the musician friends that were interviewed or attempted to be interviewed know more than they've said but that what they know is simply what Chiba has told them. And I don't doubt that Chiba had relationships with and the ability to manipulate them. She has likely confided in some of them and they are on board with whatever she has said. Given Elliott's past and a history of burning bridges with many of his friends, I suspect it was easy for her to create a narrative that they would believe. They wouldn't know the whole truth, only she would, but they may know more than other people and they may have gotten similar stories from her. These stories would likely have minor details missing or different that may cast more doubt on her story, but I don't think people have compared notes in any way.*"[171]

Alyson agreed with everything Jakob had to say, and especially with the fact that, assuming Chiba did it, only a confession could close the case. Homicide detective J. King had already told her that,[88] and she was also well aware of the fact that the police would never take the risk to prosecute anyone based on what was essentially suspicious behavior and circumstantial evidence.

"*I don't think Chiba will talk to you under any circumstance*,"[171] added Jakob. Alyson had realized this very early on. Chiba had everything to lose and nothing to gain from another interview asking about the details of that tragic day. She had already done that in *Searching for Elliott Smith*. But could we even regard that as an interview?

One important point had been suggested several times by different people. If Chiba, instead of Elliott, had been found with two stab wounds in the chest after arguing with her boyfriend, Elliott would have probably been considered a suspect right away. Isn't it commonly understood by most people when a woman is found dead that the husband or boyfriend is the first suspect? She could have been the most depressed individual on the planet, or the worst junkie around, and Elliott would probably have been a suspect because, in our collective subconscious, it is much easier to imagine a man rather than a woman committing a murder.

Chiba's experience as a therapist put her in a strange position. For her supporters, she was an educated professional who could not have done the deed, but could have panicked and removed the knife. For her detractors, at the very least, she had been completely irresponsible, because she should have known better and acted very differently, due to her education and training.

"*Just because someone is a professional in their career does not mean they are not a total hot mess in their personal life,*" lawyer Lois had said. "*Therapists and psychology folks tend to pursue that career to figure their own shit out.*"[85]

For some people, the conclusion of suicide followed the Occam's razor principle, suggested by Schultz, a recurrent argument claiming that the simplest explanation should always be the best one, and that people expressing doubts should be ignored and deterred. Meanwhile, Alyson clearly found that nothing was simple in this story and that doubts were everywhere.

The statement that many people made, "*there was no doubt it was a suicide,*" was almost laughable to Alyson, as the two sides were not even equivalent. On one side, the suicide hypothesis was supported by a dubious note, Elliott's history with depression and suicidal ideation, and Chiba's story, so basically vague assumptions, speculations, and a questionable witness with an ever-changing story who had all the reasons to hide the truth. On the other hand, the homicide hypothesis was supported by a non-conclusive autopsy, forensic-literature-based solid statistics skewed toward homicide, the opinions of several forensic and psychology experts, a case left open by the LAPD for 18 years, and the fact that suicide by stabbing is a statistical oddity, while stabbing is the leading method of homicide during domestic violence. Why should we have had any doubt indeed?

"*It's breathtaking what professionals (as well as the public in general) will do to the facts in order to produce the illusion of clarity,*" the family member had written in an email. "*They define us as obfuscating when we see reality as offering little clarity and lots of questions when they are the real obfuscators.*"[80] Alyson couldn't have agreed more, as the suicide hypothesis not only gave the illusion of clarity but ignored many facts and avoided the real questions, all the questions Alyson had asked repeatedly.

Then there was the misogyny argument, the Yoko Ono effect or syndrome, heard like an echo on message boards, Twitter, and articles like this one in *Salon*[172] ("The twisted misogyny behind suicide conspiracy theories") or this other one in *Playboy*: "The lost person must be held blameless at all costs. So what people do is locate other targets. And if there is a woman even remotely involved, a basic misogyny erupts, and all the blame gets directed at this imaginary evil harpy."[173]

Alyson didn't like the amalgam created in these articles, for all the facts for each case has to be seriously examined, and it was just as stupid to suppose that all women were victims as to suppose that all women were guilty. There was nothing impressive in these articles, which were simply ignoring facts and sounding like opportunistic pompous tirades jumping on the #metoo bandwagon in order to look good for our times. It surely wasn't helping that we had now entered a "believe-all-women" era, reinforced with some fanaticism never seen before. Any human being is capable of the best and the worst, but in 2020, was it even possible to suggest that some women are liars and capable of the worst, not because they are women but because they are human beings?

The misogyny argument sounded like the last refuge of people with no real facts to provide. It was getting worn thin, and should have never been discussed when some solid arguments for murder had been seriously considered by the police and other experts. With sentences such as "*we are not investigating this case as a suicide*," and "*his case was very suspicious*,"[87] could Detective P.J. Morris, proud father of two daughters, be considered a misogynist?

Could misogyny even be in the picture when talking about someone who had made a career of being Elliott Smith's post-mortem-fiancée, with a three-year-long lawsuit, a magazine interview, a movie, and a book? Even if Reyes's documentary had never found distribution, the *SPIN* magazine interview has been referenced by many as the definitive nail in Elliott's coffin.

Despite her positive communication with the police, Alyson couldn't stop thinking about the probable lack of investigation in the early moments of the tragic event, and the holes in the narration. Some fans had even suggested that Elliott's brawl with the police during the Beck/Flaming Lips concert in 2002 could have influenced the police's behavior immediately after the stabbing. However, this was a stretch. How could the police have connected the two stories right away? The police officers who arrived at the scene were very probably unaware of Elliott's identity and semi-famous status.

After all of Alyson's research, we are indeed left with little clarity and lots of questions.

Musician Alec, who had known Elliott for a long time and had hung out with him very shortly before his death, said:

"Three or four days before his death, it seemed to me that killing himself was probably the farthest thing from his mind.[86] *I mean, he was a kind of dramatic sort, so I can imagine that maybe he got swept up in some kind of drama in his mind and it got the better of him. He talked about suicide a lot. But he had told me 'I still have some more work to do, I'm gonna hang around.' I always felt like it was probably part of his neuroses and part of what fueled his inspiration was toying with the idea of leaving the planet."*[86]

If this declaration may have appeared ambiguous at first, it was actually a real insight into Elliott's mind. Elliott was toying with the idea of suicide as philosophers do, and in particular as existentialists have contemplated it. Philosophical thoughts have never implied acting on them, and Alyson liked that term "toying" because it was exactly this and it had never meant anything more than that.

Elliott had a degree in philosophy. He was the author of an undergrad thesis entitled *Toward a Poststructuralist-Feminist Critique of Law*, and he loved Kierkegaard so much he had named one of his albums after one of the philosopher's most famous books. The cleverness of Elliott's multi-meaning metaphorical lyrics demonstrated how well read and how seriously involved in existentialist philosophy he was.

"There is not a single human being who does not despair at least a little, in whose innermost being there does not dwell an uneasiness, an unquiet, a discordance, an anxiety in the face of an unknown something,"[174] wrote Kierkegaard in *Sickness Unto Death.* According to Kierkegaard's philosophy, suicide was a non-defendable act, and not a possible response to the absurd. The melancholy of "Either/Or" could have never led to the psychological abyss of suicide; this rejection of oneself, this neglecting of one's responsibilities. It was clear that Kierkegaard rejected and condemned suicide; it would have been a mutiny against God, a detachment from any spiritual authority, and probably Elliott's "Easy Way Out." Would Elliott, a man so well-versed in Kierkegaard's philosophy that he had named one of

his albums after Kierkegaard's philosophy of "*Either*/Or," have committed suicide and negated his profound admiration? Elliott was more interested in how to live his life (*Either/Or*) than how to end his life.

If it could be very naïve to confound art or philosophy with life—how could Elliott have thought about Kierkegaard's philosophy in the middle of a fight with his girlfriend, someone could claim—this argument was as valid as the one advanced by people who thought his alleged suicide was the "*most romantic*" suicide ever, the most Romeo and Juliet suicide ever. How could Elliott have thought about Shakespeare at this moment?

"*Perfection is for the gods,*"[1] Elliott had once written on his message board. "*I liked the idea of a self-contained, endless pursuit of perfection,*" he had also declared to the *Boston Herald*, echoing the same train of thought while describing the thematic idea behind his album *Figure 8*.[175] "*But I have a problem with perfection. I don't think perfection is very artful. But there's something I liked about the image of a skater going in a twisted circle that doesn't have any real endpoint. So, the object is not to stop or arrive anywhere; it's just to make this thing as beautiful as they can.*"[175]

This declaration was the perfect illustration of Elliott's vision for life and had all the marks of *The Myth of Sisyphus*,[176] an endless repetition and a desire to search for meaning and happiness in the work itself, while not looking for its real finality. Do people have such short vision they cannot imagine Elliott happy?

There are enough examples in his lyrics to realize that Elliott's work could not be reduced to one feeling, especially sadness. Anger and irony are present too, with sometimes a touch of nihilism, plenty of self-sabotage, but also moments of hope, solace, and freedom. And if metaphors can lead to resurging traumas, songs were a way for Elliott to overcome and exorcise them. There is not one Elliott Smith song that can be about a single thing or feeling, as each one will bring a myriad of thoughts and a kaleidoscope of sentiments and states of mind, often expressed by different people about the same song.

Elliott wrote songs with titles such as "Going Nowhere," "The Ballad of Big Nothing," and "Everything Means Nothing to Me," but he also wrote "Say Yes," "Happiness," and "Independence Day." It had never been about one direction, one idea, one thought, one goal; Elliott's songs were about life, about the anxious journey of existence and its choices. They were often about Kierkegaard's "*dizziness of freedom*,"[177] a very existentialist thought indeed. It's safe to say that the fallen bodies featured on the artwork of Elliott's self-titled album were not chosen to suggest suicide. They were probably another Kierkegaard reference, the perfect illustration of a Kierkegaardian anxiety, described as a person standing on the edge of a tall building or cliff. But far from being a negation of life, anxiety and dizziness were experienced as empowering and as a way to drive creativity. Never had bodies flying from tall buildings illustrated so well a combination of anxiety, freedom, and the visceral experience of losing yourself in creation. In short, they had nothing to do with suicide.

Elliott was a philosopher. He had ambitions for his songs, and what he accomplished with them was way above your average pop-rock tune. One of the best-known definitions of the poet is this passage in Kierkegaard's *Either/Or*,[178] but the irony may escape a few:

"*What is a poet? An unhappy man who in his heart harbors a deep anguish, but whose lips are so fashioned that the moans and cries which pass over them are transformed into ravishing music. His fate is like that of the unfortunate victims whom the tyrant Phalaris imprisoned in a brazen bull, and slowly tortured over a steady fire; their cries could not reach the tyrant's ears so as to strike terror into his heart; when they reached his ears they sounded like sweet music. And men crowd around the poet and say to him, 'Sing for us soon again'—which is as much as to say, 'May new sufferings torment your soul, but may your lips be fashioned as before; for the cries would only distress us, but the music, the music, is delightful.' And the critics come forward and say, 'That is perfectly done—just as it should be, according to the rules of aesthetics.' Now it is understood that a critic resembles a poet to a hair; he only lacks the anguish in his heart and the music upon his lips. I tell you, I would rather be a swineherd, understood by the swine, than a poet misunderstood by men.*"[178]

Kierkegaard wrote a thesis on irony,[179] and if most people will agree that all great art stems from suffering, there is a large part of irony in this long quote. Who was Elliott? A singer-songwriter misunderstood by most? The fact that he recorded "Suicide Machine" (at New Monkey Studio) just a few days before he died is sadly ironic.[180] It also echoes a statement made by Kill Rock Stars founder Slim Moon: "*I also really want him to be remembered for his humor, warmth, and absurdist sense of irony.*"[181]

The best way to learn more about Elliott is probably to stop writing about him and listen to him, since he gave enough interviews to have a good idea of who he was. In interviews, he often made allusions to the public's obsession with associating songs with the author's life:

"*Possibly so far I've been misunderstood by people who think that all the sad things I've written are autobiographical. I noticed that sometimes they felt sorry for me because of my lyrics, and this ended up disturbing me. I hate self-pity, and I don't like people who play with that, it is often dishonest. In the new album the lyrics are more imprecise, they come in general from dreams I had, so there's no use in trying to associate them with real things,*"[2] Elliott stated in an interview with Les Inrockuptibles in 2000.

"*People are forever trying to interpret my songs as if they are all particularly revealing about my life,*" he also declared to *Q* magazine in 2000. "*If I experiment with certain things, that's my business. People can look all they want into my lyrics but often my songs don't really mean anything. they are just snapshots of life—but not necessarily my life. I think the suggestion that all my songs are personal is insulting because that assumes that I just have a bunch of issues that I feel the need to unload on strangers. That is not the case. It also assumes that I just talk about myself the whole time which, again, is not true… songs for me are about mystery. Their charm is that they are open-ended.*"[182]

This is often the case with songwriters, that they are the authors of a song and people assume they are writing about themselves. It's an easy assumption just because there is basically no filter, no intermediate between a songwriter and his songs, but people rarely commit the same mistake when talking about a writer and his murder-mystery novel or a filmmaker and his movie about a serial killer or a depressed junkie.

Elliott was well aware of the cartoon character the public and media had invented for him: "*People tell me it sounds happier,*" he explained to Nigel Williamson, for UK magazine *Uncut* around the release of his album *Figure 8*. "*But it seems you've got to be the angry punk guy, or the depressed interior person or the ebullient pop star. There are different cartoons and you're bound to end up in one of them. So, on this record some part of my brain was trying to get out of the cartoon I'm in.*"[183]

Elliott repeatedly said in interviews that he had no desire to convey his life to people, that it would have been self-pity, something he despised, and he was finding it insulting that all his songs were often interpreted at a personal level. He wanted to get rid of this depressed-tortured portrait the media had drawn about him and his work. He was interested in words, feelings, and life experiences and the abundance of ways of expressing and describing them without ever giving definitive meaning to a word. He was always more interested in describing a feeling than a precise person or situation. He was imagining his songs as dreams and fragmented stories, unfinished narratives imbued with Portland's rain or soaked with Los Angeles's sun. They were pieces of himself, but also pieces of other people and pieces of imagination. Elliott was always blurring the lines between the three with remarkable precision at the risk of confusing everyone.

Jonathan Valania asked Elliott for *Magnet* magazine in 2001: "*Do you think suicide is courageous or cowardly?*" Elliott replied: "*It's ugly and cruel and I really need my friends to stick around but dying people should have that right.... I was hospitalized for a little while and I didn't have that option, and it made me feel even crazier. But I prefer not to appear as some kind of disturbed person. I think a lot of people try to get mileage out of it, like, 'I'm a tortured artist' or something. I'm not a tortured artist, and there's nothing really wrong with me. I just had a bad time for a while.*"[184]

Elliott's case may look like a lost cause to the eyes of many people, but it is important to report the correct narrative. Additionally, there's not one lost cause that is not worth fighting for, and it matters that Sisyphus never gave up.

I will let Elliott have the last words:

"*Everybody gets a tag. If you listen to a Velvet Underground record, you don't think, 'Godfathers of Punk,' you just think, 'This sounds great.' The tags are there in order to help try to sell something by giving it a name that's going to stick in somebody's memory. But it doesn't describe it. So 'depressing' isn't a word I would use to describe my music. But there is some sadness in it—there has to be, so that the happiness in it will matter.*"[186]

Notes

(1) Elliott used to post on Sweet Adeline, his fan message board, under the name (h)hhelliott

(2) "The Eighth Heaven," "Elliott Smith, Le huitième ciel," by Christophe Conte, Les Inrockuptibles, April 4, 2000 https://www.lesinrocks.com/2000/04/18/musique/musique/elliott-smith-le-huitieme-ciel/ translation here: http://www.sweetadeline.net/inrock00.html

(3) "Beck pays tribute to Elliott Smith," NME October 30, 2003 https://www.nme.com/news/music/beck-89-1379784

(4) Private conversation with Deanna (not her real name), an Elliott Smith fan who had corresponded with Chiba

(5) Sweet Adeline, Elliott Smith's fan message board (now defunct)

(6a) Christine Pelisek's article in the LA Weekly: "The Elliott Smith Mystery" She is the first one who broke the news Chiba removed the knife from Elliott's chest https://www.laweekly.com/the-elliott-smith-mystery/

(6b) Christine Pelisek's article in the LA Weekly: "The Final Moments of Elliott Smith's Life" https://www.laweekly.com/the-final-moments-of-elliott-smiths-life/

(6c) Christine Pelisek's article in the LA Weekly: "Another view of Elliott Smith" https://www.laweekly.com/another-view-of-elliott-smith/

(7) Christine Pelisek's short bio http://www.christinepelisek.com/about.php

(8) The Smoking Gun published parts of the autopsy report in January, "Rocker's Autopsy Doesn't Rule Out Homicide" http://www.thesmokinggun.com/documents/crime/rockers-autopsy-doesnt-rule-out-homicide

(9) "Coroner: Elliott Smith death open question" CNN, December 31, 2003 https://www.cnn.com/2003/SHOWBIZ/Music/12/31/smith.reut/index.html

(10) All Tomorrow's Parties 2003: https://www.atpfestival.com/artist/elliottsmithtribute

(11) Posted on Sweet Adeline by Deanna (not her real name)

(12) Posted on Sweet Adeline by Caroline S. who was renting/owning the studio next to New Monkey (Elliott's studio)

(13) Email exchange with the new owner of the New Monkey studio

(14) A comment left on Blogcritics: "Smith's Girlfriend Speaks." The article is offline but it can be found on web archive: https://web.archive.org/web/20151115162719/https://blogcritics.org/smiths-girlfriend-speaks/

(15) Jennifer Chiba's LinkedIn page: https://www.linkedin.com/in/jennifer-chiba-ab6a6737/?originalSubdomain=uk

(16) Institutions where J. Chiba worked: 5 Acres (https://5acres.org) and Maryvale (https://www.maryvale.org/)

(17) Private conversation with a Cedars Sinai therapist

(18) Email from Robin Smith Jurado, Assistant Director of Human Resources, Volunteers and Recruitment - Five Acres

(19) MTV News: "Elliott Smith's Girlfriend Insists no Involvement in Death" January 9, 2004 http://www.mtv.com/news/1484246/elliott-smiths-girlfriend-insists-no-involvement-in-death/

(20) MTV News: "Elliott Smith's Family to Girlfriend: Don't Speak for Us" http://www.mtv.com/news/1484342/elliott-smiths-family-to-girlfriend-dont-speak-for-us/

(21) The Oregonian in 2010 (offline) "The Truth about Elliott Smith." By Margie Boulé

(22) Private email from J. Chiba to Deanna (not her real name)

(23) Chiba v. Greenwald: https://www.courtlistener.com/opinion/2290940/chiba-v-greenwald/ https://casetext.com/case/chiba-v-greenwald

(24) Email exchanges with Ruth (not her real name)

(25) Posted by Elliott and Valerie on Sweet Adeline

(26) Under The Radar: Interview: "Elliott Smith, Better Off Than Dead" http://www.undertheradarmag.com/interviews/elliott_smith

(27) The Lummox Journal: "Coast to Coast: Elliott Smith, a Personal Account" by Nelson Gary http://www.lummoxpress.com/journal/j002/smith.php

(28) Email exchange with Nelson Gary

(29) Message exchange with Elizabeth (not her real name)

(30) Conversation with Plasticsoul, a musician who was working with David McConnell at Satellite Park Studio.

(31) Message exchange with Josie Cotton

(32) Magnet: "Q&A with Josie Cotton" http://magnetmagazine.com/2009/03/23/qa-with-josie-cotton/

(33) Andrew Morgan's Soundcloud page: https://soundcloud.com/andrewmorgan-1-1

(34) Posted on the news of Sweet Adeline, after Elliott's injury at the Beck/Flaming Lips concert: http://www.sweetadeline.net/april03.html

(35) Exchange on YouTube with Ross Harris

(36) Email exchange with Lonnie (not her real name), a nurse with a long experience in the E.R.

(37) "Elliott Smith: Mr. Misery" by Liam Gowing SPIN magazine December 2004 pages 80-92 https://books.google.com/books?id=_jMs8xO7QE4C&pg=PA15&dq=Elliott+Smith+Gowing&hl=en&sa=X&ved=2ahUKEwir6aDXwInrAhUD26wKHQmSDRAQ6AEwA3oECAEQAg#v=onepage&q=Elliott%20Smith%20Gowing&f=false https://www.SPIN.com/2013/10/elliott-smith-mr-misery-10-year-anniversary-death/

(38) Email exchange and phone conversation with Liam Gowing

(39) Phone conversation with the Disney Cottages neighbor

(40) NME: "Stranger Than Fiction: Elliott Smith: The Life and Music of a Tragic Hero" by Barry Nicolson, 30 October 2010 pages 20-25 https://www.nme.com/blogs/nme-blogs/elliott-smith-archive-interview-there-has-to-be-darkness-in-my-songs-782397

(41) Email from Dr. Lisa Scheinin

(42) "Searching for Elliott Smith": documentary by Gil Reyes, 2009 https://www.imdb.com/title/tt1500885/

(43) "Searching for Elliott Smith" Should Actually Be Called The Vindication of Jennifer Chiba" October 26, 2009 https://microphonememoryemotion.wordpress.com/2009/10/26/searching-

for-elliott-smith-should-actually-be-called-the-vindication-of-jennifer-chiba/

(44) Phone call between my editor at rocknyc.live, Iman Lababedi, and Gil Reyes

(45) Message posted by Larry Crane on his message board Tape Op, October 22 2003: https://messageboard.tapeop.com/viewtopic.php?printertopic=1&t=4998&postdays=0&postorder=asc&&start=75&sid=7a9f2fc2b7da075cd204be4b29fa7513

(46) Chiba Q&As after the screening of "Searching for Elliott Smith," May 2011

(47) Interview of Dr. Scheinin at the Los Angeles Coroner, April 28, 2011

(48) Full autopsy and police report. You can order the autopsy report from the Los Angeles County Coroner.

(49) San Francisco Weekly: "Stiffed" by John Geluardi, September 10, 2008: https://www.sfweekly.com/news/stiffed/

(50) Email exchange with Kaitlyn (not her real name), a forensic behavioral psychologist

(51) "Homicidal and suicidal sharp force fatalities: Autopsy parameters in relation to the manner of death" by Christophe Brunel, Christophe Fermanian, Michel Durigon, Geoffroy Lorin de la Grandmaison, Forensic Science International 198 (2010) 150–154 https://pubmed.ncbi.nlm.nih.gov/20219299/

(52) Email exchange with one of the co-authors of the forensic article, "Homicidal and suicidal sharp force fatalities: Autopsy parameters in relation to the manner of death"

(53) Email exchange with a forensic pathologist, ex-president of the American Academy of Forensic Sciences and the American College of Legal Medicine, ex-head of the board of trustees of the American Board of Legal Medicine

(54) "Criminal investigation" by Christine Hess Orthmann, Kären M. Hess, 2009

(55) "Sharp Edged and Pointed Instrument Injuries" by William A. Cox, M.D. Forensic Pathologist/Neuropathologist (2011)

(56) "CDC Study: More men than women victims of partner abuse" by

Bert H. Hoff, J.D. http://www.saveservices.org/2012/02/cdc-study-more-men-than-women-victims-of-partner-abuse/

(57) "The Risk of Serious Physical Injury from Assault by a Woman Intimate: A Re-Examination of National Violence Against Women Survey Data on Type of Assault by an Intimate." B. H. Hoff (2001), MenWeb on-line

(58) "Suicide by self-stabbing" by R.D. Start, C.M. Milroy and M.A. Green, (1992) Forensic Science International vol. 56 September 1992 pages 89-94

(59) "Homicide-Suicide by Stabbing Study Over 10 Years in the Toulouse Region" by V. Scolan, N. Telmon, A. Blanc, J. P. Allery, D. Charlet, and D. Rouge, Am. J. Forensic Med Pathol (2004) 25: 33–36

(60) "Retrospective study on suicidal cases by sharp force injuries" by Setsuko Fukube, Takahito Hayashi MD, Yuko Ishida PhD, Hitoshi Kamon, Mariko Kawaguchi, Akihiko Kimura PhD, Toshikazu Kondo PhD, MD, Journal of Forensic and Legal Medicine 15 (2008) 163–167

(61) "Homicidal and suicidal sharp force fatalities in Stockholm, Sweden. Orientation of entrance wounds in stabs gives information in the classification" T Karlsson Forensic Sci. Int. April 22, 1998; 93(1): 21-32 https://pubmed.ncbi.nlm.nih.gov/9618908/

(62) "Non-fatal suicide attempt by intentional stab wound: Clinical management, psychiatric assessment, and multidisciplinary considerations" by James M Badger, Shea C Gregg, Charles A Adams, Journal of Emergencies, Trauma and Shock 2012 Volume 5 issue 3 page 228-232 http://www.onlinejets.org/article.asp?issn=0974-2700;year=2012;volume=5;issue=3;spage=228;epage=232;aulast=Badger

(63) "Homicide-Suicide by Stabbing Study Over 10 Years in the Toulouse Region V." Scolan, N. Telmon, A. Blanc, J. P. Allery, D. Charlet, and D. Rouge Am J Forensic Med Pathol 2004, 25: 33–36

(64) "Patterns in sharp force fatalities – a comprehensive forensic medical study: part 2. suicidal sharp force injury in the Stockholm area" by Karlsson T, Ormstad K, Rajs J., 1972–1984. J Forensic Sci (1988) 33: 448–61.

(65) "Sharp injury fatalities in New York City" by Gill JR, Catanese C. J Forensic Sci (2002) 47: 554–7.

(66) "Suicides by sharp force: typical and atypical features" by Karger B, Niemeyer J, Brinkmann B. Int. J Legal Med (2000) 113:259–62.

(67) "Tentative injuries in self stabbing", Vanezis P, West IE. Forensic Sci. Int. (1983) 21:65–70.

(68) "Criteria for homicide and suicide on victims of extended suicide due to sharp force" by Dettling A, Althaus L, Haffner HT. injury. Forensic Sci Int. (2003) 134:142–6.

(69) "Suicidal and homicidal sharp force injury: a 5-year retrospective comparative study of hesitation marks and defense wounds" by Stephanie Racette, Celia Kremer, Anne Desjarlais, Anny Sauvageau, Forensic Sci Med Pathol (2008) 4:221–227

(70) "Sharp edged and Pointed Instrument Injuries" by William A. Cox, M.D. Forensic Pathologist/Neuropathologist (2011)

(71) Email from a woman from Sacramento (Elliott's extended family)

(72) "Wineks' Drug & Chemical Blood-Level Data 2001" Prepared by: Charles L. Winek, Ph.D., Wagdy W. Wahba, Ph.D., Charles L. Winek, Jr., B.S. (Pharm.), M.S., and Tracey Winek Balzer B.S. (Pharm.), M.S. https://abmdi.org/documents/winek_tox_data_2001.pdf

(73) "Drug concentrations in post-mortem femoral blood compared with therapeutic concentrations in plasma" by Terhi Launiainen* and Ilkka Ojanperä - Published online in Wiley Online Library: 23 July 2013 https://www.ncbi.nlm.nih.gov/pmc/articles/PMC4237191/pdf/dta0006-0308.pdf?fbclid=IwAR1OyF4xC7AgRcc10HDzAnJV1Oz-66le7peDw4o9GhdviTZ1EP5MAsCLEJw

(74) "Drug Interactions between gabapentin and Remeron" https://www.drugs.com/drug-interactions/gabapentin-with-remeron-1147-0-1640-1015.html

(75) "Adderall Withdrawal: what you should know" https://www.webmd.com/add-adhd/adderall-withdrawal

(76) "Should I Be Concerned About Strattera Crash?" https://www.healthline.com/health/adhd/managing-strattera-crash#effectiveness

(77) "Strattera Withdrawal and Detox" https://www.therecoveryvillage.com/strattera-addiction/withdrawal-detox/

(78) Email exchange with Dwain Fuller F-ABFT, TC-NRCC, Board Certified Forensic Toxicologist

(79) Email exchange with Forensic Toxicologist Justin Brower

(80) Email exchange with a family member. This person was very close to Elliott

(81) J. Chiba's DUI see Appendix #1

(82) Torment Saint: The Life of Elliott Smith by William Todd Schultz, 2013, Bloomsbury

(83) "The mysterious death of Mr. Misery" by Alexis Petridis, March 18, 2004, The Guardian: http://www.theguardian.com/music/2004/mar/19/popandrock.elliottsmith

(84) Blogcritics: "Smith's Girlfriend Speaks" by Marty Dodge. The article is off line but can be found in the web-archives:https://web.archive.org/web/20151115162719/https:/blogcritics.org/smiths-girlfriend-speaks/

(85) Message exchange with Lois (not her real name), a lawyer who had experience with therapy as a teenager

(86) Message exchange with Alec (not his real name) a musician who knew Elliott very well

(87) Phone conversation and email exchange with LAPD homicide detective P.J. Morris

(88) Phone conversation and email exchange with LAPD homicide detective J. King

(89) "Basic CPR doesn't help gunshot wounds" by Jeremy Samuel Faust, Slate, March 26, 2018: https://slate.com/technology/2018/03/basic-cpr-doesnt-help-gunshot-wounds-rick-santorum.html

(90) "Triumph of the Transient: A Band of Horses Road Log," by Pat McGuire, Filter Magazine February 1, 2008

(91) "Some Characteristics of Genuine versus simulated suicides notes," by Daniel M. Ogilvie, Philip J. Stone, and Edwin S. Shneidman. Page 404 - The Content Analysis Reader Klaus Krippendorff SAGE, 2009 - Language Arts & Disciplines. http://books.google.com/books?id=-y1KEoBSqHMC&dq=%22suicide+notes%22+genuine+simulated&source=gbs_navlinks_s

(92) "The Language of Suicide Notes" by Jess Jann Shapero - A thesis submitted to the University of Birmingham for the degree of Doctor of Philosophy quote of Shneidman (ibid., p.151). p 68

https://etheses.bham.ac.uk/id/eprint/1525/1/Shapero11PhD.pdf

(93) "Linguistic Manifestations Of Power In Suicide Notes: An Investigation Of Personal Pronouns" by Susan M. Roubidoux, A Thesis Submitted in Partial Fulfillment of the Requirements for the Degree of Masters of Arts- English, at the University of Wisconsin Oshkosh, Wi, 2012 p. 68 https://minds.wisconsin.edu/bitstream/handle/1793/62261/RoubidouxSusan.pdf?sequence=3&isAllowed=y

(94) SPIN's 1999 Profile of Elliott Smith: "He's Mr. Dyingly Sad, and You're Mystifyingly Glad" by RJ Smith, February 26, 2017 https://www.SPIN .com/2017/02/elliott-smith-either-or-reissue-archives-feature/

(95) "Elliott Smith – "I don't feel any sadder than anybody else I know": a classic interview from the vaults" by RJ Smith – October, 16 2013 From Rock's Backpages Elliott Smith https://www.theguardian.com/music/2013/oct/16/elliott-smith-rocks-backpages

(96) "Elliott Smith and the Big Nothing" by Ben Nugent – Da Capo, 2004

(97) "Elliott Smith: Last word on a tormented rock hero" by Gillian Orr – Independent November 2013 https://www.independent.co.uk/arts-entertainment/music/features/elliott-smith-last-word-on-a-tormented-rock-hero-8915555.html

(98) Conversation with Abigail Russell. She had been around the Silverlake scene since 1999

(99) Email from one of Abigail's friends

(100) Encounter with Elliott and Chiba in October 2002 after the show at the Echo.

(101) "5 more reasons your therapist won't see you now" by John M. Grohol, Psy. D. 8 July 2018 https://psychcentral.com/blog/5-more-reasons-your-therapist-wont-see-you-now/

(102) "The Lost Boy" by Keith Cameron, Q magazine, January 2011

(103) Jennifer Chiba in Weezerpedia: https://www.weezerpedia.com/wiki/Jennifer_Chiba

(104) Message exchange with Seth (not his real name) a musician who was living in Silverlake at the time of Elliott's death

(105) Message exchange with Rick (not his real name) a sound-engineer who recorded at Elliott's studio in 2002

(106) Message exchange with a fan from Florida

(107) W. T. Schultz's signing of "Torment Saint" at Skylight books on October 12, 2013

(108) Short oral exchange with Autumn de Wilde at her signing "Elliott Smith" November 2007

(109) Twitter exchange with W. T. Schultz

(110) "From a Basement": Elliott Smith's Posthumous Gift" by Elizabeth Blair (NPR segment) https://www.npr.org/templates/story/story.php?storyId=4109711

(111) "Keep the things you forgot: An Elliott Smith oral history" by Jayson Greene Pitchfork, October 2013 https://pitchfork.com/features/article/9246-keep-the-things-you-forgot-an-elliott-smith-oral-history/

(112) Flaming Lips concert at the Hollywood Forever Cemetery. Wayne Coyne's quote

(113) Heaven Adores You by Nickolas Rossi - Screening at the Regent, February 14, 2012

(114) Conversation with Gil Reyes during W. T. Schultz's signing of "Torment Saint" at Skylight books on October 12, 2013

(115) Cardinal Times, Lincoln High's school paper (https://cardinaltimes.org) – 2005 article offline

(116) Conversation with J. Chiba during W. T. Schultz's signing of "Torment Saint" at Skylight books on October 12, 2013

(117) Email exchange with Serena, Elliott's college friend at Hampshire College in Amherst, Massachusetts

(118) Incident at the Music Box on January 31, 2003 with Valerie Deerin

(119) "Blue Spark, Part III" by Nelly Reifler, September 27, 2013 https://theweeklings.com/nreifler/2013/09/27/blue-spark-part-iii/

(120) Elliott Smith Foundation: See Appendix #2: https://ca.ltddir.com/companies/elliott-smith-foundation

(121) Phone call with Jerry Schoenkopf, Elliott's drug counselor

(122) Phone conversation and email exchange with Sybil (not her real name), a musician from New Orleans. She had lived in Portland and Los Angeles

(123) Message exchange with B., a musician who had played with a local band, and was close to Elliott

(124) Posted by Ashley, Elliott's half-sister, on Sweet Adeline

(125) interview of Johan Wohlert, of Danish indie band Mew

(126) Second lawsuit: Jennifer Chiba v. Ron Gold: See Appendix #4 https://justiceforelliottsmithcom.wordpress.com/jennifer-chiba/jennifer-chibas-lawsuit-against-ron-gold-lawyer-at-oldman-cooley-sallus-gold-birnberg-coleman-l-l-p/

(127) "La mort du chanteur Elliott Smith conserve une part de mystère, quinze and après les faits" by Ana Benabs, France 24, October 22, 2018 https://www.france24.com/fr/20181019-elliott-smith-mort-suicide-rock-musique-quinze-ans-mystere

(128) Email exchange with Ana Benabs

(129) Message exchange with a fan who had stayed at J. Chiba's house after Elliott's death

(130) "Romantic relationships in recovery" http://alcoholrehab.com/addiction-recovery/romantic-relationships-in-recovery/

(131) Chiba's Therapist licenses https://search.dca.ca.gov see Appendix #5

(132) Exchange of emails with Steve Hanft, film and video director (Strange Parallel)

(133) "Elliott Smith: La cicatrice intérieure" Voxpop #13 Mars-Avril 2010 offline, can be found in web archives https://web.archive.org/web/20160226185829/http://www.voxpopmag.com/le-magazine/16358-elliott-smith-la-cicatrice-interieure/

(134) Message exchange with a recording engineer who had worked with Elliott

(135) Message exchange with Karrie, one of Chiba's friends

(136) Message exchange with musician Lou Barlow

(137) Email exchange with Robin Peringer, a drummer who played with Elliott during his last shows in 2003

(138) Anonymous neighbor comment found on a website

(139) Email exchange and conversation in person with Mark, an independent journalist

(140) Phone conversation with one of founders of Vice magazine

(141) Message exchange with a podcaster

(142) Message exchange with Susie, a woman who had been around the LA music scene

(143)"The Other Way" song by Weezer 2003 (Make Believe album) https://www.weezerpedia.com/wiki/The_Other_Way

(144) "I'll Think About You" song by Rivers Cuomo 1994 (Alone II) https://www.weezerpedia.com/wiki/I%27ll_Think_About_You

(145) "Oh Jonas" or Maria's Theme song by Rivers Cuomo, 1995 Alone II: the Home Recordings of Rivers Cuomo https://www.weezerpedia.com/wiki/Oh_Jonas

(146) Posted on the news of Sweet Adeline in October 2003 http://www.sweetadeline.net/oct03.html

(147) Ticket of the show at the Henry Fonda Theatre on November 3, 2003 see Appendix #6

(148) Email exchange with the Steffens (Chiba's next door neighbor)

(149) Email exchange with Richard Cromelin (LA Times journalist living across the street)

(150) Message exchange with Rosa, a neighbor who was living just across the street.

(151) Conversation in person with Joey, a neighbor who was living next door, and was in his backyard on October 21, 2003

(152) Residential eviction lawsuit against Chiba https://unicourt.com/case/ca-la12-gerstein-adam-vs-chiba-jennifer-1032161

(153) Comment left by Larry Crane (Elliott Smith's archivist) after an article mentioning his re-mastering of Elliott's album and his "suicide."

(154) "The dreams I did not expect. They hadn't come with any of" Seattle Weekly, October 16, 2013 https://www.seattleweekly.com/music/the-dreams-i-did-not-expect-they-hadnt-come-with-any-of/

(155) "The Seven Major Mistakes in Suicide Investigation," By Vernon J. Geberth, M.S., M.P.S. Homicide and Forensic Consultant 2013 https://www.practicalhomicide.com/Research/7mistakes.htm

(156) "Smith's girlfriend won't collect," by Leslie Simmons, Hollywood Reporter, October 17, 2007 https://www.hollywoodreporter.com/news/smiths-girlfriend-wont-collect-152763

(157) "Stunner guilty of trying to kill boyfriend" by Rebecca Rosenberg, NY Post November 21, 2013 https://nypost.com/2013/11/21/latvian-beauty-yekaterina-pusepa-guilty-of-attempted-murder/

(158) Melters' Blog, "Suicide or homicide. When the lines are blurred," by Daniel Melters

https://meltersblog.wordpress.com/category/eline-melters/

(159) "He wanted to invite his ex to the wedding, so his bride grabbed a steak knife, police say" The Kansas City Star by Lisa Gutierrez, July 25, 2018 https://www.kansascity.com/news/nation-world/article215485870.html

(160) "No charges filed against bride-to-be arrested for fiancé's death," by KKTV

October 19, 2018 https://www.kktv.com/content/news/No-charges-filed-against-bride-to-be-arrested-for-fiances-death-498076371.html

(161) "Last chance appeal for Donna Vasyli over murder of orthotics tycoon husband Phil" by Duncan McNab, Crime Editor, 7news Australia, September, 15, 2019

https://7news.com.au/original-fyi/crime-story-investigator/last-chance-appeal-for-donna-vasyli-over-murder-of-orthotics-tycoon-husband-phil-c-446851

(162) "Dpp Wants New Trial For Vasyli" by Rashad Rolle, Tribune 242, June 9, 2020 http://www.tribune242.com/news/2020/jun/10/dpp-wants-new-trial-vasyli/?news

(163) "Feds charge Army wife with stabbing husband and warn of domestic violence amid pandemic," by Kyle Rempfer, Armytimes May 19, 2020 https://www.armytimes.com/news/your-army/2020/05/19/feds-charge-army-wife-with-stabbing-husband-and-warn-of-domestic-violence-amid-pandemic/

(164) "André Fortin: meurtre ou suicide? le coroner ne peut rien confirmer," by Jean-François Guérin, TVA Nouvelles, May 10, 2000 https://www.tvanouvelles.ca/2000/05/10/andre-fortin-meurtre-ou-suicide-le-coroner-ne-peut-rien-confirmer

(165) "Dédé Fortin (1962 -2000)" by A-J Charron, Guitar Noise http://www.guitarnoise.com/blog/dede-fortin/

(166) "Suicide by self-inflicted stab wound to the heart: a rare case of suicide from Nepal" S Jha, Sudhir Raman Parajuli, Nuwadatta Subedi, Journal of College of Medical Sciences-Nepal 10(2) July 2015 https://www.researchgate.net/publication/281807685_Suicide_by_self-inflicted_stab_wound_to_the_heart_a_rare_case_of_suicide_from_Nepal

(167) "Dying Transfixing His Own Heart A Rare Case of Suicide by Stabbing," by Alessandra Pentone, Liliana Innamorato, Francesco Introna, The American Journal of Forensic Medicine and Pathology: official publication of the National Association of Medicine https://www.researchgate.net/publication/258281483_Dying_Transfixing_His_Own_Heart_A_Rare_Case_of_Suicide_by_Stabbing

(168) "Non-fatal suicide attempt by intentional stab wound: Clinical management, psychiatric assessment, and multidisciplinary considerations," by James M Badger, Shea C Gregg, Charles A Adams Journal of Emergencies, Trauma, and Shock 2012, Volume: 5, Issue: 3 pages 228-232: http://www.onlinejets.org/article.asp?issn=0974-2700;year=2012;volume=5;issue=3;spage=228;epage=232;aulast=Badger

(169) You Made It Weird With Pete Homes Podcast, guest Mark Flanagan, October 28, 2015 http://youmadeitweird.nerdistind.libsynpro.com/mark-flanagan

(170) "The Long Slow Death Of Elliott Smith" by Ariel Levy 2004, originally in Blender http://ronfordrites.blogspot.com/2004/01/my-last-goodbye.html

(171) Message exchange with criminal attorney Jakob (not his real name)

(172) "Courtney didn't kill Kurt: The twisted misogyny behind suicide conspiracy theories," by William Todd Schultz, Salon, May 17, 2015 https://www.salon.com/2015/05/17/courtney_didnt_kill_kurt_the_twisted_misogyny_behind_suicide_conspiracy_theories/

(173) "The Aftermath of the Celebrity Suicide Lingers," by Leigh Kunkel, Playboy, June 29, 2018 https://www.playboy.com/read/the-misogynistic-aftermath-of-celebrity-suicide

(174) Sickness Unto Death by Søren Kierkegaard 1849

(175) Elliott Smith's interview in Boston Herald May 11, 2000

(176) "The Myth of Sisyphus," 1942 philosophical essay by Albert Camus

(177) "Kierkegaard on why anxiety powers creativity rather than hindering it" by Maria Popova, Brainpickings https://www.brainpickings.org/2013/06/19/kierkegaard-on-anxiety-and-creativity/

(178) Either/Or, by Søren Kierkegaard, 1843

(179) On the Concept of Irony with Continual Reference to Socrates by Søren Kierkegaard's 1841 doctoral thesis under Frederik Christian Sibbern.

(180) "Suicide Machine": first recorded in October 1998 at Abbey Road Studios, London, England, UK - Place Pigalle Demos – instrumental, unofficially circulating as "Tiny Time Machine." Recorded on October 19-20, 2003 at New Monkey Studios, Los Angeles, CA - Final Recordings - unofficially circulating (vocals and additional drum tracking)- Alphabet Town, An exhaustive guide to the music of Elliott Smith. Song guide https://songs.alphabet-town.com/songguide

(181) Kill Rock Stars founder Slim Moon's quote from an email for the promotion of the "Elliott Smith: Expanded 25th Anniversary Edition" released August 28 2020, on Kill Rock Stars

(182) by Nick Duerden, Q magazine August 2000 http://www.sweetadeline.net/q00.html

(183) "The Twisted Circle," by Nigel Williamson, Uncut June 2000 http://www.sweetadeline.net/uncut00.html

(184) "Emotional Rescue" by Jonathan Valania, taken from Magnet Jan/Feb 2001 http://magnetmagazine.com/2001/01/02/elliott-smith-emotional-rescue/

(185) "A Comparison of Self-Inflicted Stab Wounds Versus Assault-Induced Stab Wounds" by Sanghyun Ahn, Dong Jin Kim, Kwang Yeol Paik, Jae Hee Chung, Woo-Chan Park, Wook Kim, and In Kyu Lee, Trauma Mon. November 2016; 21 (5):e25304 https://www.ncbi.nlm.

nih.gov/pmc/articles/PMC5292019/pdf/traumamon-21-05-25304.pdf

(186) "Flashback: Elliott Smith Plays Stripped-Down 'Figure 8' Songs on "The Jon Brion Show" by Hank Shteamer, Rolling Stone April 18, 2020 https://www.rollingstone.com/music/music-features/elliott-smith-figure-8-jon-brion-show-984798/

Appendix #1: Jennifer Chiba's DUI

Booking No.: **7821135** Last Name: **CHIBA** First Name: **JENNIFER** Middle Name: **RIE**

Sex: **F** Race: **O** Date Of Birth: **06/17/1967** Age: **36** Hair: **BRO** Eyes: **BRO** Height: **505** Weight: **115**

Charge Level: **M (Misdemeanor)**

ARREST

Arrest Charge: **23152(A)VC** Charge Description: **DRUNK DRIVING ALCOHOL/DRUGS**

Arrest Date: **08/30/2003** Arrest Time: **0108** Arrest Agency: **9975** Agency Description: **CHP-GLENDALE/VERDUGO HILLS STATION**

Date Booked: **08/30/2003** Time Booked: **0214** Booking Location: **1925** Location Description: **PD - GLENDALE**

BAIL

Total Bail Amount: **15,000.00** Total Hold Bail Amount: **0.00** Grand Total: **15,000.00**

HOUSING LOCATION

Housing Location: Module:

Permanent Housing Assigned Date: **08/30/2003** Assigned Time: **0214** Visitor Status: **N**

Facility:
Address: City:

Public Visiting Guidelines

For County facility visiting hours, Please call (213) 473-6080 at Inmate Information Center.

COURT

Next Court Code: **GLN** Next Court Date: **09/02/2003** Next Court Time: **0900** Next Court Case: **9999999999**

Court Name: **GLENDALE MUNICIPAL COURT**
Court Address: **600 E. BROADWAY** Court City: **GLENDALE**

RELEASE

Actual Release Date: **08/30/2003** Release Time: **1400**

CASE INFORMATION

(Click on specific Case No. for detailed info.)

Case No.	Charge No.	Level	Court Name	Court Address	Court City	Bail Amt.	Fine Amt.	Court Date
9999999999	23152 (A)VC	M				15,000.00	.00	09/02/2003

Appendix #2: Elliott Smith Foundation

Company Name:	ELLIOTT SMITH FOUNDATION		
Status:	Suspended	Filing Date:	10/01/2003
Entity Type:	Corporation	File Number:	C2525773
Filing State:	California (CA)	Qualifying State:	
Company Age:	9 Years, 2 Months	List Due Date:	
Principal Address:	[redacted] Malibu, CA 90265	Mailing Address:	
Registered Agent:	Jerry Schoenkopf [redacted] Malibu, CA		

Appendix #3: First Lawsuit Marta Greenwald versus Jennifer Chiba

Miles E. Locker, CSB #103510
DIVISION OF LABOR STANDARDS ENFORCEMENT
Department of Industrial Relations
State of California
455 Golden Gate Avenue, 9th Floor
San Francisco, California 94102
Telephone: (415) 703-4863
Fax: (415) 703-4806
Attorney for State Labor Commissioner

BEFORE THE LABOR COMMISSIONER

STATE OF CALIFORNIA

MARTA GREENWALD, as personal representative of the Estate of ELLIOT SMITH aka STEVEN PAUL SMITH, deceased, Petitioner, vs. JENNIFER CHIBA, Respondent.	No. TAC 03-05 DETERMINATION OF CONTROVERSY

The above-captioned matter, a petition to determine controversy under Labor Code §1700.44, came on for telephonic pre-hearing conference on July 13, 2005, and following that pre-hearing conference, the parties agreed that the Labor Commissioner could adjudicate the controversy without a live hearing, but rather, on the basis of evidence to be submitted by declaration and/or through the submission of Respondent's prior deposition testimony in a related action. Pursuant to this agreement, the parties, through their respective counsel, Roy G. Rifkin for the petitioner, and Eric S. Jacobson and Ronald Gold for the respondent, simultaneously filed opening papers on August 2, 2005, and reply papers on August 16, 2005. Having reviewed the evidence and argument submitted, the Labor Commissioner hereby adopts the following decision.

FINDINGS OF FACT

1. Petitioner Marta Greenwald is the administrator of the estate of Elliott Smith. The estate is being administered in a probate action that is pending in the Los Angeles County Superior Court. Prior to his death on October 21, 2003, Smith resided in Los Angeles, California. Smith was a well-known composer, singer and musical recording artist.

2. Respondent Jennifer Chiba is a resident of Los Angeles. She met Smith during the summer of 1999, and began a romantic relationship with him. On August 26, 2002, Smith moved into Chiba's apartment, and they resided together from then until his death. Chiba has never been licensed by the State Labor Commissioner as a talent agency.

3. On July 28, 2004, Chiba filed a creditor's claim, which was subsequently amended, against Smith's estate in the probate matter. On July 30, 2004, Chiba filed an action against Greenwald in Los Angeles Superior Court, alleging, *inter alia,* that in August 2002 she and Smith entered into an oral agreement under which "the parties agreed that they would live together, cohabitate and combine their efforts and earnings and would share equally any and all property accumulated as a result of their efforts whether individual or combined....and that Plaintiff would render her services as a homemaker, housekeeper, and cook to the decedent, and that Plaintiff would further forego any independent

career opportunities to devote her full time to decedent as a homemaker, housekeeper, cook, secretary, bookkeeper, and financial counselor to the decedent, in consideration for which decedent agreed to provide for all of plaintiff's financial needs and support for the rest of her life." The complaint further alleged that as part of this oral agreement, "plaintiff would also act as decedent's manager and agent for the purposes of arranging the booking and scheduling appearances for musical performances by decedent ... in consideration for which Plaintiff would be specifically entitled to 15% of the proceeds earned and received on all such performances...."

4. On November 1, 2004, before any responsive pleading had been filed, Chiba filed a First Amended Complaint, which omitted any allegation that she had agreed to act or acted as Smith's manager or agent for the purposes of arranging the booking and scheduling appearances for his musical performances, and omitted any claim for any commissions on his earnings for such musical performances. The First Amended Complaint retained all of the other allegations detailed above regarding the parties' oral agreement and her performance of services as a homemaker, housekeeper, cook, secretary, bookkeeper, financial counselor, and added to this list her services as a "personal and career manager to the decedent." In her court action, Chiba alleges that Greenwald, as the administrator of Smith's estate, breached this agreement to provide for her financial needs and support for the rest of her life, resulting in damages in excess of $1,000,000.

5. By order dated January 10, 2005, the Los Angeles Superior Court stayed the civil action pending the reference of this matter

to the Labor Commissioner for determination of issues under the Talent Agencies Act (Labor Code §1700, *et seq.*). On January 14, 2005, Greenwald filed this petition to determine controversy, seeking a determination that pursuant to her oral agreement with Smith, Chiba procured performing engagements for Smith, and since she did so without the requisite talent agency license, the oral agreement is void in its entirety from its inception, and that Chiba has no enforceable rights under that agreement. Chiba filed an answer to the petition, denying that she procured the engagements that were alleged in the petition, and seeking a determination that her oral agreement with Smith is not void, invalid or unenforceable under the Talent Agencies Act.

6. During a deposition that was taken on September 29, 2004 in connection with the parties' civil action, Chiba testified that she and Smith entered into the oral agreement that is the subject of the lawsuit sometime between August 26 and August 31, 2002, during a conversation in her home, and that during this conversation, she agreed to help him by becoming his manager and agent for the purpose of arranging the booking and scheduling appearances for Smith's musical performances, for which she would receive commissions on his entertainment earnings. Chiba testified that this discussion did not take place separately from the discussion about the other matters included in the alleged oral agreement, such as Smith's promise to provide for her financial needs and support her, and her promise to perform housekeeping, cooking, secretarial, bookkeeping, and financial counseling services for Smith. There was just one conversation during which all of these matters were discussed, and, according

to Chiba, the parties reached one oral agreement regarding all of these matters. Following this discussion, Chiba became involved in arranging the booking and scheduling Smith's performances for every one of his engagements. He performed at 20 engagements from the end of August 2002 until his death. Chiba testified that for some of these engagements, she initiated contact with the venue where the performance ultimately took place in order to procure the booking for Smith, and that for the others, she received telephone calls from persons requesting that he perform at their venue, and in those instances, she communicated with these callers to agree to and schedule the performances. She testified that for all of these engagements, she was involved in negotiations for Smith's fee.

7. No evidence was submitted that contradicts or casts any doubt upon Chiba's testimony as outlined above, so we rely on this testimony in deciding this case.

LEGAL ANALYSIS

1. Smith is an "artist" within the meaning of Labor Code §1700.4(b).

2. Labor Code §1700.4(a) defines "talent agency" as "a person or corporation who engages in the occupation of procuring, offering, promising, or attempting to procure employment or engagements for an artist or artists, except that the activities of procuring, offering or promising to procure recording contracts for an artist or artists shall not of itself subject a person or corporation to regulation and licensing under this chapter." The term "procure," as used in this statute, means "to get possession of: obtain, acquire, to cause to happen or be done: bring about."

Wachs v. Curry (1993) 13 Cal.App.4th 616, 628. Thus, under Labor Code §1700.4(a), "procuring employment" is not limited to initiating discussions with potential purchaser's of the artist's services; rather, "procurement" includes any active participation in a communication with a potential purchaser of the artist's services aimed at obtaining employment for the artist, regardless of who initiated the communication. *Hall v. X Management* (TAC No. 19-90, pp. 29-31.) The Labor Commissioner has long held that "procurement" includes the process of negotiating an agreement for an artist's services. *Pryor v. Franklin* (TAC 17 MP 114). Significantly, the Talent Agencies Act specifically provides that an unlicensed person may nevertheless participate in negotiating an employment contract for an artist, provided he or she does so "in conjunction with, and at the request of a licensed talent agent." Labor Code §1700.44(d). This limited exception to the licensing requirement would be unnecessary if negotiating an employment contract for an artist did not require a license in the first place. The uncontradicted evidence here plainly establishes that Chiba promised to procure employment, and did procure employment for Smith, so that she acted as a "talent agency" within the meaning of Labor Code §1700.4(a).

3. Labor Code §1700.5 provides that "[n]o person shall engage in or carry on the occupation of a talent agency without first procuring a license . . . from the Labor Commissioner." The Talent Agencies Act is a remedial statute that must be liberally construed to promote its general object, the protection of artists seeking professional employment. *Buchwald v. Superior Court* (1967) 254 Cal.App.2d 347, 354. For that reason, the overwhelming

weight of judicial authority supports the Labor Commissioner's historic enforcement policy, and holds that "even the incidental or occasional provision of such [procurement] services requires licensure." *Styne v. Stevens* (2001) 26 Cal.4th 42, 51. "The [Talent Agencies] Act imposes a *total* prohibition on the procurement efforts of unlicensed persons," and thus, "the Act requires a license to engage in *any* procurement activities." *Waisbren v. Peppercorn Productions, Inc.* (1995) 41 Cal.App.4th 246, 258-259; see also *Park v. Deftones* (1999) 71 Cal.App.4th 1465 [license required even though procurement activites constituted a negligible portion of personal manager's efforts on behalf of artist, and manager was not compensated for these procurement activities].

4. Of course, an artist who procures employment for him or herself does not act as a "talent agency," and need not be licensed, in that the activity of procuring employment under the Talent Agencies Act refers to the role an agent plays when acting as an intermediary between the artist whom the agent represents and a third-party employer. See *Chinn v. Tobin* (TAC No. 17-96), *Bautista v. Romero* (TAC NO. 3-04). But a spouse, or live-in boyfriend or girlfriend of an artist, who procures employment for that artist falls under the statutory definition of a "talent agency," as there is no exemption that would exclude such persons from the definition. The artist's spouse, or significant other, must be licensed as a talent agency to procure employment for the artist, in the same way that a license to practice law would be required to represent the person's spouse or significant other in a court trial.

5. An agreement that violates the licensing requirement of the Talent Agencies Act is illegal and unenforceable. "Since the clear object of the Act is to prevent improper persons from becoming [talent agents] and to regulate such activity for the protection of the public, a contract between an unlicensed [agent] and an artist is void." *Buchwald v. Superior Court, supra,* 254 Cal.App.2d at 351. Having determined that a person or business entity procured, promised or attempted to procure employment for an artist without the requisite talent agency license, "the [Labor] Commissioner may declare the contract [between the unlicensed agent and the artist] void and unenforceable as involving the services of an unlicensed person in violation of the Act." *Styne v. Stevens, supra,* 26 Cal.4th at 55. "[A]n agreement that violates the licensing requirement is illegal and unenforceable . . . ." *Waisbren v. Peppercorn Productions, Inc.,* supra, 41 Cal.App.4th at 262.

6. The Labor Commissioner has exclusive primary jurisdiction to determine all controversies arising under the Talent Agencies Act. "When the Talent Agencies Act is invoked in the course of a contract dispute, the Commissioner has exclusive jurisdiction to determine his (or her) jurisdiction in the matter, including whether the the contract involved the services of a talent agency." *Ibid.* at 54. This means that the Labor Commissioner has "the exclusive right to decide in the first instance *all the legal and factual issues on which an Act-based defense depends.*" *Ibid.,* at fn. 6, italics in original. In doing so, the Labor Commissioner will "search out illegality lying behind the form in which a transaction has been cast for the purpose of concealing such

illegality," and "will look through provisions, valid on their face, and with the aid of parol evidence, determine [whether] the contract is actually illegal or part of an illegal transaction." *Buchwald v. Superior Court, supra,* 254 Cal.App.2d at 351.

7. California courts have uniformly held that a contract under which an unlicensed party procures or attempts to procure employment for an artist is void *ab initio* and the party procuring the employment is barred from recovering payments for *any* activities under the contract, including activities for which a talent agency license is not required. *Yoo v. Robi* (2005) 126 Cal.App.4th 1089, 1103-1104; *Styne v. Stevens, supra,* 26 Cal.4th at 51; *Park v. Deftones, supra,* 71 Cal.App.4th at 1470; *Waisbren v. Peppercorn Productions, supra,* 41 Cal.App.4th at 1470. The courts have also unanimously denied all recovery to personal managers even when the overwhelming majority of the managers' activities did not require a talent agency license and the activities which did require a license were minimal and incidental. *Yoo v. Robi, supra,* 126 Cal.App.4th at 1104; *Park v. Deftones, supra,* 71 Cal.App.4th at 1470; *Waisbren v. Peppercorn Productions, supra,* 41 Cal.App.4th at 250, 261-262. The rationale for denying a personal manager recovery even for activities which were entirely legal, where that personal manager also unlawfully engaged in employment procurement without the requisite talent agency license, is based on the public policy of the Talent Agencies Act to deter unlicensed persons from engaging in activities for which a talent agency license is required. This rationale is not limited to actions for breach of contract; it also applies to actions seeking recovery on theories of unjust

enrichment or quantum meruit. *Yoo v. Robi, supra,* 126 Cal.App.4th at 1104, fn. 30; *Waisbren v. Peppercorn Productions, supra,* 41 Cal.app.4th at 250, fn. 2. Knowing that they will receive no help from the courts in recovering for their legal activities undertaken pursuant to an agreement under which they also engaged in unlawful procurement, personal managers are less likely to enter into illegal arrangements. *Yoo v. Robi, supra,* 126 Cal.App.4th at 1104; *Waisbren v. Peppercorn Productions, supra,* 41 Cal.App.4th at 262, citing *Lewis & Queen v. N.M. Ball Sons* (1957) 48 Cal.2d 141, 150. In *Waisbren,* the court observed that one reason the Legislature did not enact criminal penalties for violations of the Talent Agencies Act was "because the most effective weapon for assuring compliance with the Act is the power ... to declare any contract entered into between the parties void from the inception." *Waisbren v. Peppercorn Productions, supra,* 41 Cal.App.4th at 262, quoting from a 1985 report issued by the California Entertainment Commission.

8. Here, Chiba argues that with the filing of her First Amended Complaint in the superior court action, she abandoned any prior claim for compensation for her procurement activities, so that she is now seeking recovery only for those activities for which she did not need a talent agency license, and that the Talent Agencies Act cannot apply to deny her right to recovery for activities that are not covered by the Act. This argument was made and rejected in *Yoo v. Robi:* "The fact that procuring recording contracts without a license does not in itself violate public policy is not determinative. The same thing could be said about numerous other activities personal managers engage in which

do not require a license such as counseling artists in the development of their professional careers, selecting material for their performances, managing their money, and the like. Engaging in those activities without a talent agency license does not violate public policy but those activities are nevertheless noncompensable if they are mixed in with activities which do require a license because of the overriding public policy of deterring unlicensed activities." *Yoo v. Robi, supra,* 126 Cal.App.4th at 1105. The fact that Chiba has abandoned her prior claim for commissions for her procurement activities is essentially irrelevant to the validity and enforceability of the alleged oral agreement between her and Smith. What matters is not whether or not she is seeking recovery for procurement activities, but whether she engaged in such activities without a talent agency license pursuant to an agreement under which she agreed to perform (and did perform) many other activities for which a license is not required. The evidence here is that there was but one integrated oral agreement, and that pursuant to that agreement, she performed unlawful procurement activities "mixed in" with activities for which a license was not required. As a result, the oral agreement is void from its inception, in its entirety, and Chiba has no enforceable rights thereunder. Whether or not, under the facts herein, this is a harsh result we cannot say, as it is the result that is unquestionably mandated by the line of cases interpreting the Talent Agencies Act.

ORDER

For all of the reasons set forth above, IT IS HEREBY ORDERED that the August 2002 oral agreement between Jennifer Chiba and

Elliott Smith is void from its inception, in its entirety, and that Chiba has no enforceable rights thereunder.

Dated: 10/20/05

MILES E. LOCKER
Attorney for the Labor Commissioner

ADOPTED AS THE DETERMINATION OF THE LABOR COMMISSIONER:

Dated: 11/16/05

DONNA M. DELL
State Labor Commissioner

STATE OF CALIFORNIA
DEPARTMENT OF INDUSTRIAL RELATIONS - DIVISION OF LABOR STANDARDS ENFORCEMENT

CERTIFICATION OF SERVICE BY MAIL
(C.C.P. §1013a)

(Marta Greenwald for Elliott Smith, etc. v. Jennifer Chiba)
(TAC 03-05)

I, MARY ANN E. GALAPON, do hereby certify that I am employed in the county of San Francisco, over 18 years of age, not a party to the within action, and that I am employed at and my business address is 455 Golden Gate Avenue, 9th Floor, San Francisco, CA 94102.

On November 22, 2005, I served the following document:

DETERMINATION OF CONTROVERSY

by placing a true copy thereof in envelope(s) addressed as follows:

ROY G. RIFKIN, ESQ.
Wolf, Rifkin, Shapiro & Schulman, LLP
11400 West Olympic Boulevard, 9th Floor
Los Angeles, CA 90064-1582

RONALD GOLD, ESQ.
MEREDITH C. LEVY, ESQ.
Oldman, Cooley, Leighton, Sallus,
Gold & Birnberg
16133 Ventura Blvd., Penthouse Suite A
Encino, CA 91436-1818

ERIC S. JACOBSON, ESQ.
EDWIN M. ROSENBERG, ESQ.
3435 Wilshire Boulevard, Suite 2360
Los Angeles, CA 90010

and then sealing the envelope with postage thereon fully prepaid, depositing it in the United States mail in the city and county of San Francisco by ordinary first class mail.

I certify under penalty of perjury that the foregoing is true and correct. Executed on November 22, 2005, at San Francisco, California.

Mary Ann E. Galapon
MARY ANN E. GALAPON

CERTIFICATE OF SERVICE BY MAIL

Appendix #4: Second Lawsuit Chiba versus Ron Gold

Sep 23 2008 10:41AM David Alden Erikson 323-465-3177 p.2

David Alden Erikson, California Bar No. 189838
200 North Larchmont Blvd.
Los Angeles, California 90004
Telephone: (323) 465-3100
Facsimile: (323) 465-3177

Attorney For Plaintiff Jennifer Chiba

FILED
LOS ANGELES SUPERIOR COURT
SEP 2 3 2008
JOHN A. CLARKE, CLERK
BY SHAUNYA WESLEY, DEPUTY

SUPERIOR COURT OF THE STATE OF CALIFORNIA

FOR THE COUNTY OF LOS ANGELES, CENTRAL DISTRICT

JENNIFER CHIBA, an individual, Plaintiff, vs. RON GOLD, an individual ,OLDMAN, COOLEY, SALLUS, GOLD, BIRNBERG & COLEMAN, L.L.P., a California Limited Liability Partnership, and DOES 1 through 100, Defendants.	BC398671 Case No. COMPLAINT FOR ATTORNEY MALPRACTICE (PROFESSIONAL NEGLIGENCE, BREACH OF FIDUCIARY DUTY AND CONSTRUCTIVE FRAUD) DEMAND FOR TRIAL BY JURY

Plaintiff Jennifer Chiba ("Jennifer" or "Plaintiff") hereby complains against Defendants Ron Gold ("Gold") and Oldman, Cooley, Sallus, Gold, Birnberg & Coleman, ("Oldman Cooley"), and Does 1 through 100 (collectively referred to as "Defendants") as follows:

GENERAL ALLEGATIONS

1. Jennifer was the long-time romantic partner of musician Elliott Smith ("Elliott") at the time of his suicide in 2003. The two essentially lived together as husband and wife.

CIT/CASE: BC398671 LEA/DEF#:
RECEIPT #: CCH465980049
DATE PAID: 09/23/08 02:58:25 PM
PAYMENT: 331.00
RECEIVED:
CHECK:
CASH:
CHANGE:
CARD: 331.00

DQ0001

2. When Smith died, his step-mother Marta Greenwald (from whom Elliott was long estranged, and who was made the personal representative of his estate because Elliott had left no instructions to the contrary) opportunistically sought to assert total control over Elliott's assets and affairs. It became clear to Jennifer that Greenwald wanted to take control of Elliott's intellectual property and master tapes (including unreleased work) and maximize their commercial appeal for monetary gain.

3. Blindly blaming Jennifer for the tragedy, Greenwald undertook a vindictive campaign to rewrite Elliott's history with Jennifer excised. Part of this effort involved denying her certain legal rights that she would otherwise hold as a result of her relationship with Elliott. Because Greenwald was obviously adamant about cutting Jennifer completely out of the picture, Jennifer was forced to sue Greenwald. The lawsuit sought monetary damages, as it must have, but also involved deeply emotional matters for Jennifer. For one, she felt responsible for protecting the artistic integrity of Elliott's work. In addition, the lawsuit would have essentially been a referendum on the truth and significance of her relationship with Elliot, especially in light of Greenwald's efforts to publicly denigrate it and even accuse Jennifer of his murder.

4. Jennifer's claims against Greenwald were very strong, as evidenced in part by Defendants' eagerness to pursue the case on a contingency basis. Indeed, they offered to assert Jennifer's claims against Greenwald, as personal representative of the estate, for 45% of any monetary recovery (after initially taking the case on an hourly basis). On June 17 2004, Chiba hired Defendants to prosecute her clearly meritorious legal claim against Greenwald. Defendants accepted this engagement and agreed to perform these services for Jennifer. Defendants drafted Jennifer's lawsuit and filed it on July 30, 2004.

5. But incredibly, no judge or jury ever decided the merits of Jennifer's claims. Jennifer was denied her day in court. The reason was Defendants' egregious professional negligence. One example of such malpractice was sloppily adding superfluous

and untrue allegations to the lawsuit that effectively left it no chance of reaching a jury—when any competent practioner (or anyone who researched applicable law) would have known the allegations would vitiate an otherwise valid claimed. Defendants even failed to realize this mistake as the litigation proceeded, when Greenwald's attorneys were obviously maneuvering to exploit it. Greenwald did in fact exploit Defendants' mistake and a result managed to have the case dismissed without the merits or factual allegations ever being addressed.

6. In addition to this and other elements of professional negligence, Defendants went further and actually breached the fiduciary duties of fidelity, care and loyalty they owed to Jennifer. They did so by concealing from her their professional negligence, even as those mistakes appeared more and more likely to destroy her case—and even when they did destroy it. In fact, there was a period of time after Defendants' initial (and ultimately fatal) mistake was out in the open among the attorneys, although never explained to Jennifer, when Defendants could have remedied the situation by performing an embarrassing mea culpa—and asking the trial judge to allow them to amend their papers to remove the mistake. Such request would have been granted under clear statutory and case law, which would have allowed Jennifer's lawsuit to proceed on the merits.

7. This option, of which any competent litigator would be aware, would have been advantageous for Jennifer. Essentially, it would have allowed Defendants to go back to the drawing board in order to craft the complaint with the benefit of knowing the applicable law. But there was great risk to Defendants in this strategy: If they had admitted their mistake in this way, they would squarely open themselves to liability for malpractice.

8. Not wanting to admit their mistake, Defendants stubbornly stuck by their imprudent allegations **even though they knew the allegations were not true and fatal to Jennifer's claims,** and instead fiddled with several proposed amendments to the

Complaint in an effort to avoid the fatal effect of the original allegations. This didn't work at the trial court level, nor in the Court of Appeal.

9. After a Petition for Rehearing was denied, Defendants told Jennifer that they would file a Petition for Review with California Supreme Court. Jennifer agreed, especially given several good reasons why their appeal looked promising—such as the fact that the Court had accepted another similar case for review (and thus it seemed that there was some sentiment on the Court favorably disposed to changing the law that turned out to be so harsh for Jennifer). It is now clear that Jennifer would have prevailed at the Supreme Court.

10. But in another example of their striking malpractice, Defendants (after drafting an extensive Petition for Review and all the necessary documentation including appendices) missed the filing deadline for the Petition, solely because they made a counting mistake when they calendared the deadline. The Supreme Court thus neglected to review Jennifer's Petition, and the case was over. Defendants tried to resurrect it by applying to the Supreme Court for "Relief From Untimely Filed Petition For Review," on the grounds that calendaring mistakes can be overlooked by the court, but this Application was also denied.

PARTIES

11. Jennifer is, and at all times relevant was, an individual residing in Los Angeles, California.

12. On information and belief, Defendant Gold is an individual residing in Los Angeles County, California.

13. On information and belief, Defendant Oldman Cooley is a California limited liability partnership with principal offices in Los Angeles County, California.

14. Plaintiff is ignorant of the true names and capacities of the Defendants sued herein as Does 1 through 100, inclusive, and therefore sue said Defendants by such fictitious names. Plaintiff will amend this Complaint to allege the true names and

Sep 23 2008 10:42AM David Alden Erikson 323-465-3177 p.6

capacities when the same has been ascertained. Plaintiff is informed and believes, and thereon alleges, that each fictitiously-named Defendant is responsible in some manner for the occurrences herein alleged, and that Plaintiff's damages as herein alleged were proximately caused by their conduct.

15. Each of the Defendants acted as an agent for each of the other Defendants in doing the acts alleged and each Defendant ratified and otherwise adopted the acts and statements performed, made or carried out by the other Defendants so as to make them directly and vicariously liable to Plaintiff for the conduct complained of herein.

16. At all times mentioned herein, defendant Ron Gold and Does 1 through 50 was the agent and employee of (or a partner in) Defendant Oldman Cooley and in doing the things herein alleged was acting within the course and scope of such agency.

First Cause Of Action for Professional Negligence

(Against All Defendants)

17. Jennifer incorporates herein by this reference paragraphs 1 through 16 as if set forth in full in this cause of action.

18. Defendants (and each of them) failed to exercise reasonable care and skill in undertaking to perform legal services for Jennifer. Some examples of such malpractice are cited above, but there were others.

19. Had Defendants exercised proper care and skill in Jennifer's litigation against Greenwald, Jennifer would have prevailed and received an received the appropriate recovery.

20. As a proximate result of Defendants' negligence, Jennifer was harmed according to proof, within the jurisdiction of this Court.

Second Cause Of Action for Breach of Fiduciary Duty

(Against All Defendants)

21. Jennifer incorporates herein by this reference paragraphs 1 through 20 as if set forth in full in this cause of action.

22. By virtue of the attorney-client relationship that existed between Jennifer and Defendants, and by virtue of Jennifer's having placed confidence in the fidelity and integrity of Defendants and entrusting Defendants with her meritorious legal claims, a confidential and fiduciary relationship existed between Jennifer and Defendants and Defendants owed Jennifer fiduciary duties under the law.

23. Despite having voluntarily accepted the trust and confidence of Jennifer with regard to her meritorious legal claims, and in violation of this relationship of trust and confidence, Defendants abused the trust and confidence of Jennifer, including as alleged above (as an example).

24. As a result of Defendants' breaches of fiduciary duties, Defendants benefited in that it became less likely that their lack of reasonable care and competence and failure to know applicable law would come to light.

25. As a proximate result of Defendants' breaches of fiduciary duty, Jennifer was harmed according to proof, within the jurisdiction of this Court.

26. As a further proximate result of Defendants' malpractice, Jennifer incurred legal fees and costs in amount to be proved .

27. In doing the acts alleged herein, Defendants acted with oppression fraud and malice, and Jennifer is entitled to punitive and exemplary damages.

Third Cause Of Action for Constructive Fraud

(Against All Defendants)

28. Jennifer incorporates herein by this reference paragraphs 1 through 27 as if set forth in full in this cause of action.

29. Jennifer placed trust and confidence in Defendants until after the demise of her case, when she eventually consulted another attorney.

30. Despite having voluntarily accepted the trust and confidence of Jennifer with regard to her meritorious legal claims, and in violation of this relationship of

trust and confidence, Defendants abused the trust and confidence of plaintiff by (as an example) concealing from Jennifer their prior professional negligence.

31. As a result of Defendants' breaches of fiduciary duties, Defendants benefited in that it became less likely that their lack of reasonable care and competence and failure to know applicable law would come to light. To achieve their goal, Defendants concealed facts by refusing to address direct questions and even affirmatively misrepresented what was going on in the litigation in order to keep Jennifer in the dark. Defendants performed these acts with the intent to induce reliance by Jennifer in the continuing fidelity of Defendants as her attorneys.

32. Defendants perform the acts alleged herein with the intent to deceive and defraud Jennifer.

33. As a proximate result of Defendants' fraud and constructive fraud, Jennifer was harmed according to proof, within the jurisdiction of this Court.

34. As a further proximate result of Defendants' fraud and constructive fraud, Jennifer incurred legal fees and costs in amount to be proved.

35. In doing the acts alleged herein, Defendants acted with oppression fraud and malice, and Jennifer is entitled to punitive and exemplary damages.

Fourth Cause of Action for Intentional Infliction of Emotional Distress

(Against All Defendants)

36. Jennifer incorporates herein by this reference paragraphs 1 through 35 as if set forth in full in this cause of action.

37. As a result of the actions alleged above, Jennifer suffered serious emotional distress of a kind that an ordinary reasonable person would suffer under the circumstances.

38. As a proximate and direct result of defendant's willful conduct, Jennifer has suffered extreme emotional distress and other damages, all in an amount

Sep 23 2008 10:43AM David Alden Erikson 323-465-3177 p.9

within the jurisdiction of this Court.

39. The conduct of Defendants, and each of them, was intentional and malicious insofar as their actions were taken with knowledge that Plaintiffs emotional and physical distress would result from their conduct, but nevertheless undertook and continued such conduct with a wanton and reckless disregard of the consequences to Plaintiff.

40. The acts of Defendants, and each of them, were willful, wanton, malicious and oppressive, and justify the awarding of exemplary and punitive damages.

PRAYER

WHEREFORE, Jennifer prays judgment against Defendants as follows:

1. That Jennifer be awarded all damages, including future damages, that she has sustained, or will sustain, as a consequence of the acts complained of herein, subject to proof at trial;

2. That Jennifer be awarded her costs, attorneys' fees and expenses in this action;

3. That Jennifer be awarded pre-judgment interest;

4. That Jennifer be awarded exemplary and punitive damages;

5. That Jennifer have such other and further relief as the Court may deem appropriate;

DEMAND FOR JURY TRIAL

Jennifer hereby demands a jury trial on its claims on all issues triable by a jury.

DATED: September 23, 2008

David A. Erikson

By: ______________
David A. Erikson

Attorney for Plaintiff Jennifer Chiba

8

COMPLAINT

Sep 23 2008 10:43AM David Alden Erikson 323-465-3177 p.10

CM-010

ATTORNEY OR PARTY WITHOUT ATTORNEY (Name, State Bar number, and address):
David Alden Erikson, SBN 189838
200 North Larchmont Blvd
Los Angeles, California 90004
TELEPHONE NO.: 323-465-3100 FAX NO.: 323-465-3177
ATTORNEY FOR (Name): Plaintiff Jennifer Chiba

FOR COURT USE ONLY

FILED
LOS ANGELES SUPERIOR COURT
SEP 2 3 2008
JOHN A. CLARKE, CLERK
BY SHAUNYA WESLEY, DEPUTY

SUPERIOR COURT OF CALIFORNIA, COUNTY OF Los Angeles
STREET ADDRESS: 111 North Hill Street
MAILING ADDRESS:
CITY AND ZIP CODE: Los Angeles, California 90012
BRANCH NAME: Central District, Mosk Courthouse

CASE NAME:
Chiba v. Gold

CIVIL CASE COVER SHEET

[✓] Unlimited (Amount demanded exceeds $25,000) [ ] Limited (Amount demanded is $25,000 or less)

Complex Case Designation
[ ] Counter [ ] Joinder
Filed with first appearance by defendant (Cal. Rules of Court, rule 1811)

CASE NUMBER: BC398671
JUDGE:
DEPT:

Items 1–5 below must be completed (see instructions on page 2).

1. Check one box below for the case type that best describes this case:

Auto Tort
[ ] Auto (22)
[ ] Uninsured motorist (46)

Other PI/PD/WD (Personal Injury/Property Damage/Wrongful Death) Tort
[ ] Asbestos (04)
[ ] Product liability (24)
[ ] Medical malpractice (45)
[ ] Other PI/PD/WD (23)

Non-PI/PD/WD (Other) Tort
[ ] Business tort/unfair business practice (07)
[ ] Civil rights (08)
[ ] Defamation (13)
[ ] Fraud (16)
[ ] Intellectual property (19)
[✓] Professional negligence (25)
[ ] Other non-PI/PD/WD tort (35)

Employment
[ ] Wrongful termination (36)
[ ] Other employment (15)

Contract
[ ] Breach of contract/warranty (06)
[ ] Collections (09)
[ ] Insurance coverage (18)
[ ] Other contract (37)

Real Property
[ ] Eminent domain/Inverse condemnation (14)
[ ] Wrongful eviction (33)
[ ] Other real property (26)

Unlawful Detainer
[ ] Commercial (31)
[ ] Residential (32)
[ ] Drugs (38)

Judicial Review
[ ] Asset forfeiture (05)
[ ] Petition re: arbitration award (11)
[ ] Writ of mandate (02)
[ ] Other judicial review (39)

Provisionally Complex Civil Litigation (Cal. Rules of Court, rules 1800–1812)
[ ] Antitrust/Trade regulation (03)
[ ] Construction defect (10)
[ ] Mass tort (40)
[ ] Securities litigation (28)
[ ] Environmental/Toxic tort (30)
[ ] Insurance coverage claims arising from the above listed provisionally complex case types (41)

Enforcement of Judgment
[ ] Enforcement of judgment (20)

Miscellaneous Civil Complaint
[ ] RICO (27)
[ ] Other complaint (not specified above) (42)

Miscellaneous Civil Petition
[ ] Partnership and corporate governance (21)
[ ] Other petition (not specified above) (43)

2. This case [ ] is [✓] is not complex under rule 1800 of the California Rules of Court. If the case is complex, mark the factors requiring exceptional judicial management:
a. [ ] Large number of separately represented parties
b. [ ] Extensive motion practice raising difficult or novel issues that will be time-consuming to resolve
c. [ ] Substantial amount of documentary evidence
d. [ ] Large number of witnesses
e. [ ] Coordination with related actions pending in one or more courts in other counties, states, or countries, or in a federal court
f. [ ] Substantial postjudgment judicial supervision
3. Type of remedies sought (check all that apply):
a. [✓] monetary b. [ ] nonmonetary; declaratory or injunctive relief c. [✓] punitive
4. Number of causes of action (specify): 2
5. This case [ ] is [✓] is not a class action suit.
6. If there are any known related cases, file and serve a notice of related case. (You may use form CM-015.)

Date: September 22, 2008
David Alden Erikson
(TYPE OR PRINT NAME) (SIGNATURE OF PARTY OR ATTORNEY FOR PARTY)

NOTICE
- Plaintiff must file this cover sheet with the first paper filed in the action or proceeding (except small claims cases or cases filed under the Probate Code, Family Code, or Welfare and Institutions Code). (Cal. Rules of Court, rule 201.8.) Failure to file may result in sanctions.
- File this cover sheet in addition to any cover sheet required by local court rule.
- If this case is complex under rule 1800 et seq. of the California Rules of Court, you must serve a copy of this cover sheet on all other parties to the action or proceeding.
- Unless this is a complex case, this cover sheet will be used for statistical purposes only.

Page 1 of 2

Form Adopted for Mandatory Use Judicial Council of California CM-010 [Rev. January 1, 2006]

CIVIL CASE COVER SHEET

Cal. Rules of Court, rules 201.8, 1800–1812; Standards of Judicial Administration, § 19 www.courtinfo.ca.gov

American LegalNet, Inc. www.USCourtForms.com

Sep 23 2008 10:43AM David Alden Erikson 323-465-3177 p.11

SHORT TITLE: Chiba v. Gold	CASE NUMBER BC398671

CIVIL CASE COVER SHEET ADDENDUM AND STATEMENT OF LOCATION (CERTIFICATE OF GROUNDS FOR ASSIGNMENT TO COURTHOUSE LOCATION)

This form is required pursuant to LASC Local Rule 2.0 in all new civil case filings in the Los Angeles Superior Court.

Item I. Check the types of hearing and fill in the estimated length of hearing expected for this case:

JURY TRIAL? ✓ YES CLASS ACTION? YES LIMITED CASE? YES TIME ESTIMATED FOR TRIAL 4 HOURS/ ✓ DAYS.

Item II. Select the correct district and courthouse location (4 steps – If you checked "Limited Case", skip to Item III, Pg. 4):

Step 1: After first completing the Civil Case Cover Sheet Form, find the main civil case cover sheet heading for your case in the left margin below, and, to the right in Column **A**, the Civil Case Cover Sheet case type you selected.

Step 2: Check one Superior Court type of action in Column **B** below which best describes the nature of this case.

Step 3: In Column **C**, circle the reason for the court location choice that applies to the type of action you have checked. For any exception to the court location, see Los Angeles Superior Court Local Rule 2.0.

Applicable Reasons for Choosing Courthouse Location (see Column C below)

1. Class Actions must be filed in the County Courthouse, Central District.
2. May be filed in Central (Other county, or no Bodily Injury/Property Damage).
3. Location where cause of action arose.
4. Location where bodily injury, death or damage occurred.
5. Location where performance required or defendant resides.
6. Location of property or permanently garaged vehicle.
7. Location where petitioner resides.
8. Location wherein defendant/respondent functions wholly.
9. Location where one or more of the parties reside.
10. Location of Labor Commissioner Office.

Step 4: Fill in the information requested on page 4 in Item III; complete Item IV. Sign the declaration.

	A Civil Case Cover Sheet Category No.	B Type of Action (Check only one)	C Applicable Reasons - See Step 3 Above
Auto Tort	Auto (22)	A7100 Motor Vehicle - Personal Injury/Property Damage/Wrongful Death	1., 2., 4.
	Uninsured Motorist (46)	A7110 Personal Injury/Property Damage/Wrongful Death – Uninsured Motorist	1., 2., 4.
Other Personal Injury/Property Damage/Wrongful Death Tort	Asbestos (04)	A6070 Asbestos Property Damage A7221 Asbestos - Personal Injury/Wrongful Death	2. 2.
	Product Liability (24)	A7260 Product Liability (not asbestos or toxic/environmental)	1., 2., 3., 4., 8.
	Medical Malpractice (45)	A7210 Medical Malpractice - Physicians & Surgeons A7240 Other Professional Health Care Malpractice	1., 2., 4. 1., 2., 4.
	Other Personal Injury Property Damage Wrongful Death (23)	A7250 Premises Liability (e.g., slip and fall) A7230 Intentional Bodily Injury/Property Damage/Wrongful Death (e.g., assault, vandalism, etc.) A7270 Intentional Infliction of Emotional Distress A7220 Other Personal Injury/Property Damage/Wrongful Death	1., 2., 4. 1., 2., 4. 1., 2., 3. 1., 2., 4.
Non-Personal Injury/Property	Business Tort (07)	A6029 Other Commercial/Business Tort (not fraud/breach of contract)	1., 2., 3.
	Civil Rights (08)	A6005 Civil Rights/Discrimination	1., 2., 3.
	Defamation (13)	A6010 Defamation (slander/libel)	1., 2., 3.
	Fraud (16)	A6013 Fraud (no contract)	1., 2., 3.
	Intellectual Property (19)	A6018 Intellectual Property	2., 3.

CIV 109 03-04 (DRAFT Rev. 01/06) LASC Approved

CIVIL CASE COVER SHEET ADDENDUM AND STATEMENT OF LOCATION

LASC, rule 2.0 Page 1 of 4

Sep 23 2008 10:44AM David Alden Erikson 323-465-3177 p.12

SHORT TITLE: Chiba v. Gold	CASE NUMBER

	A Civil Case Cover Sheet Category No.	B Type of Action (Check only one)	C Applicable Reasons -See Step 3 Above
Non-Personal Injury/Property Damage/ Wrongful Death Tort (Cont'd.)	Professional Negligence (25)	✓ A6017 Legal Malpractice A6050 Other Professional Malpractice (not medical or legal)	1., (2.), 3. 1., 2., 3.
	Other (35)	A6025 Other Non-Personal Injury/Property Damage tort	2.,3.
Employment	Wrongful Termination (36)	A6037 Wrongful Termination	1., 2., 3.
	Other Employment (15)	A6024 Other Employment Complaint Case A6109 Labor Commissioner Appeals	1., 2., 3. 10.
Contract	Breach of Contract/ Warranty (06) (not insurance)	A6004 Breach of Rental/Lease Contract (not Unlawful Detainer or wrongful eviction) A6008 Contract/Warranty Breach -Seller Plaintiff (no fraud/negligence) A6019 Negligent Breach of Contract/Warranty (no fraud) A6028 Other Breach of Contract/Warranty (not fraud or negligence)	2., 5. 2., 5. 1., 2., 5. 1., 2., 5.
	Collections (09)	A6002 Collections Case-Seller Plaintiff A6012 Other Promissory Note/Collections Case	2., 5., 6. 2., 5.
	Insurance Coverage (18)	A6015 Insurance Coverage (not complex)	1., 2., 5., 8.
	Other Contract (37)	A6009 Contractual Fraud A6031 Tortious Interference A6027 Other Contract Dispute(not breach/insurance/fraud/negligence)	1., 2., 3., 5. 1., 2., 3., 5. 1., 2., 3., 8.
Real Property	Eminent Domain/Inverse Condemnation (14)	A7300 Eminent Domain/Condemnation Number of parcels_____	2.
	Wrongful Eviction (33)	A6023 Wrongful Eviction Case	2., 6.
	Other Real Property (26)	A6018 Mortgage Foreclosure A6032 Quiet Title A6060 Other Real Property(not eminent domain, landlord/tenant, foreclosure)	2., 6. 2., 6. 2., 6.
Unlawful Detainer	Unlawful Detainer-Commercial (31)	A6021 Unlawful Detainer-Commercial (not drugs or wrongful eviction)	2., 6.
	Unlawful Detainer-Residential (32)	A6020 Unlawful Detainer-Residential (not drugs or wrongful eviction)	2., 6.
	Unlawful Detainer-Drugs (38)	A6022 Unlawful Detainer-Drugs	2., 6.
Judicial Review	Asset Forfeiture (05)	A6108 Asset Forfeiture Case	2., 6.
	Petition re Arbitration (11)	A6115 Petition to Compel/Confirm/Vacate Arbitration	2., 5.

CIV 109 03-04 (DRAFT Rev. 01/08) LASC Approved

CIVIL CASE COVER SHEET ADDENDUM AND STATEMENT OF LOCATION

LASC, rule 2.0 Page 2 of 4

Sep 23 2008 10:44AM David Alden Erikson 323-465-3177 p.13

SHORT TITLE: Chiba v. Gold	CASE NUMBER

	A Civil Case Cover Sheet Category No.	B Type of Action (Check only one)	C Applicable Reasons - See Step 3 Above
Judicial Review (Cont'd.)	Writ of Mandate (02)	A6151 Writ - Administrative Mandamus A6152 Writ - Mandamus on Limited Court Case Matter A6153 Writ - Other Limited Court Case Review	2., 8. 2. 2.
	Other Judicial Review (39)	A6150 Other Writ /Judicial Review	2., 8.
Provisionally Complex Litigation	Antitrust/Trade Regulation (03)	A6003 Antitrust/Trade Regulation	1., 2., 8.
	Construction Defect (10)	A6007 Construction defect	1., 2., 3.
	Claims Involving Mass Tort (40)	A6006 Claims Involving Mass Tort	1., 2., 8.
	Securities Litigation (28)	A6035 Securities Litigation Case	1., 2., 8.
	Toxic Tort Environmental (30)	A6036 Toxic Tort/Environmental	1., 2., 3., 8.
	Insurance Coverage Claims from Complex Case (41)	A6014 Insurance Coverage/Subrogation (complex case only)	1., 2., 5., 8.
Enforcement of Judgment	Enforcement of Judgment (20)	A6141 Sister State Judgment A6160 Abstract of Judgment A6107 Confession of Judgment (non-domestic relations) A6140 Administrative Agency Award (not unpaid taxes) A6114 Petition/Certificate for Entry of Judgment on Unpaid Tax A6112 Other Enforcement of Judgment Case	2., 9. 2., 6. 2., 9. 2., 8. 2., 8. 2., 8., 9.
Miscellaneous Civil Complaints	RICO (27)	A6033 Racketeering (RICO) Case	1., 2., 8.
	Other Complaints (Not Specified Above) (42)	A6030 Declaratory Relief Only A6040 Injunctive Relief Only (not domestic/harassment) A6011 Other Commercial Complaint Case (non-tort/non-complex) A6000 Other Civil Complaint (non-tort/non-complex)	1., 2., 8. 2., 8. 1., 2., 8. 1., 2., 8.
Miscellaneous Civil Petitions	Partnership Corporation Governance(21)	A6113 Partnership and Corporate Governance Case	2., 8.
	Other Petitions (Not Specified Above) (43)	A6121 Civil Harassment A6123 Workplace Harassment A6124 Elder/Dependent Adult Abuse Case A6190 Election Contest A6110 Petition for Change of Name A6170 Petition for Relief from Late Claim Law A6100 Other Civil Petition	2., 3., 9. 2., 3., 9. 2., 3., 9. 2. 2., 7. 2., 3., 4., 8. 2., 9.

CIV 109 03-04 (DRAFT Rev. 01/06)
LASC Approved

CIVIL CASE COVER SHEET ADDENDUM AND STATEMENT OF LOCATION

LASC, rule 2.0
Page 3 of 4

Sep 23 2008 10:45AM David Alden Erikson 323-465-3177 p.14

SHORT TITLE: Chiba v. Gold	CASE NUMBER

Item III. Statement of Location: Enter the address of the accident, party's residence or place of business, performance, or other circumstance indicated in Item II., Step 3 on Page 1, as the proper reason for filing in the court location you selected.

REASON: CHECK THE NUMBER UNDER COLUMN C WHICH APPLIES IN THIS CASE 1. ✓2. 3. 4. 5. 6. 7. 8. 9. 10.			ADDRESS: [redacted] Los Angeles, CA 90026
CITY: Los Angeles	STATE: CA	ZIP CODE: 90066	

Item IV. Declaration of Assignment: I declare under penalty of perjury under the laws of the State of California that the foregoing is true and correct and that the above-entitled matter is properly filed for assignment to the Mosk courthouse in the Central District of the Los Angeles Superior Court (Code Civ. Proc., § 392 et seq., and LASC Local Rule 2.0, subds. (b), (c) and (d)).

Dated: September 22, 2008

(SIGNATURE OF ATTORNEY/FILING PARTY)

PLEASE HAVE THE FOLLOWING ITEMS COMPLETED AND READY TO BE FILED IN ORDER TO PROPERLY COMMENCE YOUR NEW COURT CASE:

1. Original Complaint or Petition.
2. If filing a Complaint, a completed Summons form for issuance by the Clerk.
3. Civil Case Cover Sheet form CM-010.
4. Complete Addendum to Civil Case Cover Sheet form CIV 109, 03-04 (use latest revision)
5. Payment in full of the filing fee, unless fees have been waived.
6. Signed order appointing the Guardian ad Litem, JC form 982(a)(27), if the plaintiff or petitioner is a minor under 18 years of age, or if required by Court.
7. Additional copies of documents to be conformed by the Clerk. Copies of the cover sheet and this addendum must be served along with the summons and complaint, or other initiating pleading in the case.

CIV 109 03-04 (DRAFT Rev. 01/08) LASC Approved

CIVIL CASE COVER SHEET ADDENDUM AND STATEMENT OF LOCATION

LASC, rule 2.0 Page 4 of 4

Appendix #5: Chiba's therapist licenses

CALIFORNIA BOARD OF BEHAVIORAL SCIENCES

ISSUANCE DATE
JUNE 28, 1995
EXPIRATION DATE
JUNE 30, 2001
CURRENT DATE / TIME
AUGUST 2, 2020
8:41:53 AM

LICENSING DETAILS FOR: 27483

NAME: CHIBA, JENNIFER RIE
LICENSE TYPE: ASSOCIATE MARRIAGE & FAMILY THERAPIST
PRIMARY STATUS: CANCELLED

ADDRESS OF RECORD
2658 GRIFFITH PARK BLVD #151
LOS ANGELES CA 90039
LOS ANGELES COUNTY
MAP

CALIFORNIA BOARD OF BEHAVIORAL SCIENCES

ISSUANCE DATE
OCTOBER 25, 2005
EXPIRATION DATE
OCTOBER 31, 2011
CURRENT DATE / TIME
AUGUST 2, 2020
8:42:03 AM

LICENSING DETAILS FOR: 49412

NAME: CHIBA, JENNIFER RIE
LICENSE TYPE: ASSOCIATE MARRIAGE & FAMILY THERAPIST
PRIMARY STATUS: CANCELLED

ADDRESS OF RECORD
2658 GRIFFITH PARK BLVD #151
LOS ANGELES CA 90039-2520
LOS ANGELES COUNTY
MAP

CA.GOV

CALIFORNIA BOARD OF BEHAVIORAL SCIENCES

ISSUANCE DATE
APRIL 6, 2011
EXPIRATION DATE
JUNE 30, 2022
CURRENT DATE / TIME
AUGUST 2, 2020
8:42:32 AM

LICENSING DETAILS FOR: 49812

NAME: CHIBA, JENNIFER RIE
LICENSE TYPE: LICENSED MARRIAGE AND FAMILY THERAPIST
PRIMARY STATUS: LICENSE RENEWED & CURRENT

ADDRESS OF RECORD
PO BOX 6431
ALTADENA CA 91003-6431
LOS ANGELES COUNTY
MAP

Appendix #6: Ticket of the tribute show at the Henry Fonda Theatre, on November 3, 2003

TICKETWEB

This is your ticket. **Present this entire page at the event.**

LEVEL	SECTION	ROW	SEAT
	GENERAL		

PURCHASED BY

CONFIRMATION NUMBER 7WKLYJQL

CREDIT CARD NUMBER Visa ************

SPACELAND PRESENTS

ELLIOTT SMITH MEMORIAL/TRIBUTE

featuring

BECK / CONOR OBERST (BRIGHT EYES) / GRANDADDY / BETH ORTON / RILO KILEY / FUTURE PIGEON / AND SPECIAL GUESTS

all proceeds go to the ELLIOTT SMITH FOUNDATION

HENRY FONDA THEATRE

6126 Hollywood Boulevard, Hollywood CA

MON 03 NOV 2003 6:00 PM

Price: U.S.$20.00

Fee: U.S.$7.55

Online

27 OCT 2003 8:30 PM

J8Q7XQ8Y

www.ingramcontent.com/pod-product-compliance
Lightning Source LLC
Chambersburg PA
CBHW062125020426
42335CB00013B/1096

* 9 7 8 1 9 4 7 5 2 1 6 8 1 *